Question&Answer

EUROPEAN UNION LAW

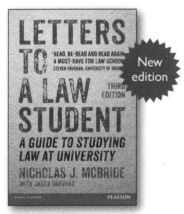

Question&Answer

EUROPEAN
UNION LAW

3rd edition

Jessica Guth
University of Bradford

Edward Mowlam
University of Bradford

PEARSON

Harlow, England • London • New York • Boston • San Francisco • Toronto • Sydney • Auckland • Singapore • Hong Kong
Tokyo • Seoul • Taipei • New Delhi • Cape Town • São Paulo • Mexico City • Madrid • Amsterdam • Munich • Paris • Milan

Pearson Education Limited
Edinburgh Gate
Harlow CM20 2JE
United Kingdom
Tel: +44 (0)1279 623623
Web: www.pearson.com/uk

First published 2012 (print)
Second edition published 2014 (print and electronic)
Third edition published 2016 (print and electronic)

ISBN: 978–1–292–06689–9 (print)
       978–1–292–06691–2 (PDF)
       978–1–292–06693–6 (eText)
       978–1–292–06692–9 (ePub)

British Library Cataloguing-in-Publication Data
A catalogue record for the print edition is available from the British Library

ARP impression 98

Front cover bestseller data from Nielsen BookScan (2009–2013, Law Revision Series).

Print edition typeset in Helvetica Neue by 71
Printed by Ashford Colour Press Ltd

NOTE THAT ANY PAGE CROSS REFERENCES REFER TO THE PRINT EDITION

Contents

Supporting resources

Visit the **Law Express Question&Answer** series companion website at
www.pearsoned.co.uk/lawexpressqa to find valuable learning material
including:

- **Additional essay and problem questions** arranged by topic for each chapter
  give you more opportunity to practise and hone your exam skills.
- **Diagram plans** for all additional questions assist you in structuring and writing
  your answers.
- **You be the marker** questions allow you to see through the eyes of the examiner
  by marking essay and problem questions on every topic covered in the book.
- Download and print all **Before you begin** diagrams and **Diagram plans** from
  the book.

Also: The companion website provides the following features:

- Search tool to help locate specific items of content.
- Online help and support to assist with website usage and troubleshooting.

For more information please contact your local Pearson sales representative or
visit **www.pearsoned.co.uk/lawexpressqa**

Acknowledgements

The authors would like to thank their families for their support throughout this project. Also, we could not have done this without the help and guidance provided by the team at Pearson. Thanks must also go to the reviewers whose comments were extremely helpful and constructive.

Publisher's acknowledgements

The publisher would like to thank Timothy Connor for his contributions as an author to the first and second editions of the book. Some of Timothy's material is still included in this edition and on the companion website. Timothy was awarded a doctorate in December 2013 and we would like to extend our congratulations to him on this achievement.

Our thanks also go to all reviewers who contributed to the development of this text, including students who participated in research and focus groups which helped to shape the series format.

We are also grateful to the following for permission to reproduce copyright material:

Figure on page 2 from http://upload.wikimedia.org/wikipedia/commons/5/56/EU_Structure_History.png, The Wikipedia Foundation (Wikipedia material is reproduced under the terms of the GNU Free Documentation Licence (GFDL); Figure on page 3 from www.ena.lu, Centre Virtuel de la Connaissance sur l'Europe (CVCE).

In some instances we have been unable to trace the owners of copyright material, and we would appreciate any information that would enable us to do so.

What you need to do for every question in EU Law

Books in the *Question and Answer* series focus on the *why* of a good answer alongside the *what,* thereby helping you to build your question answering skills and technique.

This guide should not be used as a substitute for learning the material thoroughly, your lecture notes or your textbook. It *will* help you to make the most out of what you have already learned when answering an exam or coursework question. Remember that the answers given here are not the *only* correct way of answering the question but serve to show you some good examples of how you *could* approach the question set.

Make sure that you regularly refer to your course syllabus, check which issues are covered (as well as to what extent they are covered) and whether they are usually examined with other topics. Remember that what is required in a good answer could change significantly with only a slight change in the wording of a question. Therefore, do not try to memorise the answers given here: instead, use the answers and the other features to understand what goes into a good answer and why.

EU law is not a subject enjoyed by most students but it really does not have to be difficult. Every EU law question is likely to ask you to apply your knowledge of the law to a particular context – either a practical one, as in problem questions, or a more theoretical one, as in essay questions. For both you need to remember that EU law does not exist in isolation but is inextricably linked with the national legal systems of the Member States. The interaction between European law and these systems is crucial to understanding how EU law works.

EU law is often considered in a political context. Recognising that your political stance is likely to influence your views on EU law is valuable and something which can make your answers stronger.

There are a number of issues in EU law assessment which you should look out for. Make sure you always clearly state the legal authorities on which you are basing your argument and be aware of the differences between different types of EU legal sources. You should be familiar with the treaties as a framework and you must be able to distinguish between, for example, directives and regulations, recognising that the latter are directly applicable whereas the former need implementation by the Member States.

In addition, you should be familiar with the importance of the case law of the Court of Justice of the European Union and understand that this does not set the same sort of binding precedent you know from the English legal system. In other words, you need to remember that the EU is a unique system with a unique set of institutions and unique rules of governance that do not really exist anywhere else in the world and are thus not easily compared to legal or political systems you might be more familiar with.

Finally, it is worth remembering that substantive EU law questions, for example on the free movement of goods, can also benefit from a mention of procedural legal issues where appropriate: in particular, when advising clients in problem questions. A client would want to know what their legal rights are but also how to enforce them, and this is something many EU law exam answers lack.

Good luck!

Guided tour

What you need to do for every question in EU Law

What to do for every question – Identify the key things you should look for and do in any question and answer on the subject, ensuring you give every one of your answers a great chance from the start.

HOW TO USE THIS GUIDE

Books in the *Question and Answer* series focus on the *why* of a good answer alongside the *what*, thereby helping you to build your question answering skills and technique.

This guide should not be used as a substitute for learning the material thoroughly, your lecture notes or your textbook. It will help you to make the most out of what you have already learned when answering an exam or coursework question. Remember that the answers given here are not the only correct way of answering the question but serve to show you some good examples of how you could approach the question set.

Make sure that you regularly refer to your course syllabus, check which issues are covered (as well as to what extent they are covered) and whether they are usually examined with other topics. Remember that what is required in a good answer could change significantly with only a slight change in the wording of a question. Therefore, do not try to memorise the answers given here. Instead, use the answers and the other features to understand what goes into a good answer and why.

EU law is not a subject enjoyed by most students but it really does not have to be difficult. Every EU law question is likely to ask you to apply your knowledge of the law to a particular context – either a practical one, as in problem questions, or a more theoretical one, as in essay questions. For both you need to remember that EU law does not exist in isolation but is inextricably linked with the national legal systems of the Member States. The interaction between European law and these systems is crucial to understanding how EU law works.

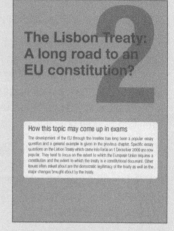

The Lisbon Treaty: A long road to an EU constitution?

How this topic may come up in exams

The development of the EU through the treaties has long been a popular essay question and a general example is given in the previous chapter. Specific essay questions on the Lisbon Treaty which came into force on 1 December 2009 are now popular. They tend to focus on the extent to which the European Union requires a constitution and the extent to which the treaty is a constitutional document. Other issues often asked about are the democratic legitimacy of the treaty as well as the major changes brought about by the treaty.

How this topic may come up in exams – Understand how to tackle any question on this topic by using the handy tips and advice relevant to both essay and problem questions. In-text symbols clearly identify each question type as they occur.

 Essay question

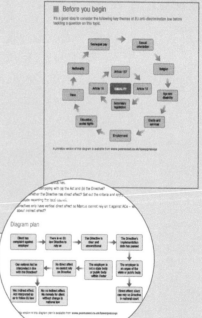 Problem question

Before you begin – Use these diagrams as a step-by-step guide to help you confidently identify the main points covered in any question asked. Download these from the companion website to add to your revision notes.

Answer plans and Diagram plans – A clear and concise plan is the key to a good answer and these answer and diagram plans support the structuring of your answers, whatever your preferred learning style.

■ Before you begin

It's a good idea to consider the following key themes of EU anti-discrimination law before tackling a question on this topic.

A printable version of this diagram is available from www.pearsoned.co.uk/lawexpressqa

Diagram plan

A printable version of this diagram plan is available from www.pearsoned.co.uk/lawexpressqa

Answer plan

→ Identify the complaints Marcus has.

→ Is the employer complying with (a) the Act and (b) the Directive?

→ Discuss whether the Directive has direct effect? Set out the criteria and apply them.

→ Conclude regarding the local council.

→ Directives only have vertical direct effect so Marcus cannot rely on it against ACo – what about indirect effect?

Answer with accompanying guidance – Make the most out of every question by using the guidance to recognise what makes a good answer and why. Answers are the length you could realistically hope to produce in an exam to show you how to gain marks quickly when under pressure.

Answer

[1] Always identify the legal issue to deal with – if you do this right at the start, the examiner can be sure you are on the right track.

The question concerns the regulation by the EU of the internal taxation of Member States.[1] The legalities of proposed changes with respect to rates of VAT on chocolate, and liquorice and doors, and rates of duty on carbonated drinks and juice, fall for consideration within the scope of Article 110 Treaty on the Functioning of the European Union (TFEU).[2] This provides that:

[1] Always identify the legal issue to deal with – if you do this right at the start, the examiner can be sure you are on the right track.

[2] Once you know the legal issue, the next logical step is stating the legal provisions which apply and then define them.

[2] Once you know the legal issue, the next logical step is stating the legal provisions which apply and then define them.

1. No Member State shall impose, directly or indirectly, on the products of other Member States any internal taxation of any kind in excess of that imposed directly or indirectly on similar domestic products.

2. Furthermore, no Member State shall impose on the products of other Member States any internal taxation of such a nature as to afford indirect protection to other products.[3]

Article 110 applies where the charges are levied as part of a general system of internal dues applied systematically to categories of products. Both VAT and duty levied in Denmark fall into general system of

criteria clearly and illustrates with case examples, so you are highlighting the clarity of your understanding and can then move on to analysis.

[1] This sentence is a lead-in to the more analytical discussion of direct effect which then begins by examining directives in this context, which is where most of the issues can be illustrated most clearly.

en Loos dealt with vertical direct effect, the question of whether provisions could also be horizontally directly effective was not answered until the case of *Defrenne v Sabena (No. 2)* (1976) in which an air stewardess brought a claim against her employer. The ECJ's judgment clarifies that European law provisions are enforceable by individuals against other individuals, a position which has since been confirmed in cases such as *Walrave v Koch* (1974), *Thieffry v Paris Bar Association* (1977) or *Brasserie de Haecht* (1973).[4]

While the direct effect of directly applicable EU law such as treaty articles and regulations has been relatively uncontroversial, the application of the doctrine to directives has been more problematic.[5]

Case names clearly highlighted – Easy-to-spot bold text makes those all important case names stand out from the rest of the answer, ensuring they are much easier to remember in revision and an exam.

Make your answer stand out – Really impress your examiners by going the extra mile and including these additional points and further reading to illustrate your deeper knowledge of the subject, fully maximising your marks.

✓ Make your answer stand out

- State more clearly the importance of indirect effect and state liability, in particular as a tool of interpretation which seeks to preserve primacy of EU law. Note in particular the role of the ECJ in developing these principles.
- Explain further why the ECJ took it upon itself to develop the principle.
- Speculate in more detail on whether or not the principle would have developed without the ECJ's impetus.
- Further academic commentary, such as De Witte, B. (1999) Direct Effect, Supremacy and the Nature of the Legal Order, in P. Craig and G. De Burca (eds) *The Evolution of EU Law*, Oxford: Oxford University Press, and Lenaerts, K. and Courthaut, T. (2006) Of Birds and Hedges: The Role of Primacy in Invoking Norms of EU Law, *EL Rev*, 31, 287, would strengthen the answer further.

Don't be tempted to – Points out common mistakes ensuring you avoid losing easy marks by understanding where students most often trip up in exams.

! Don't be tempted to . . .

- State the law and jump straight to the conclusion. You must apply the law to each of the scenarios.
- Write a general answer about customs duties and free movement of goods; stick with the scenario and focus on what is relevant.
- Repeat the detail of the legal provisions for each section; you will run out of time if you do that.
- Base your answer on just the treaty provisions; you need to highlight how they have been interpreted with reference to case law.

Bibliography – Use this list of further reading to really delve into the subject and explore areas in more depth, enabling you to excel in exams.

Bibliography

Arnull, A. (2003) From Charter to Constitution and Beyond: Fundamental Rights in the New European Union, *Public Law*, 774.

Barnard, C. (2013) *The Substantive Law of the EU: The Four Freedoms*, 4th edn, Oxford: Oxford University Press.

Guided tour of the companion website

Book resources are available to download. Print your own **Before you begin** and **Diagram plans** to pin to your wall or add to your own revision notes.

Additional Essay and Problem questions with **Diagram plans** arranged by topic for each chapter give you more opportunity to practise and hone your exam skills. Print and email your answers.

You be the marker gives you a chance to evaluate sample exam answers for different question types for each topic and understand how and why an examiner awards marks. Use the accompanying guidance to get the most out of every question and recognise what makes a good answer.

All of this and more can be found when you visit
www.pearsoned.co.uk/lawexpressqa

Table of cases, legislation and conventions

Cases

▮ Primary Legislation

■ Secondary Legislation

▉ Conventions

The origins and institutions of the EU

1

How this topic may come up in exams

The origins and historical development of the EU are often seen as background information and are rarely examined other than in a very general sense. Questions in this area tend to focus on the roles and functioning of the institutions or their historical development. As such, problem questions are very rare and most questions are essay-type questions. Answers in this area are often far too descriptive and do not apply the knowledge or answer the question set in an analytical and critical way. To make the most of this topic, you need to avoid pure description as much as possible.

Before you begin

It's a good idea to consider the following key themes of the origins and institutions of the EU before tackling a question on this topic.

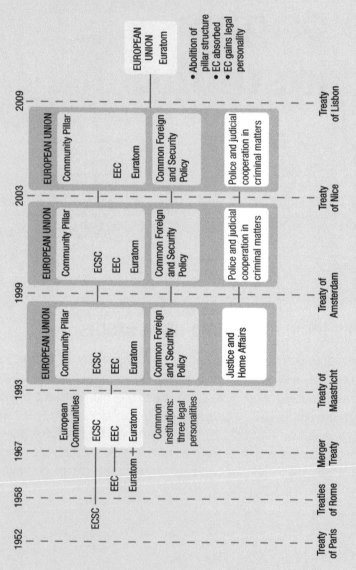

Source: http://upload.wikimedia.org/wikipedia/commons/5/56/EU_Structure_History.png Wikipedia material is reproduced under the terms of the GNU Free Documentation Licence (GFDL).

A printable version of this diagram is available from www.pearsoned.co.uk/lawexpressqa

**Institutions of the European Union
(simplified diagram)**

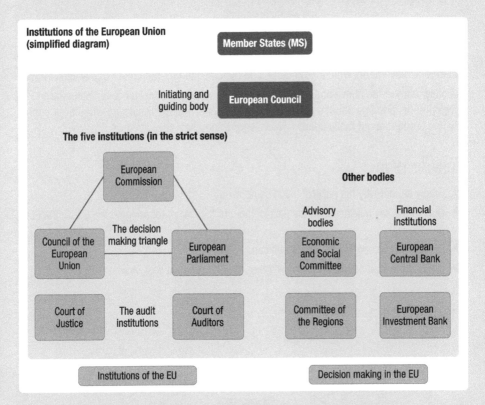

Source: Centre Virtuel de la Connaissance sur l'Europe, **www.ena.lu** Reproduced with permission.

A printable version of this diagram is available from **www.pearsoned.co.uk/lawexpressqa**

Question 1

'Europe will not be made all at once, or according to a single plan. It will be built through concrete achievements which first create a de facto solidarity.' (Schuman Declaration 1950)

Critically analyse the above statement by examining what you consider to be the major developments bringing about a political union in Europe, and by discussing whether or not this has brought about the solidarity which Robert Schuman envisaged.

Answer plan

➡ Briefly set out why the political union came about.

➡ Outline the key milestones in the development of the Union, focusing on the ECSC, the EEC and the EU.

➡ Discuss the Lisbon Treaty and its ratification process.

➡ Discuss the idea of solidarity, and whether or not it exists in your view.

Diagram plan

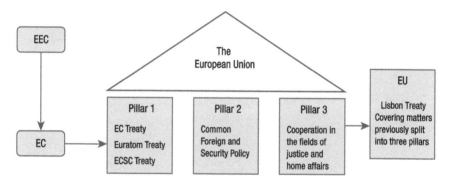

A printable version of this diagram plan is available from **www.pearsoned.co.uk/lawexpressqa**

[1] This question is quite wide-ranging. It is asking you to explain the historical origins of the European Union, its development thereafter and then to comment on the current state of the Union as it is perceived by its citizens and Member States.

Answer

This essay will firstly set out the purpose of bringing the nations of Europe together into a political union and will chart its evolution through to the present day, before comment will be made on whether or not a 'de facto solidarity' currently exists among the citizens and Member States of the European Union (EU).[1]

² It makes sense to start with Robert Schuman in the context of this question. There are many starting points however, such as the Potsdam Conference in 1945, Churchill's Zurich speech in 1946 or the formation of the Organisation for European Economic Co-Operation in 1948 and so on. Wherever you start, be brief.

³ If you can remember quotes then use them. Do feel free to abridge long quotes, as done here, or to accurately paraphrase a quote.

⁴ You could say here that these states had already started this trend towards intergovernmental co-operation through the creation of the Netherlands–Belgium–Luxembourg Customs Convention which came into effect in 1948.

⁵ A note on the key policies created under the treaties is useful to display your wider knowledge and reading to the examiner.

⁶ This is useful as it displays an up-to-date working knowledge of the EU.

⁷ Here we are moving away from the discussion on the treaties. This is useful as it displays knowledge of the range of influences on the development of European integration.

Robert Schuman is seen as one of 'Europe's' 'founding fathers'.[2] Schuman, a French Finance Minister, and Jean Monnet, a French Civil Servant, developed a plan which became the first major intergovernmental initiative towards the system of European integration we know today as the EU. The Schuman Plan recommended that coal and steel production and distribution in France and Germany should be placed under a common High Authority to allay 'French fears of emerging German industrial might' (Chalmers et al., 2014). Permanently ending the hostilities between these countries was key to the plan. Schuman continued, '. . . solidarity in production [means] that any war between France and Germany becomes not merely unthinkable, but materially impossible'.[3] In this singular aspect, Schuman's vision of solidarity has been a complete success.

The Schuman Plan was accepted by Germany and, along with Italy, Belgium, Luxembourg, the Netherlands[4] and France, these six nations ratified the Treaty Establishing the European Coal and Steel Community (ECSC) in 1951. The Pleven Plan followed in 1952 to hastily arrange the six into a European Defence Community (EDC) in the face of the threat of the Soviet Union. The EDC fell apart soon after and attention was focused, by way of the Spaak Report in 1956, on the creation of a wider supranational entity to develop economic cooperation among the ECSC six. A year later the Treaties of Rome were signed and the European Economic Community (EEC) was established in 1958 along with the European Atomic Energy Committee.

The EEC Treaty created a customs union, abolishing duties on intra-community trade, and a common external tariff on imports. It also created a free-trade area to remove restrictions on the free movement of goods, people, services and capital.[5] Other policies were created to enforce fair competition, to prevent states from discriminating against non-domestic products and to standardise trade deals with non-EEC countries. The Common Agricultural Policy was set up to 'Europeanise' state intervention in the agricultural sector. To oversee these policies, the EEC Treaty formed three institutions which still exist to this day: Commission, Council and Assembly (now Parliament).[6]

Another of the EEC's institutions, the Court of Justice, made its mark in the 1960s,[7] widening the supranational reach of the Community. The Community was described as a 'new legal order', which 'limited the sovereign rights' of the states. The decision in **Van Gend en**

8 You could also mention
Declaration 17 of the Lisbon
Treaty here, which confirmed
the primacy of EU law.

Loos (1963) established the principle of direct effect and gave full legal authority to the EEC Treaty. This began a flurry of activity in the Court of Justice, creating a number of judgments and bringing about further European integration, such as the supremacy of European law as stated in *Costa v ENEL* (1964).[8]

Europe's economic fortunes were on the rise, and a number of countries applied to join the EEC. The UK joined in 1973 and five other Member States entered by 1986. These enlargements and other matters required several changes to the EEC Treaty. The Single European Act of 1986 called for work to be done to complete the internal market. It also increased the powers of the European Parliament and introduced Qualified Majority Voting so that legislation could more easily be voted through the Council. The EEC went into a legislative frenzy and by 1992 the internal market was said to be complete.

The Treaty on the European Union (TEU) was also signed in 1992. This established the European Union, incorporating within it the ECSC, Euratom and the European Community. These three entities formed the first pillar of the new EU structure. The second pillar gave rise to the common foreign affairs and security policy and the third pillar concerned police and judicial cooperation in criminal matters. The latter two pillars substantially extended the EU's legislative remit.[9] The TEU brought about a number of significant changes, adding such matters as social policy, public health and industrial policy to a wide list of Union competencies. The framework for economic and monetary union (EMU) was laid down in the TEU, and EU citizenship was created and bestowed upon all nationals of the Member States.

9 You should look to provide a
comment on the effect of the
changes under TEU.

The changes planned under TEU were designed to cultivate a greater sense of a collective identity without the traditional confines of the nation state. This drew some hostile criticism and resulted in a much toned down Treaty to that envisaged by the drafters.[10] The second and third pillars were made to remain intergovernmental in nature as opposed to supranational; the subsidiarity principle was developed to limit the role of the Union; and the UK and Denmark were allowed to opt out of the EMU.

The Treaty of Amsterdam followed in 1997, developing the powers of the Union and the structure of the institutions. The Treaty of Nice then looked towards enlargements of the Union, after negotiating an initial rejection from the people of Ireland. A plan for a Constitutional Treaty (CT) was then conceived to put an end to the succession of treaty reforms. The CT was designed to develop the EU into a constitutional democracy, complete with a Foreign Minister, legal personality and many of the trappings of statehood. This plan was rejected by the French and Dutch electorate. The citizens of Europe seemingly did not identify with the notion of a European citizenry, or feel any overwhelming sense of solidarity for the European project.[11]

[11] Again we are building towards our conclusion regarding the solidarity envisaged by Schuman.

The Lisbon Treaty continued the evolutionary process which then stalled after the rejection of the CT. It brought the three pillars of the TEU together, further expanded the EU's competencies, increased the involvement of the Parliament and created a President for the European Council and a High Representative for foreign affairs and security policy. Again, the Lisbon Treaty was initially rejected by the Irish, before a second vote approved the Lisbon Treaty.

[12] You can conclude this essay briefly as comment on European solidarity has already been made above, so it would be appropriate to draw upon what you have already said.

The path towards European integration has been long and often arduous. As seen in the EMU, the nation states often refuse to move at the same speed. With regard to the citizens of Europe, it is common for the voters to reject the plans for closer integration.[12] The EU has faced significant problems in its attempts to cultivate a shared European identity. This is something which is reflected in the Eurobarometer opinion polls which shows that voter trust for the EU is low, particularly after the crisis in the Eurozone, and European election turnout is falling consistently. While Schuman may well have fostered a real sense of solidarity within the walls of the EU institutions, the same cannot be said in any general sense of the people of Europe, or of its Member States.

 Make your answer stand out

- Add further details about the changes each treaty brought about.
- Provide more detail on the historical origins of the Union. See to this effect Ward, I. (2009) *A Critical Introduction to EU Law*, 3rd edn, Cambridge: Cambridge University Press.
- Add a little more detail about the failed CT and the negotiation and ratification of the Lisbon Treaty.
- Discuss what is meant by 'solidarity'. see; Sangiovanni, A. (2013) Solidarity in the EU, *Oxford Journal of Legal Studies*, 1–29.

> ## ❗ Don't be tempted to . . .
>
> - Just list the treaties, you need to say a little bit about them.
> - Outline each treaty and the changes brought about in detail. You will not have time and therefore must select those issues you think are most important.
> - Focus simply on the Lisbon Treaty (or one of the others) without mentioning the others; the question specifically asks for an outline of the history with reference to the key treaties, so you do need to mention them.

✒ Question 2

The European Union is inherently undemocratic. Explain, giving reasons, whether you agree or disagree with this statement.

Diagram plan

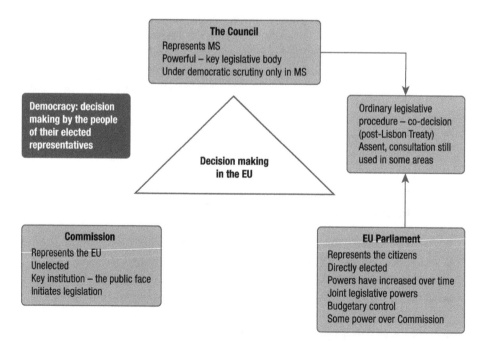

The Council
Represents MS
Powerful – key legislative body
Under democratic scrutiny only in MS

Democracy: decision making by the people of their elected representatives

Ordinary legislative procedure – co-decision (post-Lisbon Treaty)
Assent, consultation still used in some areas

Decision making in the EU

Commission
Represents the EU
Unelected
Key institution – the public face
Initiates legislation

EU Parliament
Represents the citizens
Directly elected
Powers have increased over time
Joint legislative powers
Budgetary control
Some power over Commission

A printable version of this diagram plan is available from **www.pearsoned.co.uk/lawexpressqa**

Answer plan

➜ Briefly explain the institutional structure of the EU and the institutions' law making power.

➜ Briefly consider the elements necessary for democracy.

➜ Consider the extent to which the institutional structure is democratic.

➜ Consider the extent to which law making procedures reflect democratic values.

➜ Outline any other factors contributing or mitigating the EU's democratic deficit.

Answer

¹ This introductory paragraph sets out clearly what you intend to do in this essay and thus guides the reader into it.

² You are making clear from the start that you are concentrating on these three and then going on to explain them.

³ Make sure you know the difference between the Council of the European Union and the European Council. If it helps to avoid confusion, feel free to call this Council the 'Council of Ministers'.

⁴ This comment shows that you have kept up to date and are aware of how the institutions have developed over time and in particular with the latest treaty.

⁵ You are highlighting here that you need to explain what you mean by democracy so you can assess whether or not the EU structure lives up to that ideal.

⁶ This sentence reminds the reader what it is you are doing in this essay, what the question you are trying to answer is. It helps present your argument logically.

This essay considers the extent to which the EU's institutional structure and law making procedures render it undemocratic. It first outlines the institutional structure of the EU and briefly explains the law making powers given to each of the key institutions before examining the elements necessary for democratic governance in this context.¹

The EU is made up of five key institutions, three of which form what can be termed the 'decision making triangle'.² The Commission, which comprises one Commissioner from each Member State and is supported by approximately 25,000 civil servants, acts as the main initiator of legislation. The Council,³ made up of relevant ministers from each Member State, is the main legislative body, with the European Parliament (EP), the only directly elected body of the EU, taking a supporting role in the legislative process. The European Council, which is made up of the Heads of State of EU Member States and has formal institutional status⁴ following the implementation of the Lisbon Treaty and the European Court of Justice (ECJ), have additional important roles to play in shaping policy and the application of European law respectively.

In order to assess whether or not the EU is rendered undemocratic by its institutional structure, it is essential first to understand what the EU is to be measured against.⁵ Democracy suggests that decisions on important issues such as policy direction and law making should be made by the people. Rarely does this idea extend to putting legal proposals to referendums, truly allowing the people to decide. In most cases democracy indicates some kind of parliamentary democracy, with citizens voting for representatives who are then entrusted with carefully regulated law making powers. The question in this context is therefore whether the people of Europe have sufficient scrutiny of and control over the EU institutions and the making of EU law.⁶

The EU only has one directly elected body, the EP, and therefore arguably does not effectively capture the wishes or needs of EU citizens. The other key institutions are not democratically elected, or at least not directly. The Council is of course made up of elected ministers from each of the Member States and therefore subject to the democratic processes within Member States. The Commissioners are put forward by the governments of the Member States which are open to scrutiny at the national level, and the President of the Commission as well as the Commissioners are accountable to the EP which not only has to approve them but may also question them in writing and orally.[7] The downfall of the Santer Commission serves as a useful reminder that the Commission cannot simply do as it pleases and that its Commissioners are, to some extent at least, accountable. More recently the Commission forced some Commissioners to withdraw before the Juncker Commission could take office in 2014.[8] One particularly egregious case concerned the Commissioner nominated for Slovenia, the former Prime Minister Alenka Bratusek. In a broadly anti-democratic move, she secured for herself her country's nomination just before the Slovenian electorate voted her out of office. She was later rejected by the EP because of a lack of experience.

While there are arguments to be made that the EU institutions should be subject to a more democratic process in terms of their membership, it is the balance of power between those institutions which proves problematic for democratic legitimacy of the Union.[9]

In a democratic system, one might expect the most democratic of the institutions to have the most power in shaping policy and making law, whereas one might expect the least democratic of the bodies to exercise little power. However, this is not the case in the EU. The institution which is arguably least democratic, the Commission, has the power to initiate legislation and indeed almost all proposals must come from the Commission. Legally, therefore, the Commission, in practice completely unelected and to a certain extent made up of unaccountable civil servants, is responsible for drafting all legislative proposals in the EU, thus allowing them to push forward certain agendas while neglecting others. Meanwhile the EP is a parliament without the power to initiate legislation which is 'an absurdity' (Ward 2009).[10] Once a proposal has been made, the Council remains the key legislative body, even post-Lisbon. The interests of the Member States are thus placed above the interests of the EU citizens.[11] In spite of the EP gaining in strength and legislative competence with every

[7] In this section you briefly set out how, if at all, each of the three institutions are democratic in terms of their membership.

[8] These two examples show that you are familiar with the Parliament actually exercising the power it has been given.

[9] Your first mini-conclusion, which then leads you into your next point which shows the examiners that you have a clear structure in mind and that your argument flows logically.

[10] While it is probably not sensible to try and learn lots of lengthy quotes, it can be useful to remember one or two little phrases such as this one to evidence your wider reading and knowledge.

[11] Here you again highlight that you understand how the institutional structure works and whose interests are represented.

new treaty, its role still remains far from that of an equal partner in the legislative process. The Lisbon Treaty makes the co-decision procedure, which provides for a joint decision by the Council and the EP, the main legislative procedure but the treaty provides for exceptions in key areas. The EP's legislative competence therefore does not extend across all policy areas and is completely excluded in some very important respects such as matters related to foreign affairs and security policy.

[12] You are now leading into a brief discussion of other factors to consider, which you must do as the question requires you to conclude whether or not it is the institutional structure which renders the EU undemocratic. If there are other factors, they need consideration too.

However, it is not only the institutional structure and balance which threatens the democratic legitimacy of the EU.[12] The fact that the EU institutions conducted most of their business behind closed doors was cause for major concern. To some extent this has been addressed by the Lisbon Treaty forcing greater transparency in the work of the Commission and even the Council must now meet in public, thus being opened up to increased public scrutiny.

The voting procedure adopted by the Council also attracted criticisms for its undemocratic nature. While some decisions require unanimity, many can be decided using qualified majority voting (QMV) which is based on each Member State having an allocated number of votes which are roughly based on population size but weighted in favour of the smaller states. Where unanimity applies, one Member State can effectively veto a piece of legislation even if all others agree (and indeed this was the UK's hope in relation to the Working Time Directive (2000/34), which they argued should have been brought under a legal base requiring unanimity rather than QMV). The Lisbon Treaty made some changes to the voting system which came into force in November 2014 and significantly extends the areas where QMV applies.

The lack of involvement in EU law making by national parliaments was a further concern, in particular because it meant that scrutiny in relation to subsidiary and proportionality were often lacking in areas of EU competence. The Lisbon Treaty, and, in particular, the protocols relating to the involvement of national parliaments and the application of subsidiarity and proportionality, might, if used effectively, alleviate some of the concerns in this area.[13]

[13] Highlighting possible solutions to problems you have identified shows the examiners that you have a full grasp of the area of law and also that your knowledge is up to date.

The final issue is the fact that if the EU is to be democratic, the people of Europe must make their voice heard. Voter turnout in European elections has been notoriously low in many Member States, and, as long as this is the case, it is hard to see how the perception of the EU as an undemocratic entity imposing its views on the unwilling citizens of Member States will change.

[14] Always state your conclusion and refer back to the question asked: otherwise your answer is incomplete!

In conclusion, the EU is often perceived as undemocratic, and the institutional set-up as well as the balance of power between those institutions do little to challenge that perception. However, the statement given is only partly accurate as there are other factors which influence the extent of the democratic deficit, one of the most important being voter turnout, particularly in EP elections.[14]

✓ **Make your answer stand out**

- Add additional references to the academic debates for example, Petersen, J. and Shackleton, M. (eds) (2006) *The Institutions of the European Union*, 2nd edn, Oxford: Oxford University Press; Rittberger, B. (2005) *Building Europe's Parliament. Democratic Representation Beyond the Nation-State*, Oxford: Oxford University Press.
- Add a little more detail about the historical development of EP power.
- Expand further on the law making procedures and the democratic merits of each.
- Consider issues beyond institutional structure and law making powers to show a wider awareness of the issues arising.

❗ **Don't be tempted to . . .**

- Describe each of the institutions in detail; the question requires a consideration of the institutional structure in relation to democracy rather than a description of institutions.
- Sit on the fence. You need to agree or disagree with the statement and it must be clear from your answer why you do so.
- Focus on only one of the institutions. Many students try to learn answers and then adapt them for the question set. It is actually easier to work on understanding a topic, then you can answer any question set with relative ease.

📰 Question 3

What is the role of the European Parliament in the institutional balance of the EU? How has it developed since the inception of the Union and how might it develop in the future?

Diagram plan

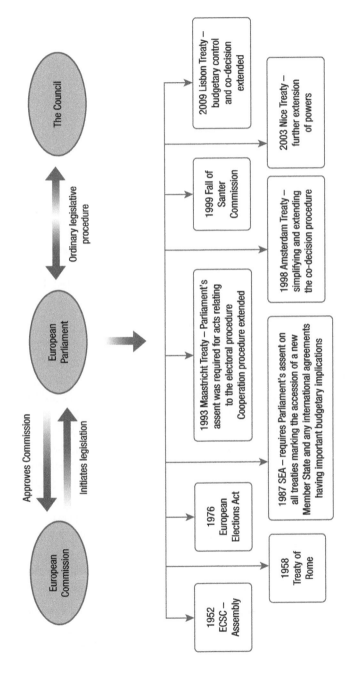

The Council

European Parliament

European Commission

Ordinary legislative procedure

Approves Commission

Initiates legislation

1952 ECSC – Assembly

1958 Treaty of Rome

1976 European Elections Act

1987 SEA – requires Parliament's assent on all treaties marking the accession of a new Member State and any international agreements having important budgetary implications

1993 Maastricht Treaty – Parliament's assent was required for acts relating to the electoral procedure Cooperation procedure extended

1998 Amsterdam Treaty – simplifying and extending the co-decision procedure

1999 Fall of Santer Commission

2003 Nice Treaty – further extension of powers

2009 Lisbon Treaty – budgetary control and co-decision extended

A printable version of this diagram plan is available from www.pearsoned.co.uk/lawexpressqa

13

Answer plan

→ Briefly outline the EU's institutional structure, focusing on the role of the Parliament.

→ Consider how the Parliament's role has developed over time, noting in particular the extension of its powers with each new treaty.

→ Outline what you consider to be the remaining issues in relation to the institutional balance (e.g. a continuing democratic deficit).

→ Suggest how the role of Parliament and the institutional balance as a whole may be developed in the future.

Answer

[1] From the start you are indicating that you have understood the question and are setting out why the EP is an important institution to consider.

[2] Here you are recognising that you cannot consider the EP in isolation but need to examine it in the context in which it operates.

[3] It is useful to provide a brief summary of how the EP started out so its development can be appreciated.

[4] You are displaying your historical awareness, showing the examiner your in-depth knowledge of this area of law.

[5] You do not need to say any more about the cases; you are just citing your authority for the point you are making about the EP's role.

[6] You are now moving from a general consideration which gives a very brief overview of the history into a more detailed discussion of the role of the EP; it is useful to signal this to the reader with a short introductory sentence.

This essay considers the role of the European Parliament (EP) in the institutional structure of the EU. As the only directly elected institution, the EP is the institution representing the EU citizens and arguably the institution giving the EU its democratic legitimacy.[1] The other key institutions making up the 'decision making triangle' of the EU are the Commission representing the interests of the EU and the Council looking after the Member States' interests.[2]

The Parliament's role has developed significantly over the history of the EU, more so than that of any other institution. Initially named the Assembly, it was envisaged as a body which would give advisory opinions on legislative matters or at most give its assent. It was not to be heavily involved in the making of legislation and had no place in the formation of policy.[3] With every new treaty the role of the EP has increased,[4] resulting in a number of possible law making procedures, ranging from mere consultation through cooperation and assent to co-decision. Case law confirms that whatever the procedure, the EP's role must be taken seriously. Two cases relating to the consultation procedure illustrate the point. In both the Council adopted a regulation without awaiting the Parliament's opinion and the ECJ held this to be unlawful (*Roquette Freres v Council* (1980)).[5] The Treaty of Nice extended the co-decision procedure to new areas, and the Lisbon Treaty specified the co-decision as the normal legislative procedure, thus extending Parliament's role in the legislative process significantly.

The Parliament's role and duties can be broken down into involvement in law making, as illustrated above, holding the Commission accountable and exercising budgetary control. They will be considered in turn.[6]

While the Commission remains the main initiator of legislation in most areas of EU law and the Council is still considered the main legislative body, the EP is now a more active player in the legislative process. The normal legislative procedure requires both the Council and the EP to approve a legislative proposal. Following the EP's opinion, the Council will prepare a common position which the EP can adopt or reject. If rejected, the measure fails. The EP can also suggest amendments by absolute majority. These amendments will then be considered by the Council which can approve them and adopt the measure. If there is no agreement a conciliation committee is convened which will also involve the Commission and may result in the eventual adoption of the measure. The power of the EP has therefore increased significantly and it is now a key player in the legislative process.

[7] You have already said that the powers have increased and you should also consider any remaining limitations on the EP's powers to make sure you give a balanced view.

However, there are still a number of very important areas of law where the EP is given no law making competence at all.[7] For example, matters related to foreign affairs and security policy will not be considered by the EP but will be left to be considered at intergovernmental level. Furthermore, even in relation to the areas that do fall within the EP's legislative competency, a special legislative process allows the EP's role to be sidestepped by relegating it to a body which merely has to be consulted.

The EP also has a role to play in holding the Commission to account. First the EP must be consulted and give approval to the nomination of a President and members of the Commission. The Commission is required under Article 230 TFEU to reply orally and in writing to questions posed by the EP. The Council can also be asked to respond to questions although the EP has no formal supervisory power over the Council. Furthermore, the EP can pass a motion of censure on the Commission under Article 17(8) TEU and Article 234 TFEU obliging the entire Commission to resign. While the EP has never done so, there are examples of the EP putting significant pressure on the Commission. In 1999, although narrowly avoiding a motion of censure, the Santer Commission resigned following pressure from the Commission following allegations of corruption.[8] The EP, as an elected body, does therefore scrutinise and hold to account the Commission as an unelected body.[9]

[8] Using examples always makes your answer more interesting and shows that you have an appreciation as to how some of these rights and powers might play out in practice. Stories such as this one also make the provisions easier to remember!

[9] It is useful to end each section with a mini-conclusion for the point discussed to clarify your key points to the examiner.

The case of **Roquette** established the EP's competence to intervene in legal proceedings before the ECJ, and **European Parliament v**

Council (1985) confirmed that it also has the competence to bring actions for failure to act under Article 265 TFEU. The Treaty of Nice eventually gave the EP the same power as the Commission and Council to challenge the legality of any legislative acts before the ECJ, finally recognising it as an institution on equal footing with the others. This was a significant step forward. The EP now had significant legislative power as well as the right to challenge the legality of acts after they had been passed, thus giving it some power in areas where it could still be excluded from the law making process.[10]

[10] Without this sentence, the paragraph would be very descriptive and not much use in analytical terms. Try to be as analytical as possible throughout.

The EP's role in the institutional set-up of the EU is therefore an important one. It represents the people of Europe and as such gives the EU its democratic legitimacy. It now plays an important role in the making of EU law and in addition exercises some scrutiny over the Commission, thus holding it accountable. Its role in relation to the EU budget further highlights its importance.[11] Following the Lisbon Treaty, the EP's role was further strengthened so that many of the criticisms levelled at the institutional structure have been addressed.[12] However, there are elements which require further consideration. First, as mentioned above, there are still areas of EU policy which exclude the EP from the law making process or limit its involvement to mere consultation. Although these areas can be described as policy areas which are particularly important to Member States, they are also areas which arguably are also important to EU citizens and should therefore be open to scrutiny at EU level rather than being simply left to intergovernmental decision making.

[11] Mentioning the budget here is not ideal as it has not been mentioned before and nothing else is said. However, sometimes in exams you need to make decisions on where to cut corners to finish in time and this might be a corner that can be cut.

[12] Here you are recognising that the criticisms levelled at the EP have been dealt with a little bit with each treaty and that many of the concerns no longer hold true, thus demonstrating your understanding of how things have developed.

The question of democratic legitimacy has also been posed in relation to participation in parliamentary elections in the EU. Although the EP is directly elected and thus represents the interests of EU citizens, the extent to which it does so can be questioned, given the low (and declining) voter turnout at such elections. The democratic legitimacy of the Union could be enhanced by increased participation but, of course, how to achieve such participation is a rather complex question beyond the scope of this essay.

[13] Your conclusion, dealing with both the role and its development, highlights to the examiner that you have understood and answered the question fully.

The EP's role has developed from a marginal one to an important one and it is likely its area of influence will increase in the future as the scope of EU competence increases. It also seems likely that the ordinary legislative procedure will be extended further into more areas of EU policy making and will in time really be the norm rather than the exception in EU law.[13]

Make your answer stand out

- Add additional references to academic debate. See, for example, Craig, P. (2006) *EU Administrative Law*, Oxford: Oxford University Press or Petersen, J. and Shackleton, M. (2006) *The Institutions of the European Union*, 2nd edn, Oxford: Oxford University Press.
- Expand on the law making procedures to highlight how the EP's power has increased, thus increasing the democratic legitimacy.
- Add a little more detail on the powers of the EP, using more examples such as the EP's concerns over the 2004 proposed Barroso Commission.
- Consider the possible future of the EP in more depth, drawing on recent commentary. Check your lecture notes for details if you have covered this.

 Don't be tempted to . . .

- Say too much about each institution; that is not what the question is asking you.
- Just focus on the EP; you need briefly to consider the other institutions too so as to make sense of the institutional structure as a whole.
- Simply chronologically explain the additional powers given to the EP with each new treaty. You must be more analytical than that.

www.pearsoned.co.uk/lawexpressqa

Go online to access more revision support including additional essay and problem questions with diagram plans, You be the marker questions, and download all diagrams from the book.

The Lisbon Treaty: A long road to an EU constitution?

2

How this topic may come up in exams

The development of the EU through the treaties has long been a popular essay question and a general example is given in the previous chapter. Specific essay questions on the Lisbon Treaty which came into force on 1 December 2009 are now popular. They tend to focus on the extent to which the European Union requires a constitution and the extent to which the treaty is a constitutional document. Other issues often asked about are the democratic legitimacy of the treaty as well as the major changes brought about by the treaty.

■ Before you begin

It's a good idea to consider the following key themes of the Lisbon Treaty before tackling a question on this topic.

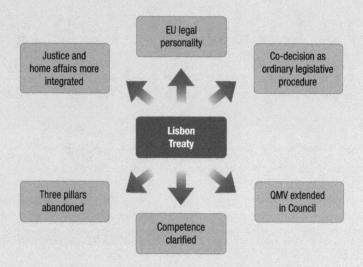

A printable version of this diagram is available from **www.pearsoned.co.uk/lawexpressqa**

 Question 1

The ratification and implementation of the Lisbon Treaty were of vital importance in the development of the EU. Critically evaluate this statement.

Answer plan

→ Give a very brief introduction to EU, focusing on the Lisbon Treaty as the latest treaty.

→ Explain the major changes brought about by the Lisbon Treaty such as:

– Legal personality

– Clarification of competence

– Restructuring of institutions

– The ordinary legislative procedure

– Fundamental rights

– Any others.

→ Discuss the problems with ratification and the implications for the treaty's legitimacy.

→ Conclude that, although it is an important treaty, it is not one without problems.

Diagram plan

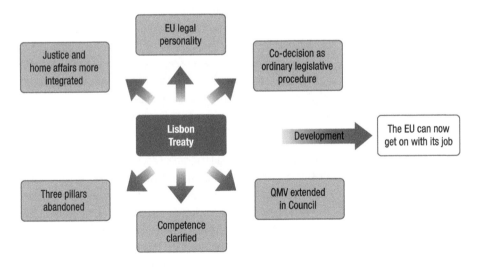

A printable version of this diagram plan is available from **www.pearsoned.co.uk/lawexpressqa**

Answer

[1] This is important because it explains why we still have two treaties and why the Lisbon Treaty itself is completely unreadable as a standalone document.

The Treaty of Lisbon is the latest in a line of treaties amending the legal framework of the European Union (EU). The Lisbon Treaty, like most EU treaties before it, is an amending treaty.[1] The changes brought about can now be found in the Treaty on European Union (TEU) and the Treaty on the Functioning of the European Union (TFEU).

[2] A useful justification for why we needed the treaty in the first place, which shows your understanding of the historical context and development of the EU.

The Treaty of Lisbon was finally to make the changes required for an efficient working of the EU following its significant expansion in 2004 and 2007. The existing structures were simply not set up to cope with now 28 Member States.[2] The Constitutional Treaty should have addressed these issues but following its failure the EU was arguably left in limbo. The first important category of changes to consider is therefore changes made to EU institutional powers as well as law making processes which are designed to ensure the efficient working of an enlarged EU.[3]

[3] Setting out clearly what you are going to consider first and why shows the examiner that you have a clear structure in mind and understand what the question is about.

[4] It is useful to state the change and then comment on it straight away. It helps you to avoid getting too descriptive.

The key change here is the extension of qualified majority voting in the Council, meaning that fewer areas of law require unanimity. While laws are now passed more easily, Member States have lost their veto in areas important to them, causing controversy across the EU.[4] The Lisbon Treaty had originally been intended to reduce the size of the Commission so that only two-thirds of EU members would be represented by a Commissioner at any one time from 2014. However, these proposals were scrapped following negotiations with Ireland during the ratification process. Changes have, however, been made to the institutions, with the European Parliament's position being further strengthened and the European Council being listed as a formal institution.

[5] This is the implication of the change. The next sentence is your comment on that change. Setting out the law or issue, the implication of it and your view on it shows the examiner that you have done more than simply learn the law and that you understand how it works and have an opinion on it.

The extension of European Parliament powers relate mainly to the law making procedures to be used. In most cases now the co-decision process should be used and the Lisbon Treaty renamed it the 'ordinary legislative procedure' to emphasise that point. In so far as most law making is concerned, the European Parliament is therefore put on an equal footing with the Council.[5] This is one step closer to fully addressing the issues concerning the democratic deficit in the EU.

As the Lisbon Treaty abolished the EU's three pillar structure, decisions on justice and home affairs policy are now subject to the co-decision procedure and QMV.⁶ Foreign policy decisions, however, are still to be decided unanimously. Logically, the ECJ now also has full jurisdiction over justice and home affairs for the first time, and, although the UK secured an opt-out in relation to police cooperation and the option to opt in to legislation relating to judicial issues, the ECJ may, in practice, make these exceptions of symbolic value only. The ECJ role in developing legal principles in this area is likely to be significant and expansive.

In order to clarify the limits of EU power the Lisbon Treaty has set out clearly for the first time the distribution of competence. It states in which areas the EU is solely responsible and in which areas competence is shared with Member States.⁷ It also gives Member State parliaments the opportunity to become more involved in EU law making by providing the option of them raising concerns in relation to EU legislation they believe not to conform with the principle of subsidiarity. How well this process works remains to be seen.⁸

Under the Lisbon Treaty, the EU gained a legal personality. The implications are perhaps not of immediate concern to individuals save in one important area. The EU now has the ability to sign up to the European Convention on Human Rights and indeed the Lisbon Treaty foresees that it will do so. This is in addition to the Charter of Fundamental Rights being given full legal status equivalent to that of the treaties.⁹

In summary, therefore, it seems that the Lisbon Treaty went some way to clarifying and simplifying administrative and institutional matters within the EU which allow the more efficient working of it while at the same time continuing to take fundamental rights seriously. Of course it also has its critics, particularly those who argue that it further undermines the sovereignty of Member States.¹⁰

However, it seems that the treaty is of significant importance for the development of the EU.¹¹ The institutional change required following enlargement has now been brought about and governance of the Union has been clarified. It therefore puts the Union in a position from which it should be able simply to get on with the tasks the Member States have entrusted it with. It no longer needs to worry about further widening of the Union as those countries currently in negotiations about membership are likely to be some years off actual accession. It also does not need to worry about deepening the Union. Further integration and expansion of areas of competence seem unlikely, given the difficulties experienced in relation to the Constitutional and Lisbon Treaties. Arguably, then, Lisbon is important because it brings the EU legal framework up to date and puts in place the rules, processes and procedures which should allow it to get on with the job at hand.

✓ Make your answer stand out

- There is a significant amount of academic commentary on the Lisbon Treaty. Consider adding some, for example Craig, P. (2008) The Lisbon Treaty: process, architecture and substance, *EL Rev*, 33, 137.
- Consider the new positions created by the treaty: High Representative of the Union for Foreign Affairs and the European President.
- Set out at the beginning what the aims and objectives of the EU are in your view and then consider throughout the essay the extent to which the Lisbon Treaty has helped reach those aims and objectives. This would pull your argument together more strongly.
- Tie your conclusion more explicitly to the question asked and refer directly back to the statement given.

! Don't be tempted to . . .

- Simply list the changes made by the treaty; you need to consider what this means for the development of the Union.
- Spend a significant amount of time on the history of the EU; the question isn't really about the history generally but more about the contribution of the Lisbon Treaty.
- Compare the Constitutional Treaty and the Lisbon Treaty. That is a different question, and as the CT was never in force it adds nothing to your discussion here.

Question 2

To what extent do we now have a United States of Europe which conforms to a federal structure with the Lisbon Treaty as the Constitution?

Diagram plan

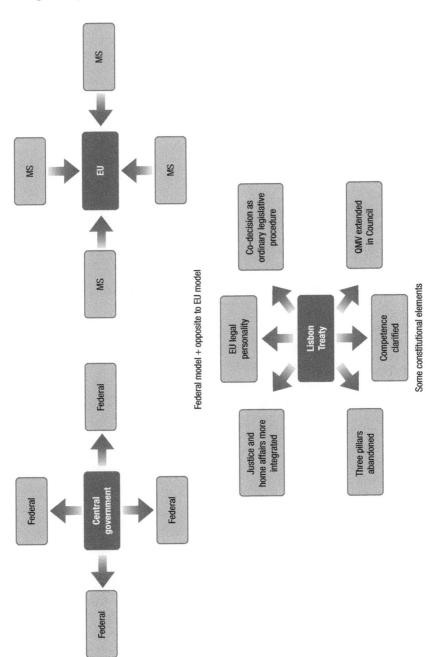

Federal model + opposite to EU model

MS

MS

MS

MS

MS

EU

Federal

Federal

Federal

Federal

Central government

Co-decision as ordinary legislative procedure

QMV extended in Council

EU legal personality

Lisbon Treaty

Competence clarified

Justice and home affairs more integrated

Three pillars abandoned

Some constitutional elements

A printable version of this diagram plan is available from **www.pearsoned.co.uk/lawexpressqa**

Answer plan

➡ Very brief introduction to EU.

➡ Definition of federalism/federalist state.

➡ EU not federal – power to delegate is the wrong way round.

➡ The EU does have some federal features.

➡ Briefly explain the Lisbon Treaty in a constitutional context.

➡ Conclusion: Union with some federalist features. Lisbon as a treaty which has constitutional features?

Answer

The European Union (EU) is the political, economic and monetary union of 28 Member States. Over the years the EU has grown in size and power, consequently various treaties have been signed to work towards an economic, monetary and political union. The most recent treaty is the Lisbon Treaty, which was signed on 13 December 2007 and ratified in December 2009.

[1] If you want to examine the extent to which the EU is a federal state, you need to define what you mean by federalism.

A federal state is one 'that utilizes a central government to represent the common interests of all its civil divisions, but which allows those civil divisions substantial freedom to manage their local affairs.'[1] Some might therefore argue that the EU is indeed moving towards federalism, with the EU institutions forming the central government and the Member States making up the civil divisions. However, a genuinely federal Europe would need to be a politically united Europe to a much greater extent than it is now, and the European institutions would have to be the central reference point for all law and policy making, with power being devolved to the Member States.[2]

[2] It is useful to be clear about what you think from the start. You can expand your argument as you go through.

[3] Notice here that you are not giving one view and then another but you are stating what you think. It makes your argument much more convincing.

Although EU institutions have many federal characteristics, Member States retain key powers which make a European United States unlikely.[3] The Council of Ministers is federal in the sense that it consists of representatives of the Member States who act together to perform their legislative role; they create rules which bind the constituent Member States. However, national interests prevail and the process of policy and law making in the Council remains intergovernmental. While the Commission represents the Union

4 This shows your knowledge is up to date and that you have an understanding of the historical development too. Both are important and should show the examiner that you have engaged with this topic fully.

5 This is a strong statement which you need to explain. It is good to be bold in stating your academic view but make sure you back it up and explain it fully.

6 This sentence states why the EU is not federal in the traditional sense. While that might seem obvious from your explanation before, to highlight your argument and understanding, make sure you make important points, such as this one, explicit.

7 Just because you are stating your argument throughout does not mean you can ignore opposing views of possible contradictions. Your argument has to be based on your understanding of all the issues and factors and this is what you are showing here.

8 A quote can be a useful way of illustrating a point you are making, but do not worry if you struggle to remember the exact words: you can paraphrase.

9 Demonstrating awareness of the political context as well as legal developments shows the examiner that you appreciate that EU law and its development operate in a political context; this shows more detailed engagement.

perspective and interest and has the power to propose legislation, it does so within established limits which are ultimately set by the Member States. It could be argued that the most federal institution of the EU is the European Parliament, which has nearly all powers of a federal house of the citizens and it co-decides with the Council of Ministers. The Treaty of Maastricht introduced a co-decision procedure by which the parliament enjoys an ultimate power of veto over proposed legislation; this power further increased when the Lisbon Treaty came into force by making this procedure the normal legislative procedure.[4]

The Lisbon Treaty clarified areas of competence, setting out clearly where the EU had exclusive competence, shared competence or supporting powers. The provisions relating to competence clearly show that the EU is some way off becoming a truly federal Union.[5] For that to happen, the power of delegation and assigning of competence would have to be reversed. In a federal state, central government would be expected to have the power to define the limits within which the individual units operate. In the EU the separate units define the limits within which the supranational element may operate.[6]

However, it may of course be argued that, in those areas where the EU has exclusive competence in particular, we have a system akin to federalism.[7] Member States have given up their sovereignty and accept Brussels law making in those areas and must then abide by such law under the principle of supremacy of EU law. As the then German Foreign Minister Joschka Fischer stated in the *Financial Times* in 2000: 'We already have a federation. The 11, soon to be 12, Member States adopting the Euro have already given up part of their sovereignty, monetary sovereignty, and formed a monetary union, and that is the first step towards a federation.'[8]

So while there is no United States of Europe, the EU does have elements of a federal system and as an economic, political and social Union must be governed by a set of rules applicable across all Member States. This has been the role of the treaties. Talks in 2001 changed the focus from treaty revision to the creation of a constitution. However, referendums in the Netherlands and France showed clearly that EU citizens did not want a European constitution.[9]

A new treaty was, however, needed and the Lisbon Treaty was drafted. Many argue that regardless of the change in the style and language of the reform treaty to the unsuccessful constitution, the effects of the two documents are identical.[10]

[10] This paragraph gives a very brief overview of the situation leading up to the Lisbon Treaty. If there is time, this could be expanded upon.

The Treaty of Lisbon strengthens the role of the European Parliament, expands the role of national parliaments, amends the political structure of the EU, clarifies areas of competence and sets out a broad legal framework on a great number of issues in a variety of policy fields.[11] It also incorporates the Charter of Fundamental Rights and gives the EU a legal personality. If considered in this way, the treaty, as perhaps the treaties before it, is not dissimilar to a constitutional document. EU citizens and perhaps also EU Member States, however, do not want a constitution. A constitution is seen as something tied to the nation state, giving citizens rights which cannot be taken away and which are of fundamental importance. Allowing the EU to have a constitution therefore, for many, signifies the end of nation states and a complete transfer of sovereignty and power to Brussels. Symbolically it may be one step too far. However, if it is accepted that a constitution is simply a legal framework governing the political structure and fundamental rights and responsibilities applicable in a given area, the Lisbon Treaty is indeed a constitution: a constitution of a unique, possibly quasi-federal Union of Member States.[12]

[11] This summary of the Lisbon Treaty changes limits itself to aspects which might be considered constitutional and thus keeps the focus on the question set.

[12] This conclusion follows on logically from what you have said before, allowing the examiner to see that you have answered the question fully and that your argument has led logically to your conclusion, which is the key to a good essay.

 Make your answer stand out

- Add more detail about changes brought about by the Lisbon Treaty which support federalism: for example, the abolition of the three pillar structure.
- There is a lot of academic commentary on the Lisbon Treaty as well as on the question of the EU as a federal state. Consider references from your lecture notes and textbooks.
- Try to minimise the descriptive elements further and really focus on analysis and commentary.
- Build your argument about the symbolic nature of having a constitution and why the Constitutional Treaty was rejected.

! Don't be tempted to . . .

- Focus solely on the Lisbon Treaty; you need to deal with the idea of a federal Europe too.
- Go through the Lisbon Treaty and the changes it made in detail; you only need to consider issues relevant to the question set.
- Simply compare the Lisbon Treaty and the Constitutional Treaty; the latter is only really relevant as to why it failed.

www.pearsoned.co.uk/lawexpressqa

 Go online to access more revision support including additional essay and problem questions with diagram plans, You be the marker questions, and download all diagrams from the book.

Sources of EU law

How this topic may come up in exams

This topic is mainly examined in essay-style questions although problem questions are also possible. Questions tend to focus on general law making principles and their effectiveness or differences between different types of legislation. You might also get questions considering the law making procedures and so there is sometimes some overlap with questions on the role of the institutions. As the principles in this area are very much linked, try not to see them in isolation but recognise the links between them.

■ Before you begin

It's a good idea to consider the following key themes of sources of EU law before tackling a question on this topic.

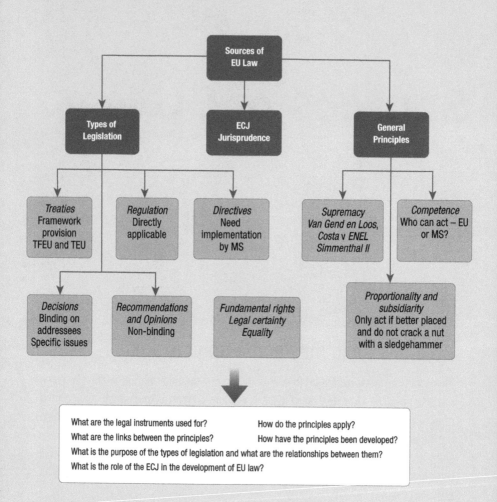

A printable version of this diagram is available from **www.pearsoned.co.uk/lawexpressqa**

 Question 1

Critically assess the effectiveness of the following legal principles:

1   Subsidiarity
2   Proportionality
3   Competence
4   Supremacy of EU law.

Answer plan

→ Identify the four principles as a framework in which law is made.

→ Discuss each principle, defining it first and then considering the effectiveness.

→ Subsidiarity: consider it as a vague principle which is interpreted differently by Member States.

→ Proportionality as a simple concept closely linked to subsidiarity.

→ Competence and supremacy also as simple but linked concepts without which EU law would make little sense.

Diagram plan

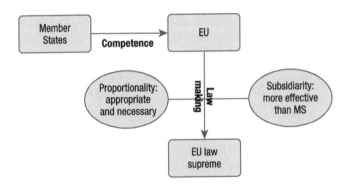

A printable version of this diagram plan is available from **www.pearsoned.co.uk/lawexpressqa**

[1] This introduction sets out clearly what the examiner is to expect and also makes clear from the start that the links between the principles under discussion are important. This shows detailed understanding.

Answer

This essay considers four of the EU's fundamental law making principles and assesses their effectiveness. The principles are discussed in turn but the links between them are important in ensuring their effectiveness and the principles should therefore not be considered in isolation from each other.[1]

[2] It is useful to give a really brief explanation of what the principles mean at the start – it shows you are clear in your mind and it means you can then quickly get on with the analysis.

[3] If you can remember it, quoting a short section from the relevant treaty article helps to make your point succinctly. If you do not have that kind of memory, just say it in your own words. If you are allowed to use a statute book in the exam, it could be useful for this sort of thing.

[4] Using case law examples is a good way of illustrating the effectiveness of principles as well as the way problems arise in practice. It also shows that your knowledge extends further than merely defining the principles.

[5] It is OK to refer the examiner to a later section rather than repeat information. In fact it shows you have your answer planned out from the start.

[6] Here you can explicitly show off your knowledge of the links and interaction between the principles.

The principle of subsidiarity proposes to ensure that law making decisions are taken as closely as possible to the citizens (Article 5 TEU). Actions should not be taken at Union level unless it is more effective than actions taken at national, regional or local levels.[2] Proportionality supports subsidiarity by stating that 'any action of the community shall not go beyond what is necessary to achieve the objectives of the treaty' (Article 5 TEU).[3] Initially there was little guidance on the application of either principle but the Treaty of Amsterdam introduced the Protocol on the Application of the Principles of Subsidiarity and Proportionality which requires each proposed piece of legislation to state how it complies with the principles. The ratification of the Lisbon Treaty has further boosted subsidiarity and proportionality because it provides for the involvement of national parliaments in the legislative process, allowing them to state their view on whether the principles have been upheld.

The case law also suggests that subsidiarity and proportionality are important concepts in EU law. In *FEDESA* (1990)[4] the ECJ held the least burdensome measure must be selected where there are several appropriate options, and *Bouchereau* (1977) confirmed that any penalty must be proportionate to the gravity of the offence. *Man (Sugar)* (1985) is a further example of the application of the principle where the loss of an entire deposit under an EU regulation because of a four-hour delay in applying for a licence was not proportionate. The principles seem on the face of it effective, in particular proportionality is used extensively by the ECJ to curb Member States' powers in applying EU law (see, for example, the free movement of goods cases such as *Rau* (1982)). However, there are problems in relation to the principles and we will return to them shortly.[5]

The distribution of the law making powers between the European Union and its Member States relies on the distinction between the different types of competences. Exclusive competence permits the European Union to make legislation and decisions regarding certain areas on its own; the Member States cannot interfere with these affairs. Toth (1992) notes that 'where the competence of the community begins, that of the member state ends'. Exclusive competence allows important EU measures to be dealt with across the Union and allows the EU to legislate on matters where it is better placed to do so. However, where exclusive competence applies, the principles of subsidiarity and proportionality become meaningless and ineffective:[6] '. . . subsidiarity and proportionality perform poorly as devices for restraining the political instinct to exercise a competence once granted' (Weatherill,

2005). While the EU must, of course, respect the limits of the powers conferred on it by its treaty, once competence has been granted there appears to be little consideration of whether a proposed measure complies with subsidiarity or proportionality. There is not yet any evidence of major change following the Lisbon Treaty and the greater involvement of national parliaments in the legislative process.[7]

On the other hand, the more common form of competence is shared competence, where both the EU and Member States have the power to make law. Shared competence enables legislation and decisions to be tailored to suit each Member State, taking into account its individual circumstances, history and culture. The principle of subsidiarity has a much clearer role in such cases as it will be the application of the principle which determines whether or not the EU is to act.

The final principle which we will examine is the legal doctrine of Supremacy of EU law, which means that European law will always prevail and will always take precedence over any national law as evident in the case of *Internationale Handelsgesellschaft* (1970): '. . . the law born from the Treaty, the issue of an autonomous source, could not, by its very nature, have the courts opposing to it rules of national law of any nature.' In *Van Gend en Loos* (1963) the ECJ stated '. . . the Community constitutes a new legal order of international law for the benefit of which the states have limited their sovereign rights . . .' and in the case of *Costa v ENEL* (1964) the ECJ expressed with regards to the treaty: '. . . has created its own legal system which . . . became an integral part of the legal systems of the member states and which their courts are bound to apply.'[8] The case law clearly sets out that all Member States are obliged to apply EU law in full. The development of the doctrine of direct effect by the ECJ (*Van Gend en Loos*) as well as indirect effect (*Von Colson* (1984), *Marleasing* (1991)) and state liability (*Francovich* (1991)) add further strength to the notion that EU law must be supreme and accessible to citizens of Member States.[9]

As should be evident from the preceding discussion, the principles examined are inextricably linked to one another, and logically so. Member States agreed to give up some of their sovereignty to the EU, and, in those areas where it does so and confers competence to the EU, it is only logical that EU law should be supreme, otherwise there would be little point in transferring competence in the first place. However, in order to protect Member States' interests, it is also important to consider the limitations on EU power to make law, and the principles of proportionality and subsidiarity provide a framework in which those limitations can be considered. However, these principles are not always as effective as perhaps they could be. Both are open to different interpretations. In relation to subsidiarity, it is for example unclear who decides whether the EU or Member States are best placed to legislate (Ward, 2009). The principle of proportionality leaves room for argument as to what is appropriate and necessary in any given case.

[10] In this conclusion you are reiterating the point you made at the beginning, showing how your argument has followed logically and that you have done what you set out to do. This demonstrates your ability to think coherently.

The most effective principle of the four discussed here is the supremacy of EU law. It has been developed through the case law of the ECJ and is supported by other doctrines such as direct and indirect effect and state liability. It is now one of the most well established and probably most controversial principles of EU law. Overall, however, it is the interaction of all four principles which creates a framework in which EU law making can take place and in which it can also be evaluated.[10]

✓ Make your answer stand out

- Include references to academic debate; see, for example, Dani, M. (2009) Constitutionalism and Dissonances – Has Europe Paid Off its Debt with Functionalism?, *European Law Journal*, *25*, 324–50.
- You could change the order and start with competence as that is the logical starting point – you do not have to stick to the order set in the question.
- You could add further case examples, for instance in relation to competence disputes.
- Spend more time considering the interplay between the principles. Ask yourself how each one would operate in isolation and then draw out the added value of seeing them all together. This would highlight a really comprehensive understanding.

! Don't be tempted to . . .

- Merely describe each principle in turn; you need to focus on effectiveness.
- Focus on the principle you know most about and ignore the others – you should talk about all four.
- Describe in detail the protocols, the case law or other measures setting out the principles – focus on their use.

 Question 2

EU Law is supreme because the ECJ decided it should be. Critically examine this statement.

Answer plan

→ Explain what supremacy of EU law means.

→ Discuss the case law which developed supremacy into a legal principle: *Van Gend en Loos*; *Costa* v *ENEL*; *Internationale Handelsgesellschaft*; *Simmenthal II*.

→ Outline the treaty provisions relating to supremacy.

→ Evaluate the contribution made by the ECJ based on the discussion above and state whether you agree or disagree with the statement.

Diagram plan

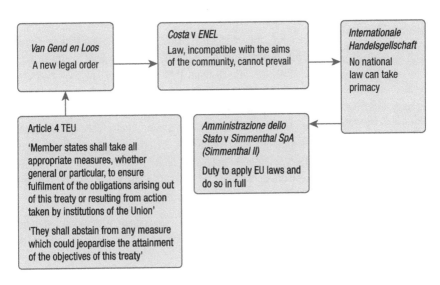

A printable version of this diagram plan is available from **www.pearsoned.co.uk/lawexpressqa**

Answer

The doctrine of supremacy of EU law was not something initially laid down in the treaties. There was little to suggest that Member States were signing up to anything other than an, albeit detailed and comprehensive, international treaty. However, the creation of the European Court of Justice (ECJ), with its powers to guide on the interpretation of EU law, ensured that EU law soon developed into a distinct legal order (see **Van Gend en Loos** (1963)). There were to be certain seminal cases which established clearly the supremacy of EU law over the laws of Member States.[1]

Van Gend en Loos was the first. The ruling in this case stated that national courts had limited their sovereignty by joining the EU in the fields included in the treaty and that individuals could enforce their then Community law rights in their national courts, even in the face of conflicting national law.[2] The ECJ held that the Community constituted a new legal order. This legal order applied not only to the Member States but also to the citizens of those Member States. The concept of enforceable rights conferred by the treaties upon individuals is now known as the principle of direct applicability.

In 1964, the court built further on its decision in **Van Gend en Loos** by clarifying the principle of supremacy.[3] In **Costa v ENEL** (1964), the ECJ decided that Community law took precedence over national law whether the law had been passed before or after the provisions of the Community law. It stated: 'The transfer, by Member States, from their national orders in favour of the Community order of their rights and obligations arising from the Treaty, carries with it a clear limitation of their sovereign right upon which a subsequent unilateral law, incompatible with the aims of the Community, cannot prevail.'[4]

The ECJ concluded that if EU law could be varied in deference to Member State law, the attainment of the objectives of the treaty would be under threat.

The principle of supremacy is now one of the most entrenched aspects of EU law (see Eleftheriadis, 1998; Ward, 2009) and its development is a clear example of the court's dynamic approach to interpreting the treaties. In **Internationale Handelsgesellschaft** (1970) the ECJ clarified the point alluded to in **Costa** and stated that 'the law born from the Treaty [cannot] have the courts opposing to it rules of national law of any nature whatsoever . . .'. In other words, no element of national law, no matter how fundamental, could take

[1] This introduction not only indicates how you are going to answer the question but also sets out your point of view early on. You are making clear you understand the question and how to answer it.

[2] A succinct summary of each of the key cases is useful here as it sets out clearly how influential the ECJ was and allows you to focus on analysis later.

[3] This sentence makes clear that the ECJ built on existing case law and pushed the boundaries a little further with each case.

[4] This essay uses a number of quotes from the case law. They illustrate the points made but remembering the quotes can be difficult in exams, so, if this is not something that comes easily to you, focus on remembering the principles rather than the exact wording.

[5] As well as taking the cases in chronological order, you are also using them to illustrate how the idea of primacy of EU law developed incrementally and in some ways logically.

primacy over any element of Community law, irrespective of how minor that might be.[5]

Matters were taken even further again by **Simmenthal II** (1978), where the Court of Justice ruled that any national court when called upon to apply the provisions of Community law must do so and must do so in full. It neatly summed up the essence of supremacy of EU law when it stated:

> Every national court must, in a case within its jurisdiction, apply Community law in its entirety and protect rights which the latter confers on individuals and must accordingly set aside any provision of national law which may conflict with it, whether prior or subsequent to the Community rule.

These cases demonstrate how the ECJ envisaged the new legal order created by the treaties. It clearly saw it as an independent legal system, the laws of which were to take precedence over national laws and were to be applied in full. The supremacy of EU law has been restated in numerous cases and has also found expression in national case law. In the UK, for example, Laws LJ in **Thoburn v Sunderland City Council** (2002) commented that 'the specific rights and obligations which European law creates are incorporated into our domestic law and rank supreme'.[6]

[6] Cases from the national context can really help illustrate how EU law works and that you have understood the EU legal provisions you are considering in the national context in which they operate.

[7] It is useful to consider how the doctrine of supremacy of EU law is supported by the other general principles of EU law, and the ones mentioned here clearly help reinforce the idea of a separate legal order which takes precedence, so an explanation of them is important.

The supremacy of EU law is further supported by the doctrines of direct applicability, direct effect, indirect effect and state liability (Ward, 2009).[7] Direct applicability provides that certain EU legal measures apply automatically in the Member States. In the UK this happens by virtue of the European Communities Act 1972 (as amended). Treaties and regulations therefore apply in full and without any further action by Member States, reinforcing the fact that EU law is supreme. Direct effect allows citizens of the EU to rely on their EU law rights directly in certain circumstances, when the measure is directly applicable (**Van Gend en Loos**) or, in the case of directives, where certain conditions are fulfilled (**Van Duyn** (1974)). Indirect effect, as a principle of interpretation, stipulates that all national law must be interpreted in line with EU provisions wherever possible (**Von Colson** (1984), **Marleasing** (1991)); indirect effect therefore gives expression to supremacy of EU law in the tools of interpretation used in Member States.[8]

[8] Keep the focus on supremacy in your answer because that is what the questions asks. However, considering the other key principles in this way shows that you have a full understanding of how they all fit together and support each other.

The **Factortame** cases further built upon the principle laid down in the **Simmenthal II** case, stating that all provisions of EU law must be enacted as efficiently as possible and that national law must be suspended where it is incompatible with Community law. The cases also built on the idea that citizens were important actors in the new legal order by allowing actions for damages against Member States as in **Francovich** (1991) and **Factortame III** (1996). State liability, then, is the final piece in the puzzle representing the supremacy of EU law over national law and the uniform and consistent application of such law across Member States. Such application is, of course, aided by the preliminary reference procedure under Article 267 TFEU.[9]

[9] Here you are acknowledging that EU law and its operation is complex and it's the coming together of a number of principles and processes which ensures consistent application of supreme EU law. This demonstrates your full understanding on the subject.

The doctrine of supremacy of EU law has been developed almost exclusively by the case law of the ECJ.[10] There were suggestions that Article 10 EC hinted at a Member State obligation to apply EU law in full, and over and above their national provisions. It refers to Member States 'taking all appropriate measures . . . to ensure fulfilment of the obligations arising out of this Treaty' as well as to 'abstaining from any measure which could jeopardise the attainment of the objectives of this Treaty'. However, the treaties did not contain an explicit statement as to the supremacy. This changed with the ratification of the Lisbon Treaty. An Annex to the treaty contains a declaration to the effect that EU law has primacy over national law (Declaration 17). Interestingly, the failed Constitutional Treaty contained such a statement in the body of the treaty lending it the full force of EU law (Articles 1–6).[11] The Lisbon Treaty Annex is merely a political statement and as such its legal force is unclear. Given the ECJ jurisprudence, however, it seems unlikely that there is any doubt over the application of the doctrine and indeed seems merely to codify what the ECJ has clearly established.

[10] Now return more directly to the question set, that is the ECJ's role in the development of the principle.

[11] If you happen to remember the old Article of the Constitutional Treaty, this is an added bonus but most examiners would not expect you to.

In conclusion, it is clear that the doctrine of supremacy of EU law is one which has been developed by the ECJ, and without the court's involvement it is likely that the doctrine would have developed at a much slower pace and in the face of much stronger opposition.[12]

[12] Your conclusion should refer back to the question set directly. To make that even more clear, you could even use the same wording as used in the question but the point is sufficiently clear in this case.

Make your answer stand out

- State more clearly the importance of indirect effect and state liability, in particular as a tool of interpretation which seeks to preserve primacy of EU law. Note in particular the role of the ECJ in developing these principles.
- Explain further why the ECJ took it upon itself to develop the principle.
- Speculate in more detail on whether or not the principle would have developed without the ECJ's impetus.
- Further academic commentary, such as De Witte, B. (1999) Direct Effect, Supremacy and the Nature of the Legal Order, in P. Craig and G. De Burca (eds) *The Evolution of EU Law*, Oxford: Oxford University Press, and Lenaerts, K. and Courthaut, T. (2006) Of Birds and Hedges: The Role of Primacy in Invoking Norms of EU Law, *EL Rev*, 31, 287, would strengthen the answer further.

! Don't be tempted to . . .

- State facts of the cases you mention: they are totally irrelevant here.
- Merely explain what supremacy means – you need to focus on the ECJ's role in developing the doctrine.
- List every case you can think of where supremacy has been at issue – focus on the key cases which established the principle.

Question 3

Critically assess the different types of secondary legislation in EU Law.

Answer plan

→ List the different types of secondary legislation and briefly explain their use.

→ Explain the advantages and disadvantages of each.

→ Comment on why different types are necessary.

→ Comment on whether the current system as a whole is satisfactory.

Diagram plan

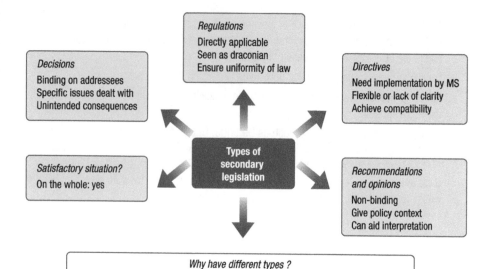

Regulations
Directly applicable
Seen as draconian
Ensure uniformity of law

Decisions
Binding on addressees
Specific issues dealt with
Unintended consequences

Directives
Need implementation by MS
Flexible or lack of clarity
Achieve compatibility

Types of secondary legislation

Satisfactory situation?
On the whole: yes

Recommendations and opinions
Non-binding
Give policy context
Can aid interpretation

Why have different types ?
Fulfil different objectives: enforce important EU measures, ensure EU policy is followed, highlight EU policy, highlight the position of an EU institution, communicate an administrative or executive decision, allow flexibility for MS, recognise diversity in MS or deal with specific situations

A printable version of this diagram plan is available from **www.pearsoned.co.uk/lawexpressqa**

Answer

[1] Starting an essay with a quote from the relevant provision indicates that you are clear in your mind about what the question is asking you to do. The introduction then sets out what you intend to cover in your answer.

[2] It is useful to spell out that EU secondary legislation pads out the framework created by the treaties – you are showing that you understand the role of the provisions you are going to discuss.

'To exercise the Union's competences, the institutions shall adopt regulations, directives, decisions, recommendations and opinions' (Article 288 TFEU).[1] This essay considers these types of legislative acts and their importance within the EU legal order. Following a brief description of each of the types of secondary legislation, this essay considers their characteristics and their advantages and disadvantages.

Secondary legislation acts as supporting legislation to the treaties and fleshes out the details necessary for the functioning of EU law.[2] The treaties provide a framework in which this secondary legislation operates. The different types of secondary legislation have different functions and characteristics. Regulations are legislative acts which have automatic and immediate effect in all Member States once implemented. They are used in areas where the uniformity of law across the Member States is imperative. Directives are a type of secondary legislation which allow Member States some degree of flexibility in relation to the exact implementation of a legal measure. Directives are binding on (generally) all Member States as to the outcome to be achieved. Decisions are legislative acts relating to a particular issue and usually addressed to a fairly narrowly defined group. The decision is binding in its entirety on all those to whom it has been addressed. Recommendations and opinions are, as their names suggest, not binding in law although they may, of course, be persuasive and some may form the basis of proposals for binding secondary legislation.[3]

[3] This whole paragraph provides an overview of the secondary legislation you intend to discuss, and by doing this you demonstrate that you appreciate the different types and their key characteristics.

There is no official hierarchy of secondary legislation although it is useful to think of them as a continuum from 'most binding' to not binding.[4] Regulations are, from a Member States' point of view, the most severe type of legislation the EU can use (Ward, 2009). They are binding on all Member States and they are binding in their entirety. They are therefore directly applicable, meaning that once they have been passed they become law in all Member States, in the UK by virtue of the European Communities Act 1972 (as amended).[5] Regulations are an important way of ensuring uniformity of EU law across Member States. In areas which are considered fundamental, regulations ensure that the law across the Union is not only similar but identical (although this, of course, does not ensure uniform application of the legal provisions) and that the law retains its EU character (***Commission v Italy*** (1973)).[6] Regulation 1612/68, for example, ensures that migrant workers have exactly the same rights regardless of which Member State they choose to work in and that these rights are clearly identifiable as EU law rights.

[4] This sentence leads nicely into a more detailed discussion of each of the types and also indicates that you understand that no one type is more important than the others.

[5] It is worth mentioning how regulations become law in your Member State – it shows you understand the relationship between national and EU law.

[6] Where you can, give one or two examples from case law that has considered the characteristics of the type of legislation you are discussing or indeed an example of such legislation as follows here.

Directives allow greater flexibility. Member States are required to achieve a certain policy objective, a result, but the means by which they achieve that result is up to them. It must, however, be a legally binding and enforceable measure (see ***Commission v Belgium*** (1986)). Directives do not make the law in the Member States the same but they do make it compatible and they ensure the policy goals of the Union are met in all Member States. Directives allow Member States the flexibility to take into account their own history, culture or tradition in areas affected by directives and are less draconian, less of 'Brussels imposing its will'. However, directives also provide less certainty and on occasion the Member States may be left trying to second guess exactly what the policy objective was and whether or not they have achieved it. Directives also require the Member States to be active and actually implement legal measures to achieve the directive's objective. In some cases this may not happen for a variety of reasons, such as lack of parliamentary time or strong national opposition.

There has been some debate as to whether a very detailed directive is in fact a directive or whether it is actually a regulation. In **Enka** (1977) the ECJ held that even though the directive contained some very precise requirements, this did not stop it from genuinely being a directive. Uniformity, it was held, was essential in the area concerned. Arguably, then, a regulation may have been more appropriate.[7]

[7] Don't be shy; state your opinion. It seems that in the case of very detailed directives the boundary between directives and regulations becomes blurred and it is worth highlighting this.

Decisions relate to specific matters and are a way of ensuring that EU law and legal measures are enforced and implemented across Member States and their institutions. Because decisions are binding on those they are addressed to, they can deal with very specific and sometimes complex or technical issues which would not apply in a more general context. They can deal with specific issues arising out of specific circumstances. However, this narrow focus can also be a disadvantage, not considering the wider implications, desired or accidental, of the decision. A useful example of a decision is a Commission decision granting exemptions from the application of competition law rules.[8]

[8] Giving examples of the types of secondary legislation makes your answer less abstract and more interesting. It also shows you really do understand the topic.

Recommendations and opinions form useful policy tools which can be used to highlight areas in need of policy development or reform. They can clarify an institution's standpoint on an issue and might then form the basis of legislative proposals. However, they have no legally binding force; they are, just as their names suggest, mere recommendations and opinions which can be discarded or ignored by the other institutions. Nonetheless, they do provide an insight into the policy objectives or goals and the considerations taken into account by the EU institutions and therefore may be useful as an aid to interpretation of the binding secondary legislation.[9] Recommendations and opinions often offer a viewpoint on a particular course of conduct. A useful example of an opinion may be a reasoned opinion under Article 226 EC. Recommendations and opinions[10] as soft law

[9] By adding your assessment of the non-legally binding measures, you are showing that you appreciate that policy and soft law can play an important part in the EU legal order. Students often miss this.

[10] As the two non-binding types of secondary legislation, it is fine to deal with recommendations and opinions together – especially given time constraints in exams.

instruments can be subject to annulment proceedings under Article 230 EC (**Grimaldi** (1989)) and preliminary references as they are acts of the institutions of the Community with Article 234(b).

The different types of EU secondary legislation allow the provisions of the treaty to be elaborated in the way most appropriate to the policy context and further allows the EU character of some fundamental areas of law to be maintained while at the same time recognising the diversity in Member States' history, culture and national legal systems in other areas. The different types of legislation fulfil different roles and aim to achieve slightly different objectives and overall seem to do so well.[11]

[11] The conclusion pulls the previous material together and comments on the overall situation. Make sure it states an opinion explicitly rather than sitting on the fence. Be confident in your opinion.

✔ Make your answer stand out

■ References to academic commentary. See, for example, Craig, P. and De Burca, G. (2011) *EU Law, Text Cases and Materials*, 5th edn, Oxford: Oxford University Press, Chapter 3.

■ This question leads to quite a descriptive answer – comment on the advantages and disadvantages as well as the overall situation as much as possible.

■ Speculate on potential problems if we only had one type of secondary legislation – for example, only regulations or only directives.

■ Discuss in more depth the sorts of issues different types are used for and use specific examples if you can think of some.

! Don't be tempted to . . .

■ Simply explain each of the types of secondary legislation.

■ List examples of each of the types – use one or two to illustrate your point.

■ Spend much time on talking about the treaties – the question is about secondary legislation.

www.pearsoned.co.uk/lawexpressqa

 Go online to access more revision support including additional essay and problem questions with diagram plans, You be the marker questions, and download all diagrams from the book.

Article 267 TFEU: The preliminary reference procedure

4

How this topic may come up in exams

The preliminary reference procedure is an important aspect of EU procedural law and is therefore a popular topic for examinations. It is also important to understand how this procedure works and what its aims are as this goes to the heart of judicial application of EU law in the Member States. Both problem and essay questions are possible. The former tend to focus on providing advice as to whether or not a reference should be made or at what point it should be made; the latter often ask for an overall assessment of the purpose of the procedure and its effectiveness.

■ Before you begin

It's a good idea to consider the following key themes of Article 267 TFEU, the preliminary reference procedure, before tackling a question on this topic.

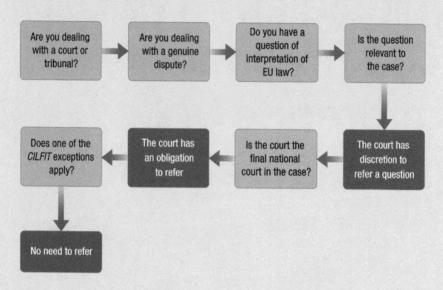

A printable version of this diagram is available from **www.pearsoned.co.uk/lawexpressqa**

Question 1

Critically assess the following statement: The preliminary reference procedure under Article 267 TFEU is of crucial importance for the consistent application of EU law across Member States.

Diagram plan

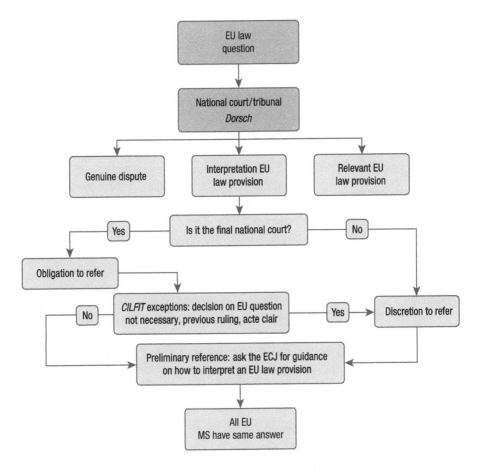

A printable version of this diagram plan is available from **www.pearsoned.co.uk/lawexpressqa**

Answer plan

→ Explain the preliminary reference procedure.

→ Highlight the issues it raises:

- Discretion to refer
- Obligations to refer
- *CILFIT* exceptions.

→ Comment on its effectiveness in ensuring consistent application.

Answer

[1] Remember this point. Students stating that individuals bring their cases to the ECJ is one of the most complained about issues among EU law teachers.

[2] By restating the problem you are going to deal with from a slightly different angle, you are showing that you have understood the question.

[3] You are again showing your clear understanding by reiterating the purpose of the procedure you are asked to evaluate.

[4] A short explanation which then allows you to go on and focus on the issues raised by the procedure – which is far more interesting.

[5] Use one or maybe two case illustrations to make your point. No more than that – it's about quality not quantity of references to case law.

Individuals do not go before the European Court of Justice to enforce their EU law rights.[1] Instead, they do this before their national courts. However, giving national courts the power to rule on matters of EU law is potentially problematic as there is then no way of ensuring that EU law is interpreted and applied in the same way across Member States.[2] In addition, national courts may need to ask for clarification of EU law matters or the compatibility of national law with EU law. The ECJ therefore has a role in assisting national courts in the interpretation of EU law and to do so has the power to hear preliminary references from national courts (Article 267 TFEU).[3]

The preliminary rulings procedure is a mechanism that allows any national court to refer a question of EU law to the ECJ and ask them for interpretative guidance. The ECJ does not rule for or against the parties: in other words, it does not apply the law to the facts; it simply interprets the law and answers the questions referred. The national courts must then apply the law and the ECJ's guidance to the factual situation before them.[4]

There are a number of issues arising out of the procedure, mainly concerned with when and what sort of questions are to be referred. First, there must be a genuine dispute. If there is not, the ECJ will refuse to accept the reference. The **Foglia** (1981) cases are a useful illustration of the need for a genuine dispute. In these cases the ECJ confirmed that it was not its job to give general abstract guidance but to contribute to real cases.[5]

The ECJ will refuse a preliminary ruling if the question referred to them by the national court is hypothetical, irrelevant or unclear. In other words, the question must be a genuine question relating to the case and not just an interesting aside that arises from the facts (**Meilicke** (2007)). It must be relevant in the sense that it must be important to the national courts' ability to decide the case. Relevance is determined by the national court making the referral (**Dzodzi** (1990)). Finally, the question put by the national court must be precisely and clearly phrased (**Telemarsicabruzzo** (1993)). If it is not clear what the Member State is asking and what point of EU law requires examination and clarification, the ECJ cannot offer interpretative guidance and thus a preliminary ruling will be refused. Given that the purpose of the preliminary reference procedure is to ensure the coherence of EU law, these restrictions make sense as in each case the coherence and uniform application of EU law is not under threat.[6]

[6] Don't simply list the conditions which give rise to a discretion to refer, but comment on them – in this case the paragraph explains why it makes sense to impose certain conditions rather than accepting any old reference.

[7] You are acknowledging a further condition here – the fact that the referring body must be a court or tribunal. If you have the time, this could be expanded on.

Once it is established that an institution is a court within Article 267 TFEU (see **Dorsch** (1997)),[7] it must be considered whether the preliminary reference procedure offers the opportunity to refer or places the court under an obligation to refer. The general rule is that any national court may bring an action. The lower courts therefore have discretion as to whether they refer a question or not on the basis that an appeal can be made where a referral should have been made. However, where a question of validity of EU law arises, this must be referred. In addition, in certain situations the court or tribunal will find itself under an obligation to refer. This applies to the highest court in the Member State for that particular case at issue. Therefore, the highest court may not necessarily be the highest court in a Member State if there is, for example, no right to appeal to that highest court.[8]

[8] This paragraph simply explains the usual discretion to refer as well as the fact that the highest court must refer, but it does so clearly and logically, which is what you should be aiming for.

[9] You have just outlined the obligation, so now turn to the exceptions so as to maintain a logical argument.

There are some exceptions to this obligation.[9] If there is a previous ruling on the same question, there is no need to refer although a reference can still be made (**Da Costa** (1963), **CILFIT** (1982)).[10] This seems to suggest a development of a doctrine of precedent in which earlier decisions of the ECJ bind the national courts. It is, however, important to remember that national rules of precedent have no bearing on the discretion or obligation to refer.[11] In other words, if the Supreme Court has ruled on an interpretation of EU law, a lower

[10] Again, use one or two case examples to make your point. You do not need to say anything about these cases, but you should refer to them to show that you are aware of them.

[11] This is a point often forgotten by students in common law jurisdiction where precedent is so vital to the way the national legal system functions, so it is worth stating this explicitly.

court can still make a reference; and if in the circumstance the lower court is the final appellate court, it will indeed be obliged to do so.

[12] Here you have moved on to the second exception – acte clair which is explained quickly and commented on straight away, highlighting your analytical skills.

If the answer is obvious under the doctrine of the acte clair (**CILFIT v Ministero della Sanità** (1982)), there is also no requirement to refer the question. However, the criteria of acte clair set out in **CILFIT** should be relatively difficult to satisfy because they require significant linguistic expertise and knowledge of European law by the national courts (see Tridimas, 2003).[12]

[13] Here you are beginning to make the real analytical comments. Without this kind of discussion, you cannot fully answer the question.

The preliminary rulings procedure has been defined as an organic connection between the national courts and the European Court of Justice (Shaw, 2000) and has been said to be essential for the preservation of the Community character of the law and has the object of ensuring that in all circumstances the law is the same in all states (**Rheinmühlen-Düsseldorf** (1974)).[13] It began as a horizontal relationship based on cooperation but arguably has developed into something rather more hierarchical. The fact that even final appellate courts are not obliged to refer matters of EU Law where there is a previous ECJ decision that can be applied suggests that the ECJ strongly encourages reliance on previous decisions even if the facts are not identical. Rather than acting as a sort of specialist partner providing each court with guidance on particular issues, the ECJ now behaves more like a superior court in the traditional sense.[14] However, given the ECJ's caseload, this makes some sense. It seems unnecessary for the ECJ to provide a preliminary ruling on a topic which it has previously ruled on, especially if that earlier ruling is recent. It is, however, important to retain the national court's discretion to ask for further clarification or pose a question which gives the ECJ the opportunity to depart from its earlier ruling.[15]

[14] Acknowledging this fact highlights your understanding of how this works in practice.

[15] Again, this is an important point often missed. The ECJ is not bound by its rulings, so, if something no longer seems to make sense, the ECJ may be grateful for the opportunity to revisit an earlier decision.

[16] Here's the answer to the question set with a small caveat which follows. Always make sure that you answer the question that was set explicitly.

Overall, the preliminary reference procedure is an important tool in ensuring that EU law is applied consistently in Member States, because it provides a connection between the national courts and the EU which can be accessed with relative efficiency and which ensures that questions of interpretation of EU law are not ultimately left to the whims of national judges.[16] However, this outcome is not guaranteed, especially where the **CILFIT** exceptions are applied broadly.

Make your answer stand out

- The first part of the essay is still quite descriptive; make sure you comment on each of the features of the preliminary reference procedure.
- Add more detail on the *CILFIT* exceptions and in particular acte clair to show you fully understand how the law here operates.
- Give some examples of inconsistent application of EU law or different application in different Member States to highlight importance of preliminary references.
- Make further reference to academic commentary. See, for example, the discussion in Craig, P. and De Burca, G. (2011) *EU Law. Text Cases and Materials*, 5th edn, Oxford: Oxford University Press, Chapter 13.

! Don't be tempted to . . .

- Simply describe the procedure in minute detail.
- Give lots of case examples: they are not necessary. Instead, use one or two to fully explore and illustrate your point.
- Provide facts of the cases: they are not relevant here; you are just citing your authority.
- Comment in detail on all aspects of the preliminary rulings procedure: focus your answer on its importance for ensuring consistent application of EU Law.

Question 2

The doctrine of acte clair allows Member States to avoid their obligations to ensure the consistent application of EU law. To what extent do you agree with that statement?

Answer plan

→ Explain what acte clair means.

→ Explain the criteria set out in *CILFIT*.

→ Explain how the ECJ guides interpretation of EU law.

→ Comment on the application of the criteria by national courts.

→ Comment on the impact of this application on the preliminary reference procedure.

→ Conclude stating the extent to which you agree with the statement.

Diagram plan

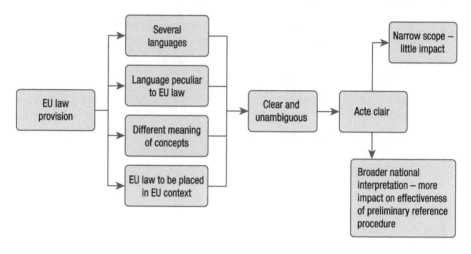

A printable version of this diagram plan is available from **www.pearsoned.co.uk/lawexpressqa**

Answer

The doctrine of acte clair refers to a situation where a national court is faced with a question of interpretation of EU law. In relation to courts with a discretion to refer it can act as guidance as to whether or not a referral is necessary and in relation to cases where there is an obligation to refer, the doctrine provides an exception to that obligation. Acte clair refers to a situation where an EU law provision is clear. The meaning of clear in this context has been examined by the ECJ. This essay firstly sets out the doctrine of acte clair and its conditions before examining the impact it has had on the uniform application of EU law across the Member States.[1]

[1] In this introduction we have explained what the doctrine is and how you are going to answer the question; straight away you have confirmed you are in control of the question.

In **CILFIT v Ministero della Sanità** (1982) the ECJ set out criteria for acte clair.[2] The matter in question must be clear to the national court and equally obvious to other national courts. In deciding whether this is the case, the national court must bear in mind that Community law is drafted in several languages; that Community law uses terminology that is peculiar to it; that legal concepts do not necessarily have the same meaning in Community law and the law of the various Member States; and that Community law must be placed in its context. If these conditions are met, the provision is acte clair and there is no need to refer the question for a preliminary ruling.[3]

[2] It is important to state the legal basis for the criteria of acte clair early on, so here we have started with it.

[3] Although this is quite descriptive, it is necessary to set this out – the analysis comes later.

In the English context, Bingham J (as he then was) pointed out that the ECJ is better placed to interpret EU law, given that it can make comparisons between EU legal texts in different language versions, has a panoramic view of the EU and its institutions and possesses detailed knowledge of EU legislation (**Samex**). As Master of the Rolls, he again referred to the ECJ's advantages in interpreting EU law and concluded that 'if the national court has any real doubt, it should ordinarily refer' (**ex parte *Else*** (1983)).[4]

Considering the **CILFIT** criteria for acte clair more closely, it seems clear that the ECJ intended them to apply in fairly narrow circumstances (see Tridimas, 2003).[5] They require a national court to have a broad overview of EU law and its application not only in their own Member States but also in others. The criteria also seems to demand a high level and sophisticated linguistic ability on the part of the national court to allow them to assess whether or not the meaning of the provision in questions is equally clear in other jurisdictions. **CILFIT** then defined the scope of this exception to the obligation to refer a question narrowly and in most cases a preliminary ruling should be necessary. **CILFIT** has been heavily criticised over the years as unworkable, and, given that the EU now has 27 Member States with 23 official languages, those criticisms are only strengthened.[6] However, the ECJ has reaffirmed the **CILFIT** line of reasoning in a number of more recent cases (**Lyckeskog** (2007), **Köbler** (2003)).

Viewed in this way, the doctrine of acte clair should have little impact on the uniform and consistent application of EU law across all Member States (see Craig and De Burca 2011).[7] It should be a useful doctrine which avoids the need for a preliminary ruling in cases where the outcome of such a ruling is obvious and clear from the outset. It is, in other words, a way of avoiding burdening the ECJ with cases where its input and guidance are actually not required. The exception makes sense in the light of the preliminary reference procedures' aims.[8] If it is to ensure that the application and interpretation of EU law is consistent in all Member States, then a provision which really is clear and unambiguous in the national as well as wider EU context does not need to be referred. Its interpretation and application does not in any way threaten the coherence of EU law and nothing is to be gained from the ECJ confirming an interpretation that is clear to all concerned.

---

[4] Using relevant examples or illustrations from your national context is often useful because it shows that you understand how EU law interacts with and works in that national context.

[5] Here the analysis starts and you are immediately stating your view and backing it up using academic authority. The extent to which you are expected to cite journals will vary, so make sure you know what is expected of you.

[6] If something has been criticised, it is worth mentioning that, even if the ECJ has reaffirmed the position as it has here (see next sentence).

[7] State your conclusion relating to the first part of your analysis to help the reader follow your structure through logically.

[8] Justify the conclusion you just made and highlight its importance. This section really shows your ability to think critically.

[9] So far we have talked about the theory. Now we need to take a look at how things actually work out in practice and that is what this next section does.

[10] It might be obvious but you still need to state that, otherwise your examiner will not know that it is obvious to you too!

[11] It is then worth explaining what you have just called obvious in a little more detail because this is really key to answering the question. You must explain why a broader interpretation of acte clair might be problematic.

[12] This conclusion simply draws together what went on before and reiterates the key points, making sure that the question set is fully answered.

However, in practice, national courts have tended to interpret acte clair more loosely,[9] allowing them to avoid references. In part, this may be simply pragmatic, the national court relying on its own interpretation which in the national context may be perfectly clear, a watered down application of **CILFIT**, perhaps. However, this may carry risks, for instance, where a national court of last resort avoided a reference by relying on acte clair, resulting in one of the parties being deprived of EU law rights. In **Köbler v Austria** (2003) and more recently **Traghetti del Mediterraneo SpA v Italy** (2006) the ECJ held that state liability in damages would arise if it was manifestly apparent that a national court had failed to comply with its obligations under (now) Article 267 TFEU, for instance by misapplying the doctrine of acte clair. In such cases the threat to the coherence of EU law is obvious.[10] If courts of last resort can sidestep their obligation to refer a question of interpretation because they hold that a measure is clear under the doctrine of acte clair, there is the potential for Member States to interpret the supposedly clear measure in different ways. National interpretation rather than EU law then reigns supreme.[11]

In conclusion, therefore, the doctrine of acte clair itself makes some sense if applied in its originally intended narrow scope. If, however, national courts are allowed to sidestep their obligation to refer a question of interpretation to the ECJ when they are acting as a court of last resort, the consistent application of EU law is threatened and the preliminary reference procedure's effectiveness is undermined.[12]

✓ Make your answer stand out

■ Add some case examples where references have been avoided – draw on your national context here, perhaps.

■ Add references to academic commentary. See Chapter 13 in Craig, P. and De Burca, G. (2011) *EU Law, Text Cases and Materials*, 5th edn, Oxford: Oxford University Press or Tridimas, T. (2003) Knocking on Heaven's Door: Fragmentation, Efficiency and Defiance in the Preliminary Reference Procedure, *CMLR*, 40, 9–50.

■ You could give more detail on *CILFIT* as this is the central case in this matter.

■ Provide further detail on the criticisms levelled at *CILFIT*, such as the difficulty in applying it.

> **!** **Don't be tempted to . . .**
>
> ■ State the facts of cases in detail: they are not relevant here.
> ■ Explain the preliminary reference procedure in detail: you are not asked about the detail of it here.
> ■ Include much, if any, detail on the other exceptions set out in *CILFIT*. Keep the focus on acte clair: that's what you are asked about.
> ■ Write about the preliminary reference procedure generally; focus your answer on the question set.

？ Question 3

Schoolplay GmbH, a German manufacturer of children's playground equipment, is contracted to supply swings to Julie, a UK retailer. The contract reserved Julie's right to reject the goods if they failed to comply with the (fictitious) Council Regulation 99/89 ('the Regulation') which requires children's playground equipment to be fitted with safety information in 'child friendly language'.

The safety information on the swings reads: 'Please use this equipment responsibly and in particular do not swing too high'. Julie refused to accept the swings because she believed they do not conform to the requirements of the directive. She brought proceedings in the High Court for return of the purchase price. Schoolplay rejected this claim on the grounds that the swings complied with the Regulation.

The High Court held that most children aged 12 and above understood the notice but that younger children were not sure what it meant, and primary-school children in particular struggled to read the words 'responsible' and 'in particular'. The court was referred to an earlier Supreme Court decision in which 'child friendly language' had been interpreted to mean language appropriate to the age group most likely to utilise the equipment in question or their parents/guardians. Schoolplay argued that children under 12 were unlikely to use the swings without supervision and therefore the parents of younger children were the intended readers of the safety notices. The High Court took the view that it was bound by the Supreme Court's interpretation and declined to make a reference to the ECJ. It gave judgment for Schoolplay.

On appeal, the Court of Appeal disagreed with the Supreme Court's interpretation, stating that the Regulation clearly intended the notice to be in a form appropriate for children using the equipment whether or not their parents were present. The court refused to make a reference to the ECJ, gave judgment for Julie and refused leave to appeal to the Supreme Court.

Consider the application of Article 267 TFEU to this situation.

Answer plan

➜ Explain the preliminary reference procedure.

➜ Explain when a reference can be made.

➜ Apply the criteria set out to the situation for the High Court in the scenario.

➜ Consider whether the Court of Appeal is the final court in this case.

➜ Consider the position of the Supreme Court as the final court in this case.

Diagram plan

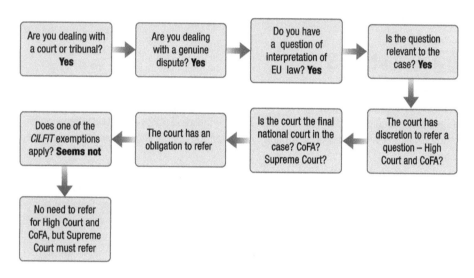

A printable version of this diagram plan is available from **www.pearsoned.co.uk/lawexpressqa**

Answer

[1] By setting out clearly from the start what the legal issue in question is, the examiner can see you have understood the question.

Under Article 267 TFEU, the ECJ has jurisdiction to give rulings on questions of interpretation of European Union law, including secondary legislation. This case concerns the interpretation of the words 'in child friendly language' in the Regulation and so the Court has jurisdiction to hear the reference.[1] In addition, there appears to be a genuine dispute between Schoolplay and Julie which requires an interpretation of the wording in the Regulation in order to solve their dispute. The matter is therefore genuine and relevant, and the ECJ would be unlikely to refuse a preliminary reference. The question that

2 You can then deal with the uncontroversial aspects of the question and set out what the real issue under consideration is. This way, you show the examiner that you understand the important issues raised and will focus on answering the question.

3 There are two courts mentioned in this question: you need to deal with both.

4 You need to identify that the High Court had discretion to refer and chose not to. You then should consider why it did not. This comes next.

5 Always comment on the reasoning of the High Court. Here you should be aware that national precedent does not affect the discretion, so it's OK to criticise the High Court for getting it wrong here.

6 You are speculating a little here, but all these issues are important and it makes sense to deal with them now and refer back to them later if necessary. It keeps the answer coherent rather than jumping about and you are still trying to establish why the High Court did not refer: something the next paragraph continues to do.

7 You do not need to spend a huge amount of time on *CILFIT* here but it does need to be mentioned as one of the key exceptions to the need to refer; it also gives useful guidance in relation to the discretion.

arises in this scenario is therefore whether or not a reference should have been made to the ECJ by the national courts.[2]

The High Court[3] in this case is not under an obligation to refer the question of interpretation arising out of this case to the ECJ. It is clearly subject to appeal to the Court of Appeal, since the question refers to such an appeal. The High Court is therefore not a 'court against whose decision there is no judicial remedy under national law' under Article 267(3). However, Article 267(2) provides that where a question of interpretation of EU law is raised before any court of a Member State, that court may, if it considers that a decision on the question is necessary to enable it to give judgment, request the ECJ to give a ruling.[4] In this case it seems the High Court does not consider it necessary and, in fact, seems to see itself bound by the Supreme Court's earlier interpretation of 'in child friendly language'.

If the High Court concluded that it could not refer the question to the ECJ because of the Supreme Court ruling, it was misguided, as the national laws of precedent have no bearing on the court's discretion to refer a question relevant to its decision in the case (*Rheinmühlen* (1974)).[5] If the High Court therefore felt that the question was relevant, it could have referred and the case of *Dzodzi* (1990) makes clear that it would have been the High Court, rather than the ECJ, that determines whether or not the question is relevant. In this case, of course, the question is not only relevant but also conclusive to the outcome of the case.

Had the High Court decided to refer, it would have been for it to determine the timing of the referral, though the facts and relevant legal issues should first be established (*Irish Creamery* (1981)). Where insufficient information is available, the ECJ has on occasions refused to accept references from national courts (*Telemarsicabruzzo* (1993)). From the information given, it appears that the facts and legal issues have been established by the High Court and it was therefore in a position to make a reference which would have been accepted.[6]

The High Court appears not to have considered whether the words in 'child friendly language' are clear and thus fall within the doctrine of acte clair. According to *CILFIT*, a provision of EU law is acte clair if it is 'so obvious as to leave no scope for reasonable doubt as to its meaning'.[7] The national court must be convinced that the matter is equally obvious to the courts of the other Member States. It must bear in mind that Union law is drafted in several languages; that Union law uses terminology that is peculiar to it; that legal concepts do not necessarily have the same meaning in Union law and the law of the various Member States; and that Union law must be placed in its context. Had the High Court considered these matters, it may well have come to the conclusion that the wording in question is not sufficiently clear to satisfy the criteria of acte clair and, as such, a referral should still have been made.

Overall, however, the case law discussed above merely provides guidance on when a referral should be made; it does not alter the fact that in EU law the High Court has a discretion to refer in this matter but is not obliged to do so.[8] The next question is therefore whether the Court of Appeal should have referred the matter. The guidance provided above applies in the same way to the Court of Appeal as it does to the High Court.[9] The only material difference between the scenarios is that the Court of Appeal interpreted the EU provision differently to the High Court, resulting in the meaning of 'child friendly language' now being disputed. This strengthens the argument that the doctrine of acte clair does not apply in this case but it does not automatically oblige the Court of Appeal to refer the matter.[10]

The question which must, however, be considered is whether the Court of Appeal is a 'court against whose decisions there is no judicial remedy under national law' under Article 267(3).[11] The Court of Appeal's decisions are subject to appeal to the Supreme Court only with leave either of the Court of Appeal or the Supreme Court. And the Court of Appeal in this case refused that leave. However, in **Lyckeskog** (2007) the fact that there was a requirement for a prior declaration of admissibility before an appeal could go to the Swedish Supreme Court did not deprive the parties of a judicial remedy and therefore the Western Sweden Court of Appeal was not the final court. In this case, therefore, the Court of Appeal is not the final court because the Supreme Court can be asked to give leave to appeal. As a result, there is no obligation on the Court of Appeal to refer the question of interpretation to the ECJ.

However, the Supreme Court is under an obligation to refer a question of EU law under Article 267(3), either at the stage of considering admissibility, so in this case when considering leave to appeal, or at a later stage, in this scenario, when hearing the full case (**Lyckeskog**).[12]

[8] This is important. Make clear that the High Court has a discretion but chose not to use it.

[9] No need to repeat what you said before, just refer to it.

[10] If two courts interpret the same phrase differently, you cannot really argue that the provision is sufficiently clear!

[11] The Court of Appeal has refused leave to appeal, so you need to consider carefully whether that means it is the court of last resort and therefore was obliged to refer.

[12] You don't need to say anything about the cases; it is OK just to list them as authorities as done here and in other sections of this answer. Check with your examiner as to how detailed a citation you are expected to give in an examination.

In conclusion, then, both the High Court and Court of Appeal legitimately exercised their discretion not to refer the question of interpretation of 'child friendly language' to the ECJ even though the guidance provided in case law might suggest that a reference would have been appropriate. However, should the case progress to the Supreme Court, it would be obliged to refer the question for a preliminary ruling.

 Make your answer stand out

- Add a little more detail on the position of the Supreme Court as the final court.
- Give more detail on whether you think the lower courts perhaps should have referred and why. Consider the fact that the courts do not agree on interpretation.
- You can add discussion of case law to illustrate how preliminary reference works in practice but you must keep this relevant to the scenario.
- Give a slightly more detailed explanation of why the provision is not acte clair (i.e. its meaning is disputed).

! Don't be tempted to . . .

- Explain the preliminary reference procedure and then state your conclusion. Integrate your application of the law to the scenario as much as possible.
- Give details of the cases referred to: you are merely illustrating your legal point.
- Spend time explaining in detail the *CILFIT* exceptions. If they do not apply, you can simply state that fact.

 www.pearsoned.co.uk/lawexpressqa

Go online to access more revision support including additional essay and problem questions with diagram plans, You be the marker questions, and download all diagrams from the book.

Enforcement in the Member States: Direct effect, indirect effect and state liability

How this topic may come up in exams

This topic is a popular one for examiners. Questions will often ask for an assessment of the effectiveness of the principles so make sure you deal with these issues rather than just describing the principles. Alternatively, essay questions might ask you to consider the development of the principles. Problem questions will require you to apply your knowledge of the enforcement of EU law in Member States to a particular scenario and you must focus your answer on that scenario rather than give a general answer. Remember that these three principles are linked, so, even if a question is predominantly about one of them, a (brief) consideration of the others is usually necessary.

■ Before you begin

It's a good idea to consider the following key themes of enforcement in the Member States (direct effect, indirect effect and state liability), before tackling a question on this topic.

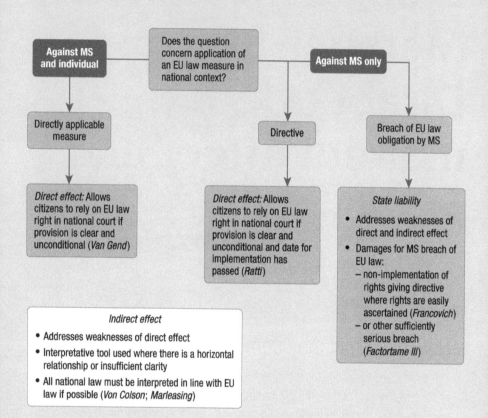

A printable version of this diagram is available from **www.pearsoned.co.uk/lawexpressqa**

❓ Question 1

Malta has failed fully to implement two recent (fictitious) directives that have now passed the date for implementation. The first relates to the consistent rating of hotel accommodation and has not been implemented at all. The second relates to the advertising of package holidays by Member States and has been partially implemented. As a result of these failures, GoMalta, the country's leading tour operator, has suffered major losses and is close to bankruptcy. Malta's government claims it has delegated implementation to the tourism board which is governmental body. In a recent judgment a Maltese court has ruled that the national law has precedence over the directive.

Advise GoMalta.

Diagram plan

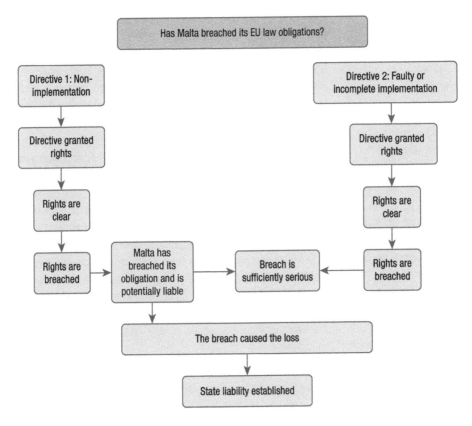

A printable version of this diagram plan is available from **www.pearsoned.co.uk/lawexpressqa**

Answer plan

→ Outline the Member States' duty to fulfil their obligations under the treaties (see Article 4(3) TEU) and the Commission's power under Article 258 TFEU.

→ Outline state liability under the *Francovich* and *Factortame* case law, setting out the requirements to be met.

→ Consider whether Malta has breached its obligations.

→ Consider whether GoMalta can bring a claim.

→ Summarise your advice.

Answer

[1] Identifying the question you are asked to deal with in the first sentence is a good way of starting answers to problem questions. It shows you understand what the issues are.

[2] These two sentences show you have a wider understanding of how EU law is enforced and therefore sets your answer in context.

[3] Please make sure you really do write causal and not casual!

[4] This paragraph sets out the relevant law briefly. This is a useful way to show that you understand the *Francovich* principle and its development. Don't do too much here, though, as it is the analysis which follows which is more important.

[5] Show clearly that you appreciate the development from *Francovich* here.

This question requires an examination of the principle of state liability and, in particular, whether or not GoMalta can claim damages against Malta.[1] Member States are under a general obligation to fulfil their obligations under the treaties under Article 4(3) TEU, and, if they fail to do so, the Commission can issue proceedings against them under Article 258 TFEU. This, however, does not help individuals who suffer loss as a result of the Member States' breach of their obligations.[2] The principle of state liability was introduced in the early 1990s and for the first time allowed national courts to award damages to individuals who have suffered loss through the actions of a Member State. This principle was first set out in **Francovich and Bonifaci v Italy** (1990) where the ECJ ruled that the effectiveness of EU law would be impaired if individuals could not claim compensation in situations where they suffer loss because of a Member State's breach of EU law. An action under the **Francovich** principle relates to a Member State's failure to implement a directive. For an individual to succeed in such a case, **Francovich** stipulates that the result prescribed by the directive in question must involve the grant of rights to individuals and the content of those rights must be clear from the directive. Furthermore, there must be a causal[3] link between the breach of the state's obligation and the damage suffered by the individual.[4]

The ECJ in **Factortame III** (1996) reformulated this test in relation to other Member State breaches of their EU law obligations[5] and ruled that where the Member State acts pursuant to a wide discretion, the state will be liable for its breach of Community law if: the breach infringes a rule of law intended to confer rights on individuals; the breach is sufficiently serious and there is a direct causal link between the breach of the state's obligation and the damage to the applicant. The ECJ went further and considered the factors to determine whether the breach would be sufficiently serious: the clarity and precision of the rule breached; the extent of any discretion left to the Member State; whether the breach was intentional or involuntary; whether the error of law was excusable or inexcusable; whether the position taken by a Community institution had contributed towards the Member State's action.[6]

[6] Succinctly setting out the legal test here allows you then to apply it systematically in the next part.

Applying the legal rules to the scenario given necessitates some speculation as little information as to the content of the directives is given.[7] For GoMalta to be able to bring a claim successfully, the directives must have involved the granting of clearly identifiable rights to individuals. We have no information in relation to this and will therefore assume, for the purposes of the discussion to come, that the directives did, in fact, confer rights and that these rights were clearly ascertainable from the text of the directives. Should this not be the case, an action would fail.[8]

[7] The scenario in this question gives you very little to go on, and it is OK to say that, as a result, you need to speculate a little.

[8] If you make an assumption such as this one, make clear what the consequences are if your presumption is wrong!

Presuming that the first two points of the *Francovich* criteria have been satisfied, we can presume that Malta has breached its obligation relating to the implementation of the directive. The ECJ confirmed in *Rechberger and others v Austria* (1999) and *Leitner v TUI Deutschland GmbH & Co KG* (2002) that the non-implementation of a directive is a serious breach of EU law.

In relation to the incomplete or faulty implementation of the second directive, it is necessary to consider the *Factortame* criteria and the question of whether GoMalta's rights have been breached and whether that breach is sufficiently serious. Again, we are given no information on these matters. We can presume that the rights have been breached or this action would not arise in the first place. Whether or not the breach is sufficiently serious to warrant an application of the principle of state liability is more difficult to speculate on. We have no information on the clarity and precision of the rule or the extent of any Member State discretion.[9] We also do not know whether the error of law was excusable or whether an EU institution contributed to the Member State's action.[10]

[9] This is the beginning of the application of the criteria for 'sufficiently serious' in *Factortame*. And even if you have little information from a scenario, you must use what you have got.

[10] Further application. You can't say much more here because the scenario gives you no information.

[11] Finally, a criterion you can say something about. The discussion which follows tries to argue that the non-implementation was intentional. You could argue the other way too, if you can use the scenario to back up your argument.

However, we do have some information regarding the intentional or involuntary nature of the lack of proper implementation of the directive in this case.[11] Malta has left the implementation to its tourism board. Arguably, therefore, the government of Malta intended to implement the directive fully and the failure to do so is not intentional. However, the responsibility to ensure correct implementation ultimately lies with the central government and the tourism board is part of the government structure, and this faulty or non-implementation is likely to be viewed in the same way as the central government's would be. Whether this is intentional or not would require further information but, in the absence of any evidence to the contrary, we can presume that it was intentional rather than by mistake or simple oversight. Further weight is added to this interpretation of the facts by the fact that a Maltese Court has recently held that national law shall prevail over this particular EU law measure. Clearly, this is in contravention of the doctrine of supremacy of EU law as established through the case law of the ECJ (*Van Gend en Loos*; *Costa v ENEL*; *Simmenthal*, etc.). Furthermore, the two directives seem to be closely linked and the first was not implemented at all. This suggests that Malta does not consider this particular EU law to be beneficial and it is therefore being at best lax and at worst obstructive.

[12] It helps coherence to sum up in between, and, as you are moving on to a new point now (causal link), it is worth doing that here.

If we presume, therefore, that there has been a sufficiently serious breach of the second directive which was to confer clear rights on individuals, then Malta seems to be in clear breach of its obligations and liable to pay damages to GoMalta.[12]

[13] Examiners tend not to set trick questions, so if you are told that the loss suffered is a result of the lack of or improper implementation then don't second-guess that.

The final hurdle for GoMalta to clear is the question of a causal link between the breach of EU law on the part of Malta and the losses suffered by GoMalta. Again, there is little information given, but the scenario does state categorically that the losses suffered by GoMalta are as a result of Malta's failure to implement the directive.[13] We must therefore presume that the causal link has been established. If our presumptions and speculations are accurate, Malta is likely to be liable to pay damages to GoMalta for breach of its obligations in EU law. However, without further details about the directive, its purpose and content, it is impossible to say with any certainty.

Make your answer stand out

- Provide more detail, using case examples of how the *Francovich* and *Factortame* criteria have been applied since their inception.
- Set out your advice directly to the client. This changes your style of writing slightly but can really show that you have fully grasped the area of law and are able to apply it to the scenario given. It also adds interests for examiners who often read very similar answers over and over again.
- Examine what the ECJ might consider to be a sufficiently serious breach so you can more easily justify your conclusion as to whether such a breach has occurred here.
- Use case law to illustrate your discussion of a possible serious breach. Consult your lecture notes for relevant examples.

! Don't be tempted to . . .

- Jump straight from the explanation of the law to the conclusion. You need to evidence your application of the principles.
- Give details about the cases mentioned. The facts are not relevant here; it is all about principles.
- Make up facts to help you answer the question. You have to work with what you're given, even if that is not much!
- Set out the law generally. You need to focus on those areas relevant to the scenario.

Question 2

The ECJ transformed the EC Treaty '. . . from a set of horizontal legal arrangements between sovereign states into a vertically integrated legal regime conferring judicially enforceable rights and obligations on all legal persons and entities, public and private, within the EC territory.' (Stone Sweet and Caporaso, 1998)

Discuss this statement with particular reference to the doctrine of direct effect.

Answer plan

→ Briefly outline the doctrine of direct effect.

→ Consider the case law on direct effect consecutively, beginning with *Van Gend En Loos*.

➡ Consider the requirements for direct effect in relation to the treaties as well as secondary legislation and directives in particular.

➡ Consider the extent to which direct effect, developed by the ECJ has transformed the treaty as indicated in the quotation.

Diagram plan

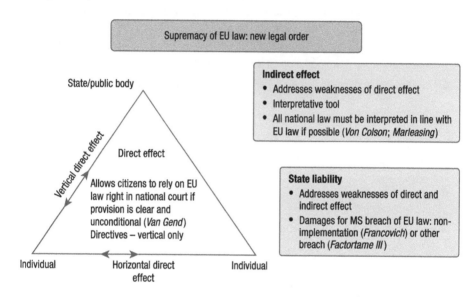

A printable version of this diagram plan is available from **www.pearsoned.co.uk/lawexpressqa**

Answer

[1] This sentence sets out what direct effect is and how it relates to the question set and thus proves from the start that you know what you're talking about.

[2] A further acknowledgement of the question set, this time in relation to the ECJ's role.

The principle of direct effect, that is, allowing European citizens to rely directly on their EU law rights rather than having to seek enforcement through the EU institutions, was a major breakthrough in the development of the EU legal order.[1] While the treaties did not foresee explicitly the direct application of its provisions to the citizens of the EU, the European Court of Justice developed a number of principles through its jurisprudence which changed the relationship between EU and national legal orders.[2] This essay shows how these principles, emanating from the doctrine of direct effect have developed and together transform the EU into a 'vertically integrated legal regime'.

The doctrine of direct effect was first articulated by the ECJ in *Van Gend en Loos* (1963), where it held that Community law imposes rights and obligations on individuals and thus should be enforceable directly in the national courts. This method of enforcement was to be in addition to the then accepted methods of Commission-issued infraction procedures. Direct effect makes considerable logical sense[3] and the doctrine's development is an example of the ECJ's pragmatic and dynamic approach to law making (Ward, 2009; Craig, 1997; Dougan, 2000, 2004). If EU law was to be enforced across all Member States, the Commission could not be expected to detect and follow up on every breach and, as such, enforcement would inevitably only be as good as the Commission's ability and resources to act as the guardian of the treaties. If, however, individuals were also given the power to enforce European law, rights in the national application of European law could become much more wholesale and uniform.

However, the ECJ did recognise that, in order for the doctrine to work effectively in practice, some limitations and guidelines would need to be provided. It therefore set out the criteria which provisions have to meet in order to be directly effective. The provision must be clear and unambiguous and its operation must not depend on further Member State action. In other words, the legal provision in question must be one that is precise and unconditional. A further distinction was drawn between vertical and horizontal direct effect, the former relating to a relationship between individuals and state institutions and the latter to a relationship existing between two individuals. While *Van Gend en Loos* dealt with vertical direct effect, the question of whether provisions could also be horizontally directly effective was not answered until the case of *Defrenne v Sabena (No. 2)* (1976) in which an air stewardess brought a claim against her employer. The ECJ's judgment clarifies that European law provisions are enforceable by individuals against other individuals, a position which has since been confirmed in cases such as *Walrave v Koch* (1974), *Thieffry v Paris Bar Association* (1977) or *Brasserie de Haecht* (1973).[4]

While the direct effect of directly applicable EU law such as treaty articles and regulations has been relatively uncontroversial, the application of the doctrine to directives has been more problematic.[5]

[3] Try to be analytical and critical from the start; this section does that by first stating your view of direct effect and then justifying that view in the rest of the paragraph.

[4] This is a fairly descriptive paragraph but it does explain direct effect and the relevant criteria clearly and illustrates with case examples, so you are highlighting the clarity of your understanding and can then move on to analysis.

[5] This sentence is a lead-in to the more analytical discussion of direct effect which then begins by examining directives in this context, which is where most of the issues can be illustrated most clearly.

The requirement for the provision to be unconditional seems to exclude directives from the scope of direct effect as they rely on Member State implementation and only the objective or result of them is binding. However, the ECJ considered the possibility of directly effective directives early on in its case law and concluded that the usefulness of directives as a legal measure would be considerably weakened if individuals were denied the opportunity to rely on them before their national courts (see **Van Duyn** (1974)). The case of **Francovich** suggests that in order to be sufficiently precise directives must identify those entitled to the right, those responsible for providing the right and ascertain the contents of the right. In addition, the date set for implementation must have passed (**Casa Pubblico Ministero v Ratti** (1979)). The ECJ has further held that directives can only be vertically directly effective and will not be enforceable against individuals (**Marshall v Southampton Health Authority** (1986); **Faccini Dori v Recreb Srl** (1994)).[6]

While the creation of direct effect was undoubtedly a big step in the creation of a new legal order[7] which differed significantly from the legal frameworks created by other international treaties, the doctrine is not without its problems.[8] First, it is difficult to know whether or not a particular provision has direct effect and the criteria can be difficult to apply in practice. For example, in **Van Duyn** the provisions relating to public policy and public security were held to be sufficiently precise even though the scope of those terms would need interpretation by the courts. Similarly in **Defrenne v Sabena (No. 2)** 'equal pay for equal work' was regarded as sufficiently clear. However, there is no guarantee that the ECJ will always take this generous approach.[9] Unless a particular provision comes before the ECJ, there is no failsafe way of determining whether or not a provision is directly effective, and the determination of these matters is therefore largely left to the chance of an appropriate case arising.[10]

A further limitation of the doctrine is the distinction drawn between vertical and horizontal relationships. In particular, directives are only vertically directly effective, leaving EU citizens unable to enforce their rights against other individuals who breach their obligations under the directive in question. The ECJ has attempted to address this weakness of the doctrine by applying a very wide definition of what constitutes 'the state' for the purposes of vertical direct effect.

[6] You do not go into detail on the cases. You have made your point and the cases just need to be listed as authority. Adding detail of the cases would not really help to illustrate your argument.

[7] Keep coming back to the question in your analysis. You have dealt with the description and explanation bit and here have the opportunity to remind the examiner that you have the question in the back of your mind and are indeed answering it.

[8] You also need to consider the limitations of direct effect – it has its critics – and this section begins to do that.

[9] Remember this principle is developed entirely by the ECJ, and the ECJ is free to change its mind about what it regards as clear and precise.

[10] This is an important point to remember and one which students often neglect. If the ECJ has not ruled, you can never say with absolute certainty whether or not a provision is directly effective.

In **Foster v British Gas** (1990) it therefore concluded that a body was an emanation of the state and thus capable of forming a vertical relationship if it provided a public service, was under state control and had special powers which went beyond those normally associated with individuals.

[11] The question asks you to write your answer with particular reference to direct effect. This does not mean that you exclude everything else. Indirect effect addresses some of the weaknesses of direct effect and, as such, adds to the creation of the new legal order. It has to be mentioned!

While a broad interpretation of the state goes some way to ensure the widest possible application and enforcement of European law, the ECJ developed the principle of indirect effect to further enhance individuals' ability to enforce their specific rights.[11] The principle simply states that any national law must be interpreted in accordance with European law and is a principle of statutory interpretation to be used in horizontal situations or in vertical situations where the provision in question is not sufficiently precise. The case of **Marleasing** (1991) confirmed that the principle of indirect effect relates to measures predating the provision in questions rather than to implementing legislation which wrongly transposes a European law measure; in such a case traditional infringement proceedings under Article 258 TFEU would have to be brought.

[12] The conclusion relates directly back to the question and follows logically from what went before, which is usually a good sign that you have not gone off track in your answer.

As is evident from the discussion above, the ECJ has been influential in creating a new legal order which is vertically integrated rather than a simple horizontal relationship between signatory states to an international treaty. Legal rights and obligations are conferred on the state as well as individuals and only few limitations regarding enforcement of those rights remain.[12]

✓ Make your answer stand out

- Include a more detailed discussion of indirect effect to show how it addresses the gaps left by direct effect and therefore ensures the legal order as a whole is effective.
- Provide a discussion of state liability as the final piece in the puzzle which ensures direct effect is backed up by sanctions against Member States which also compensate individuals.
- Explain how EU law was originally going to be enforced by the Commission and the pros and cons of that approach.
- Illustrate your further reading by referring to academic commentary to reinforce your argument.

> ## ! Don't be tempted to . . .
>
> ■ Launch into a long examination of direct effect; focus on the question asked.
> ■ List lots of case examples; one or two will do to illustrate your point.
> ■ Give the facts of cases unless you think they really help illustrate your argument.
> ■ Just explain the principles; you have to relate your answer to the question set.

📝 Question 3

The ECJ has developed a number of principles to help protect individuals' EU law rights in national courts. Critically assess these principles.

Diagram plan

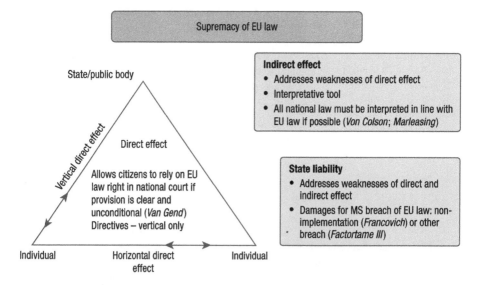

A printable version of this diagram plan is available from **www.pearsoned.co.uk/lawexpressqa**

Answer plan

➔ Introduction: identify the principles: supremacy, direct effect, indirect effect and state liability.

➔ Use the supremacy of EU law as a starting point: the principles are a way of ensuring supremacy and giving individuals access to their rights directly.

→ Direct effect: explain its development by the ECJ, pointing out the distinctions between vertical and horizontal and the issues regarding directives.

→ Indirect effect: a way of overcoming the weaknesses of direct effect; essentially a tool of interpretation.

→ State liability: the final piece in the puzzle, giving access to damages where individuals suffer loss due to a Member State breach of EU obligations.

Answer

[1] The introduction here is little more than a restatement of the question but it gets you going and tells the reader how you plan to tackle the question. If you don't know how to start in an exam, restating the question in a slightly different way can break that blank-page block.

This question requires a consideration of three principles of EU law which have been developed by the European Court of Justice (ECJ) and together ensure the functioning of the 'new legal order' (*Van Gend en Loos* (1963)) and the supremacy of EU law. This essay traces the development of the principles of direct effect, indirect effect and state liability in order to assess their importance for the protection of individuals' EU law rights in national courts.[1]

[2] We have paraphrased here; if you can remember the exact wording from the case you can also use that; but, unless you have a good memory for quotations, do not worry about memorising them too much.

In *Van Gend en Loos* the ECJ famously proclaimed that the Community constitutes a new legal order for which Member States had limited their sovereign rights.[2] As a result, EU law takes primacy over national law, as has been established in a line of case law (*Costa v ENEL* (1964); *Internationale Handelsgesellschaft* (1970); *Simmenthal* (1978); *Factortame II* (1991)).[3] This primacy of EU law provides the basis for the development of the three principles under discussion here.

[3] There is no need to give further detail about the cases: you are only giving background here.

[4] You just need to highlight that you know that there are infringement proceedings which were set in place as the method of enforcement. Do not be tempted to write about these in detail: you will run out of time.

[5] Restating a legal provision or principle shows that you really understand the provision and haven't just learned it off by heart.

The doctrine of direct effect was first articulated by the ECJ in *Van Gend en Loos* where it held that Community law imposes rights and obligations on individuals and thus should be enforceable directly in the national courts. This method of enforcement was to be in addition to the then accepted methods of Commission-issued infraction procedures.[4] However, the ECJ did recognise that, in order for the doctrine to work effectively in practice, some limitations and guidelines would need to be provided. It therefore set out the criteria which provisions have to meet in order to be directly effective. The provision must be clear and unambiguous and its operation must not depend on further Member State action. In other words, the legal provision in question must be one that is precise and unconditional.[5] A further distinction was drawn between vertical and horizontal direct effect, the former relating to a relationship between individuals and state institutions and the latter to a relationship existing between two individuals. While **Van Gend en Loos** dealt with vertical direct effect, the question of whether provisions could also be horizontally directly effective was not answered until the case of **Defrenne v Sabena (No. 2)** (1976) in which the ECJ's judgment clarifies that European law provisions are enforceable by individuals against other individuals.

[6] This is a really succinct way of highlighting that you understand how the doctrine of direct effect applies to different types of secondary legislation. It also signposts that you are going to concentrate on the controversial issues and makes your structure really clear.

While the direct effect of directly applicable EU law such as treaty articles and regulations has been relatively uncontroversial, the application of the doctrine to directives has been more problematic.[6] The requirement for the provision to be unconditional seems to exclude directives from the scope of direct effect as they rely on Member State implementation and only the objective or result of them is binding. However, the ECJ considered the possibility of directly effective directives early on in its case law and concluded that the usefulness of directives as a legal measure would be considerably weakened if individuals were denied the opportunity to rely on them before their national courts (see **Van Duyn**). The case of **Francovich** (1991) suggests that in order to be sufficiently precise directives must identify those entitled to the right, those responsible for providing the right and ascertain the contents of the right. In addition, the date set for implementation must have passed (**Casa Pubblico Ministero v Ratti** (1974)).[7] The ECJ has further held that directives can only be vertically directly effective and will not be enforceable against individuals (**Marshall v Southampton Health Authority** (1986); **Faccini Dori v Recreb Srl** (1994)).[8]

[7] The main case establishing this area of law was *Francovich*, so that is stated at the beginning of the sentence. You can then highlight extensions to those principles or cases which have consolidated it by listing them in brackets. There is no need to say more about them.

[8] The last two paragraphs may sound very familiar if you have read the answer to the previous question in this chapter. This section is pretty much identical because it deals with exactly the same material.

For the protection of individuals' rights this means that, where direct effect can be established, EU law rights are directly enforceable in national courts. However, direct effect also has its weaknesses. Until the ECJ has ruled on a particular provision, it is difficult to know whether or not it has direct effect, and directives in particular are limited to vertical direct effect, leaving those wishing to enforce their rights against another individual without a remedy.[9]

[9] This paragraph relates back to the question directly by specifically highlighting how direct effect leads to the protection of individual rights. While the explanation and, to a point, analysis of direct effect will be the same in most essay questions, the conclusions you draw from that explanation and analysis will vary depending on the question set.

While a broad interpretation of the state (**Foster**) goes some way to ensure the widest possible application and enforcement of European law under direct effect, the ECJ developed the principle of indirect effect to further enhance individuals' ability to enforce their specific rights.[10] The principle simply states that any national law must be interpreted in accordance with European law (**Von Colson**) and is a principle of statutory interpretation to be used in horizontal situations or in vertical situations where the provision in question is not sufficiently precise. The case of **Marleasing** confirmed all national law must be interpreted in line with EU law, but only 'so far as possible'. As this may not always be possible (**Wagner Miret** (1993)), the principle has its limitations but does go some way to ensuring EU rights are protected.[11]

The final piece of the puzzle is that of state liability, which is a further means of overcoming the limitations of direct and indirect effect (Ward, 2009).[12] In **Francovich** the ECJ considered damages for loss incurred as a result of a state's failure to implement a directive. It held that, where the directive entails the grant of rights to individuals; it is possible to identify the content of those rights and a causal link between the state's failure and the loss exists, damages will be payable. The doctrine was developed further in **Factortame III** where the conditions for awarding damages for other kinds of breach were set out: the breach infringes a rule of law intended to confer rights on individuals; the breach is sufficiently serious; there is a direct causal link between the breach of the state's obligation and the damage to the applicant. The ECJ went further and considered these factors to determine whether the breach would be sufficiently serious: the clarity and precision of the rule breached; the extent of any discretion left to the Member State; whether the breach was intentional or involuntary; whether the error of law was excusable or inexcusable; whether the position taken by a Community institution had contributed towards the Member State's action. The law relating to state liability has been applied in a variety of situations, such as legislation infringing Community law (**Factortame III**); incorrect implementation of a directive (**BT** (1996)); administrative breaches (**Hedley Lomas** (1996)) and incorrect interpretation of Community law by a national court of last instance (**Köbler** (2003)).[13]

In conclusion, therefore, the principles of direct effect, indirect effect and state liability which have all been developed by the ECJ, are crucially important for the protection of individuals' Community law rights in national courts as they provide a framework in which claims to enforce such rights can be brought.

Make your answer stand out

■ After each section add a little mini-conclusion as to what the principle does for the protection of individual rights. This helps clarify your structure.

■ Add references to academic commentary. For guidance, see Dougan, M. (2007) When Worlds Collide: Competing Visions of the Relationship Between Direct Effect and Supremacy, *CMLR*, 44, 931 or Drake, S. (2005) Twenty Years After Von Colson: The Impact of Indirect Effect on the Protection of the Individual's Community Rights, *EL Rev*, 30, 329–48.

■ Expand the discussion of indirect effect and state liability; there is a lot to say on direct effect so the other two are neglected a little in the answer here.

■ Make the links between the principles more explicit to show that you really understand how they form a coherent legal framework, rather than working in isolation.

! Don't be tempted to . . .

■ Just define the principles without any commentary.

■ Add lots of case details – they don't really help advance your argument in this case.

■ Focus solely on direct effect; there is a lot to say on it but you need to make sure you also say something about the other two. It is likely to be shorter but that does not mean it's not important.

■ Launch into your argument without an introduction; you need to identify the principles you will deal with at the beginning so your argument is easy to follow.

❓ Question 4

The (fictitious) Directive 2010/4051 ('the Directive') stipulates that all staff or common rooms in workplaces must be equipped with instant hot water taps and that kettles should not be used in the workplace. The Directive further states that workers should have a place on site where they can sit during the rest and lunch breaks and eat their lunch comfortably. The Directive contains an annexe which sets out examples of suitable staff rooms. The deadline for implementation of the Directive was 31 December 2012.

The (fictitious) Rest Breaks and Common Rooms Act 1980 simply states that where staff rooms are provided, any risk to health and safety should be minimised.

Marcus works for his local council in a rural office. As they are short of office space, the council is converting the staff room into further office space, leaving staff with only a small kitchen where they can make tea and coffee. The kitchen does not have sufficient space for a table and chairs. Marcus has also asked about installation of instant hot water. He is concerned about the continuing use of kettles, particularly as these are also being used in the general office space. When he raises his concerns, he is told to keep out of issues that do not concern him and is threatened with formal disciplinary procedures.

(a) Advise Marcus as to whether he has any cause of action against his employer under EU law.

(b) How would your answer differ (if at all) if Marcus was employed not by the local council but by ACo plc?

[For the purposes of this question, you are NOT required to consider any possible action for damages against the UK government.]

Answer plan

→ Identify the complaints Marcus has.

→ Is the employer complying with (a) the Act and (b) the Directive?

→ Discuss whether the Directive has direct effect? Set out the criteria and apply them.

→ Conclude regarding the local council.

→ Directives only have vertical direct effect so Marcus cannot rely on it against ACo – what about indirect effect?

Diagram plan

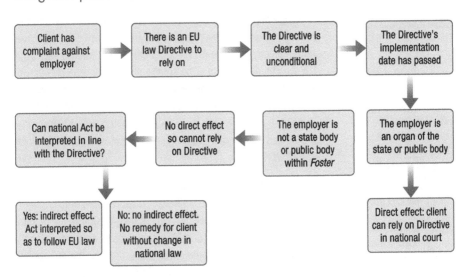

A printable version of this diagram plan is available from **www.pearsoned.co.uk/lawexpressqa**

Answer

(a) This question concerns the application of direct effect to the facts in question. In particular, Marcus requires advice on whether or not he can rely on Directive 2010/4051 and enforce his EU law rights in the national court. Marcus has two complaints. The first is the question of availability of a staff room. Second is the question of continuing use of kettles which the local council seems to be condoning.[1]

[1] In problem questions it is important to set out clearly what the issues are, and in this case your client has two complaints which need spelling out.

The council seems to have complied with the domestic law which stipulates only that, where staff rooms are available, any risk to health and safety must be minimised. The Act is silent on instant hot water provision and the use of kettles. The Act also does not stipulate that staff rooms must be available. The local council is therefore not in breach of the national provisions.[2] The Directive, however, sets out more generous provisions[3] in relation to staff rooms and more stringent provisions in relation to the use of kettles and the provision of hot water. Marcus should therefore, if possible, rely on the Directive rather than national law to make his argument that the staff room needs to be kept and an instant hot water tap needs to be installed.

[2] This is an important point to make because, if the council was in breach of the national law, a claim could be brought relying on the Act rather than EU law.

[3] If it didn't, there would be no point trying to rely on it. Still state the obvious though: otherwise, examiners will not know that you know!

In order to rely directly on the Directive, Marcus must invoke the principle of direct effect, which was established by the ECJ in **Van Gend en Loos** (1963).[4] While the direct effect of directives has been a matter of some controversy, case law has confirmed that directives can be directly effective if they meet certain conditions (**Van Duyn** (1974)). The directive must be sufficiently clear and precise as well as unconditional (**Van Gend en Loos**; **Defrenne v Sabena (No. 2)**) and the deadline for implementation must have passed (**Ratti** (1979)). In addition, directives can only be vertically directly effective: that is, they can only be enforced against a state or a public authority (**Marshall** (1986)).[5]

[4] This is such an important case that most examiners would expect you to be familiar with it and its importance.

[5] This section sets out the criteria the directive must meet in order for it to be directly effective. This paves the way for the application to the scenario.

In this case the conditions seem to be met. The Directive is clear and precise as well as unconditional.[6] It sets out the requirement to have a staff room clearly. While it might be argued that the requirement to have somewhere comfortable to sit and eat lunch is a little too vague, the Directive does give further detail in the annexe and one would argue that it therefore fulfills the requirements. It also clearly states that kettles should not be used and hot water taps

[6] While this is correct, you need to say more than this – you need to explain why you think it is clear and unconditional, to make sure you pick up all the marks for application of the principles.

are instead to be provided. There is no evidence to suggest any conditions are attached to these rights or that they are in any way ambiguous. The implementation deadline has also clearly passed. Marcus's claim is against the local authority which is clearly an organ of the state. This is not affected by the fact that in this case it acts in the capacity of an employer (**Marshall**). Marcus's claim is therefore vertical and he can rely on the Directive and the more generous rights within it in preference to the more limited provisions of the national Act.[7]

[7] Conclusion stating how you see your client's position shows you can apply the law to a given scenario.

(b) In relation to the second part of the question, the conditions for direct effect are not met because ACo is unlikely to be a public body.[8] While the conditions relating to clarity and precision as well as the passing of the implementation deadline are the same as in part (a) and are thus not reiterated here, the requirement that there exists a vertical relationship between the parties is not met in this case. ACo is not an organ of the state and it does not seem to be a public body either. Following the criteria laid down in **Foster**, a public body is one which has been given responsibility by the state for providing a public service, has special powers to do so which go beyond the normal powers of individuals and is under state control. While the scenario provides little information on these matters, the fact that ACo is a private company means it is unlikely to satisfy this test, and for that reason Marcus would not be able to rely on the Directive against ACo.

[8] As you have already set out the condition etc. above, there is no harm in going straight in with your conclusion as a lead-in to part (b). It shows you understand how parts (a) and (b) are different. You must then go on to justify that conclusion, though.

However, Marcus may be able to enforce the rights under the Directive by virtue of the principle of indirect effect.[9] This principle was created by the ECJ in **Von Colson** (1984) and requires that relevant national law be interpreted in accordance with EU law. The court held in **Marleasing** (1991) that the principle applies irrespective of whether the national provisions pre-date the EU law provisions or not, so the fact that the Act was in force long before the Directive in this case is irrelevant. While indirect effect is important in situations such as this one because it can help overcome the weaknesses of the doctrine of direct effect and in particular the fact that directives cannot have horizontal direct effect, **Marleasing** made clear that the national court's duty of consistent interpretation applies only so far as possible. In other words, there will be cases where such an interpretation is simply not possible (**Wagner Miret** (1993)) and, in particular, there is no duty to adopt an interpretation which is *contra legem*,[10] that

[9] You should recognise that even though the directive cannot be horizontally directly effective, it is still indirectly effective and that Marcus may be able to use that to aid the interpretation of the national law.

[10] Only use Latin expressions if you are sure you know what they mean. If you are not sure, it is better not to use them rather than get them wrong.

is, clearly contrary to the intention of the national law in question (***Pupino*** (2005)).

In this case the national provision is vague. While it could be argued that the installation of hot water taps and the banning of kettles could be covered by interpreting them as being part of a reduction of risk, the requirement to have a staff room cannot be read into the Act. This would likely involve a *contra legem* interpretation or at least one which goes beyond what can reasonably be read into the provisions, and the national court would not be required to adopt such an interpretation.[11]

[11] This is, of course, a matter of opinion and you might decide that the meaning is perfectly compatible, and that would be fine as long as you explain that.

In conclusion, Marcus might be able to rely on the indirect effect of the reduction of health and safety risk of the Directive, but not in relation to the provision of a staff room.

✓ Make your answer stand out

- Add some discussion about how you would interpret the relevant parts of the Directive: for example, does the kitchen count as a staff room?
- You could examine the conditions of direct effect for directives in more detail using examples if you can remember some. Check your lecture notes for cases you have covered.
- Expand your explanation of how indirect effect might apply here. You could consider how the national wording might be held to be compatible with the Directive.
- Consider what the UK would have to do if the national law is not compatible in more detail and explain that infringement proceedings are possible if it does not do so.

! Don't be tempted to . . .

- Just explain direct effect and indirect effect and then state your conclusion – you must go through the process of application.
- Roll your answer to (a) and (b) into one; this is likely to end up a little confusing.
- Do not repeat the discussion you had in (a) in your answer to (b) – refer to the earlier discussion where relevant.
- Give facts of the cases; mostly you are just citing legal authority.

📝 Question 5

Explain the concept of state liability as introduced by the Court of Justice in *Francovich* (1991). How has the Court of Justice developed that concept in subsequent jurisprudence?

Answer plan

→ Introduce the *Francovich* case.

→ Set out the *Francovich* criteria.

→ Explain the limitation of *Francovich*.

→ Outline the development of the principle in *Factortame*.

→ Illustrate the application of the principle, using examples from case law.

Diagram plan

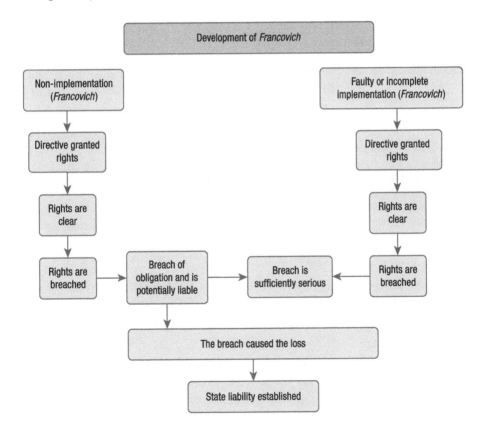

A printable version of this diagram plan is available from **www.pearsoned.co.uk/lawexpressqa**

Answer

[1] Your first sentence shows that you understand what the case you are asked to examine was about. You can then elaborate a little bit in the next sentences.

[2] Although this is a quote to show you how to use the exact provisions, there is no need to spend a long time learning provisions by rote. If you have a statute book, you could use that to check the exact wording. If you are not permitted use of a statute book, just paraphrase.

[3] You should say a little about the case, but you will see that the facts have been kept to a minimum. You do not need to show all of what happened to understand the principle established.

[4] Most examiners will accept you setting out the conditions in bullet-point style as we have done here. If in doubt, check with your examiner and, if necessary, write out the conditions in prose.

[5] The question asks about the development of the principles established, so you need to set out why the principle needed developing through the jurisprudence. This sentence signals that you are moving on to do that and shows the examiner you are taking an analytical approach.

The principle of state liability was introduced by the Court of Justice in *Francovich* (1991) ECJ.[1] The rationale behind extending liability to Member States was founded upon the obligation to implement directives under Article 288 TFEU and the general obligation under Article 4 TEU that the state 'shall ensure fulfilment of the obligations arising out of the treaties or resulting from the acts of the institutions of the Union'.[2]

In *Francovich* a group of ex-employees sought arrears of wages following the employer's insolvency.[3] The claim (inter alia) was based on the failure by Italy to implement Directive 80/987. In *Commission v Italy* (1991), Italy had previously been held to be in breach of its Community obligations with respect to its failure to implement this directive. The directive required Member States to provide a guaranteed fund to ensure the payment of arrears of wages in the event of the insolvency of the employer.

In *Francovich*, it was held that in principle the state could be liable for failure to implement an EC directive, if the following conditions were satisfied.[4]

- The result prescribed by the directive should entail the grant of rights to individuals.

- That it should be possible to identify the content of those rights on the basis of the provisions of the directive.

- That there should be a causal link between the breach of the State's obligation and the loss and damage suffered by the injured parties.

Where the three conditions of *Francovich* apply, the individual who seeks compensation as a result of the Member State failing to act in accord with European Union law may proceed directly against that state.

The implications for Member States of *Francovich* remained unclear.[5] The judgment was decided in the context of liability for the non-implementation of a directive, but it established principles that could be extended much further, to all breaches of Community law for which the state is responsible. In **Factortame** (1996) the principle of state liability was extended to all domestic acts and omissions, legislative, executive and judicial, in breach of EU law provided that the conditions in **Francovich** applied. In **Factortame** the ECJ confirmed that state liability would be found where a Member State had manifestly and gravely disregarded the limits of its discretion. The Court thus restated the need for a sufficiently serious breach in state liability cases. **Factortame** held that the factors to be taken into account in establishing whether the state had manifestly and gravely disregarded the limits of its discretion included:

> The clarity and precision of the rule breached, the measure of discretion left by that rule to the national or Community authorities, whether the infringement and the damage caused was intentional or involuntary, whether any error of law was excusable or inexcusable, the fact that the position taken by a Community institution may have contributed towards the omission, and the adoption or retention of national measures or practices contrary to Community law.

[6] Comments such as this show your analytical skills and also that you have thought about how the EU principle you are considering will affect the national context in Member States.

Bearing in mind the lack of clarity in much EU law and that Member States do not have a choice to act in breach of European Union law, it would seem that it is the *clarity and precision* of the rule breach that is important.[6] Jurisprudence has determined *how* serious the breach must be to incur liability. This approach is, for example, evidenced in **British Telecommunications plc** (1996), which involved a failed claim against the UK government concerning an alleged improper implementation of Council Directive 90/531 relating to public procurement. Despite the UK implementing regulations being contrary to the directive, this error was held excusable; the relevant provisions of the directive were sufficiently unclear. In **Brinkman** (1998)[7] an incor-

[7] Being able to set out the provisions is one thing but illustrating how they work with examples such as those here shows the examiner that you really have understood this area of law.

rect tax classification by Denmark was not sufficiently serious to found liability; the same mistake in the interpretation of the directive had been made by other Member States. Both **BT** and **Brinkman** evidence the view that where the Member State has a discretion to decide what action is to be taken in the implementation of the obligation under EU law, or where there is an excusable error in interpretation, then the standard of fault for liability will be higher. In consequence, it will be more difficult to obtain compensation. This accords with the view that

[8] Once you have made your point, conclude or summarise it as here and then move on. That helps the reader follow your structure and your argument.

[9] If you can remember examples illustrating both sides of an argument or different approaches as here, setting them out will show your full appreciation of the law and also make your argument well-rounded. Starting with phrases such as 'in contrast' highlights that you recognise the different approach.

where the obligation is much clearer, and the breach more obvious, then liability will be easier to impose on the state.[8]

By contrast, in **Hedley Lomas** (1996),[9] a different approach was adopted by the Court of Justice to the issue of state liability. Here, a UK ban on meat exports to Spain as a result of the non-compliance Spanish slaughterhouses Directive 74/577 did not comply with Union law and was held unlawful. Where the Member State 'was not called upon to make any legislative choices and had only considerably reduced, or even no, discretion, the mere infringement of Community law may be sufficient to establish the existence of a sufficiently serious breach'. This approach was adopted in **Dillenkoffer** (1996), in respect of a failure by Germany to implement Directive 90/314, designed to protect consumers in the event of a travel organiser's insolvency. This failure was held inexcusable and deemed 'sufficiently serious'. By contrast, in **Denkavit** (1996), the court followed the approach it had adopted in **BT**. In a claim for damages resulting from the faulty implementation of a directive, it was held that the relevant provisions of the directive lacked *clarity and precision* and the breach of Community law by Germany could not therefore be regarded as 'sufficiently serious' to justify liability. The approach adopted in **BT** was effectively that taken in **Lindöpark** (2001). It was noted that, given the clear wording of the VAT Directive (2006/112), Sweden was not in any position to make any legislative choices and 'had only a considerably reduced or even no discretion'. The mere infringement of the directive was therefore sufficient to create liability. Such an approach was supported in **Norbrook Laboratories Ltd** (1998) in which it was held that where a Member State was 'not called upon to make any legislative choices and had only considerably reduced, or even no, discretion, the mere infringement of Community law may be sufficient to establish the existence of a sufficiently serious breach.

 Make your answer stand out

- Include further examples from the jurisprudence in relation to the application of the principle of state liability.
- Include some academic commentary on the development of state liability. Consider the references to extra reading contained in, for example, Chalmers, D., Davies, G. and Monti, G. (2014) *EU Law. Cases and Materials*, Cambridge: Cambridge University Press.

■ Deal with the issues relating to proof of damage and causation – the condition must have been satisfied that the damage is caused by the breach and this can be difficult to show.

■ It might be helpful to set out your overall conclusion more explicitly at the end, referring back to the question.

❗ Don't be tempted to . . .

■ Spend most of the essay setting out the *Francovich* principles; you need to consider the development of the principles.

■ Set out the facts of the cases in detail – you need to give enough information to show why a breach of EU law might be sufficiently serious to give rise to state liability but you do not need to do more than that.

■ Assume that *Francovich* applied to any breach. Many students assume this, but you need to set out explicitly that *Francovich* dealt with non-implementation of a directive and the principles were extended later.

www.pearsoned.co.uk/lawexpressqa

Go online to access more revision support including additional essay and problem questions with diagram plans, You be the marker questions, and download all diagrams from the book.

Enforcement actions against Member States

How this topic may come up in exams

Almost all courses will cover enforcement actions in some detail and questions in this area are therefore common. Problem questions are popular because they are a fairly straightforward way of testing your understanding of this area of law. When answering problem questions in this area, summarise the law in the context of the question rather than generically, or, if you find that too difficult, summarise the law at the beginning and then spend the bulk of your time on application. Essay questions are, however, also possible and will tend to focus on the effectiveness of enforcement actions.

■ Before you begin

It's a good idea to consider the following key themes of enforcement actions against Member States before tackling a question on this topic.

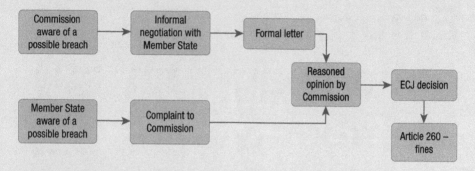

A printable version of this diagram is available from **www.pearsoned.co.uk/lawexpressqa**

❓ Question 1

In January 2014 a (fictitious) directive was issued which introduced EU rules relating to health and safety specifications for tablet computers. The date for implementation was January 2015. UK national law set out specifications for tablet computers which differ slightly from those set out by the directive in that they set more stringent requirements

Companies manufacturing tablet computers from other Member States have complained to the Commission about the difficulties of compliance with both the EU and the UK legislative regime when producing their goods for the UK market.

Two weeks ago the Commission formally opened proceedings against the UK under Article 258 TFEU by letters of formal notice.

Critically assess the procedures to be adopted together with the likely outcome if Article 258 proceedings are taken against the UK by the Commission.

Answer plan

→ Introduce Article 258 TFEU.

→ Outline the procedure in the context of the problem question:

  – Commission considers there to be a breach

  – Commission issues a reasoned opinion

  – If the UK does not comply, the judicial stage begins

  – Possible ECJ judgment with possible penalty payments for non-compliance.

Diagram plan

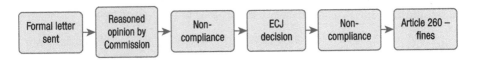

| Formal letter sent | → | Reasoned opinion by Commission | → | Non-compliance | → | ECJ decision | → | Non-compliance | → | Article 260 – fines |

A printable version of this diagram plan is available from **www.pearsoned.co.uk/lawexpressqa**

Answer

[1] Your first sentence here shows you are clear about what the question is asking you to do.

This question involves a direct action taken by the Commission under Article 258 TFEU before the Court of Justice in circumstances in which the Commission considers that a Member State has failed to fulfil an obligation under the treaties.[1] It involves a description of the procedure which would be taken by the Commission when enforcing European Union law against a Member State and an indication of the likely outcome should the Member State not comply with the ruling of the Court of Justice.

Article 258 provides:

[2] Don't worry if you cannot remember the exact wording. Paraphrasing is fine! If you are allowed to use a statute book in the exam, you could check the wording.

> If the Commission considers that a Member State has failed to fulfil an obligation under the treaties, it shall deliver a reasoned opinion on the matter after giving the State concerned the opportunity to submit its observations.[2]

> If the Member State concerned does not comply with the opinion within the period laid down by the Commission, the latter may bring the matter before the Court of Justice of the European Union.

[3] Try to highlight to the examiner that you have correctly identified the legal issue in the problem question. The more explicitly you do that, the easier the examiner can award the marks.

In this instance, the United Kingdom has failed to implement the directive introducing European standards for tablet computers.[3] It is from the non-implementation of this directive that the action by the Commission has arisen after a complaint by companies in the industry.

[4] This is a rather quick comment on the informal process which you could expand. It is focused on the context you've been given though, which is good.

It is clear from the wording of Article 258 that the Commission does not have to carry out a formal investigation, but it must 'consider' that there has been a breach of Union law. In this instance, the Commission has 'considered' that a breach exists; it has given the UK an opportunity to submit observations on the breach of European Union law that it suspects has been committed.[4] It must now deliver a 'reasoned opinion' on the matter to the UK government.

[5] This is important – the Commission must therefore make sure it includes everything and you have backed up such an important statement with case authority showing that you are aware of where the provisions come from. This makes for a solid legal argument.

The 'reasoned opinion' is a coherent statement of reasons on which it is believed that the Member State has failed to fulfil an obligation under the treaty (**Commission v Italy** (1961)). It must identify the provision, allegedly infringed, and must take into account the responses from the UK government. The Commission later cannot rely on matters not included in the reasoned opinion (**Commission v Belgium** (1987)).[5] It must detail the steps to be taken by the Member State to correct its infringement and set a time limit by which the UK must have ended that breach of EU law. The normal time period given to the Member State to respond to the 'reasoned opinion' is at least two months. Were the UK to comply within this period by implementing the directive, the Commission does not then have the power to bring the matter before the Court of Justice. If the directive has not been implemented by the date specified in the reasoned opinion, the Commission may proceed before the Court of Justice, irrespective of whether the UK subsequently implements the directive.[6]

The judicial stage

If it is held that the UK has failed to fulfil an obligation under the treaties, by not implementing the directive, the judgment under Article 258 will be 'that the state shall be required to take the necessary measures to comply with the judgment of the Court' (Article 260(1)). This means that the UK must implement the directive. In the case of infringement proceedings brought in respect of a failure to notify measures transposing a directive, the Court of Justice can impose a sanction at the same time that it rules against the Member State under Article 258. Article 260(3) provides:

> When the Commission brings a case before . . . on the grounds that the Member State concerned has failed to fulfil its obligation to notify measures transposing a directive adopted under a legislative procedure, it may, . . . specify the amount of the lump sum or penalty payment to be paid by the Member State concerned which it considers appropriate in the circumstances.[7]

The lump sum penalises an earlier non-compliance; between the original judgment (under Article 258) and the subsequent judgment (under Article 260). A periodic penalty payment on the other hand is intended to secure compliance with the final ruling under Article 260, applying in respect of each day of non-compliance with the judgment given under Article 260, continuing until eventual compliance.[8] It is clear from the judgment of **Commission v France** (1991), relating to the failure by France to comply with EU fisheries law between 1984 and 1987, that both sanctions of lump sum and penalty payments can be imposed at the same time. Should there be compliance by the Member State by the time of the judgment, the court has indicated that in these circumstances, it will not impose a penalty payment (**Commission v France** (2008)).

As to examples of sanctions that have been imposed on Member States, in **Commission v Greece** (2009), both a lump sum and penalty payment were imposed on Greece of €16,000 per day of delay in

[6] Although you are essentially setting out what the law/process is here, you are doing so in the context of the scenario set, which shows you are focused on answering the question and not just reproducing a pre-learned answer.

[7] We would not recommend learning these provisions by heart. While you might remember one or two from your course, you do not want to have to worry about getting it right in the exam. Paraphrase or, if you are allowed the use of one, consult a statute book for the exact wording.

[8] Here you are showing that you understand how the ruling can be enforced and what the purpose of different types of fines is. This shows detailed knowledge of the law which should pick up marks easily.

[9] Examples always make answers less abstract and more interesting, so it is good to include one or two where you can. It also demonstrates wider reading and knowledge.

implementing what was then a four-year-old judgment. In addition, there was a lump sum penalty of €2 million, based on the persistent failure by Greece to fulfil the obligation to implement the judgment.[9]

In ***Commission v France*** (2008) the Commission had proposed that France be ordered to pay both a lump sum and penalty payment. France, however, implemented the directive in issue before the date of judgment. It was held that the transposition of the directive would mean that France did not have to pay the penalty payment, but the Court of Justice ordered France to pay a lump sum payment of €10 million.

Make your answer stand out

- The question invites a rather descriptive answer, but the more you can comment on the provisions as you explain them, the more marks you will pick up for analysis and critical thinking.

- You could add a discussion on the informal process which should have occurred prior to starting the formal process.

- Consider the legal status of a reasoned opinion – is it binding law or 'soft law' and why might this matter.

- Comment on the level of fines that can be imposed to show your comprehensive understanding of this area.

! Don't be tempted to . . .

- Explain the procedure without reference to the problem and then draw your conclusions; this will tend to be very descriptive and you will lose marks.

- Provide an answer saying 'the Commission will do this, and then it will do this and then this . . .'. You need to back that up with authority and explore, based on case law, how the procedure would apply.

- Talk about enforcement of EU law generally – focus on the enforcement action highlighted in the problem question.

- Ignore the scenario. Even though the question is essentially about the procedure, you should locate your discussion in the context of the information you have been given.

❓ Question 2

The Polish government has received a number of complaints from Polish nationals who have been refused the right to residence and seek work in the UK. These Polish citizens report that they are either refused entry into the UK when they arrive at the border or that they are told by the UK authorities that they must leave if they have not secured a job within six weeks of arrival. The Polish government believes this to be in breach of the free movement of people provisions contained in the treaty and relevant secondary legislation and has seen a copy of a UK government memo detailing action to be taken to reduce the number of Eastern European workers in the UK. Refusing entry and asking work seekers to leave are listed as measures to be taken. None of the Polish citizens have the resources or willingness to bring their individual cases but the Polish government would like to challenge the UK's actions. Advise the Polish government.

Diagram plan

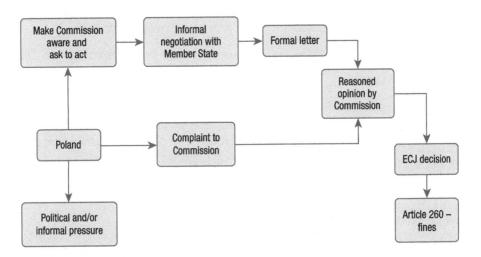

A printable version of this diagram plan is available from **www.pearsoned.co.uk/lawexpressqa**

Answer plan

→ Introduce Articles 258 and 259 TFEU.
→ Outline the procedure in the context of the problem question:
  – Ask the Commission to investigate under Article 258
  – Article 260 TFEU enforcement if necessary
  – Article 259 if Commission refuses or Poland prefers.

➡ Commission involvement in Article 259 actions.

➡ Consider the alternatives to legal process: for example, political, informal discussion.

➡ Summarise overall advice.

Answer

¹ Stating the applicable law right at the start is a really useful habit to get into because the examiner can see immediately that you have identified the correct legal issues and provisions.

² This sentence indicates that you fully understand how enforcement works and appreciate that you are asked to focus only on a particular issue to the exclusion of individual enforcement. Use all the information given to you in the scenario; it will all be there for a reason.

³ After having explained the first hurdle in the previous sentence, you now state how this applies. The next sentence explains how you came to that conclusion. The examiner can therefore see that you understand the law and how it applies in this specific case.

⁴ Here you are showing awareness of how the legal provisions work in reality. The next sentence explains why they operate in the way they do and acknowledges the political dimensions. You are highlighting that you appreciate that law always operates in context.

This problem question concerns the possibility of an enforcement action against the UK under Article 258 or Article 259 TFEU.¹ The Polish government may ask the European Commission to investigate the matter and bring Article 258 TFEU enforcement proceedings. In the event that the Commission is unwilling to do so or cannot do so in a time frame acceptable to Poland, the Polish government may also want to consider bringing an enforcement action themselves under Article 259 TFEU. As the problem question clearly indicates that the individuals concerned do not want to bring actions themselves, enforcement through individuals will not be considered here.²

Enforcement actions can be brought for any breach of EU law, but both Articles 258 and 259 TFEU are silent on what constitutes a breach. European Court of Justice jurisprudence, however, suggests that both actions and inactions are within the scope of the provisions. In this case it seems that the suspected breach is the result of action taken by the UK.³ The issuing of the government memo dealing with Eastern European workers suggests that the UK is deliberately acting in a way inconsistent with their duties under the treaty and secondary legislation as well as with their general duty of good faith under Article 4(3) TFEU.

Poland is likely to consider first initiating action under Article 258 TFEU. Although there is nothing stopping them bringing an action against the UK directly, the preferred course of action tends to be to ask the Commission to investigate matters and try and ensure compliance.⁴ This avoids the politically contentious issue of Member States taking each other to court and makes the dispute between countries less obvious. This should therefore also be Poland's first option.

If the Commission decides to investigate matters under Article 258 TFEU, it will initiate informal negotiations with the UK and notify the UK that it is suspected of not correctly fulfilling its EU law obligations. If the Commission is satisfied that a breach has indeed occurred, it will send a letter of formal notice to the UK asking for a response. Following a response or a time lapse, usually of two months within which no response has been received, the Commission would prepare a reasoned opinion. The reasoned opinion would be addressed to the UK and would set a time limit within which the UK must comply.

If it still does not do so, the action is progressed to the judicial stage where it will be considered by the Court of Justice. The UK would be compelled to comply with the judgment but there are no automatic sanctions for not doing so. If the UK still did nothing to comply with EU law and the Court of Justice judgments, the Commission could bring a further action under Article 260 TFEU which allows the Court of Justice to fine Member States for non-compliance. Both lump sums and periodic payments can be awarded.[5]

However, the Polish government should be aware that this process takes a significant amount of time[6] and there is a delay of approximately 18 months in relation to the Court of Justice hearing cases such as this one. If Poland is seeking a more speedy resolution, this procedure may not be the best option. However, only the minority of cases actually get to a judicial stage and most are resolved in the earlier stages. If this was the case here, and the UK complied with their EU law obligations as a result of the informal negotiations, the matter could be resolved relatively quickly. In addition, once the Commission has been notified of the breach, Poland cannot compel it to take action.[7] The Commission has a wide discretion to investigate matters and bring Article 258 TFEU proceedings, so if it decides not to, there is nothing Poland can do (**Star Fruit Company v Commission** (1989)). In addition, the Commission is not under a duty to inform Poland of the progress of the investigation or action although it does tend to publish its progress in the *Official Journal*.

An alternative option for Poland is to initiate proceedings against the UK under Article 259 TFEU. If this is the preferred course of action, Poland must still bring the matter before the Commission which will then ask both Poland and the UK to submit their position. On the basis of those submissions, the Commission will issue a reasoned opinion. It may even take over the action at this point (**Commission v France** (1979)).[8] This is, of course, unlikely to happen if the Commission refused to act in this matter in the first place. If no solution is found at this point or the Commission does not issue their reasoned

[5] The preceding paragraph outlines how the procedure you are considering works but, rather than writing it in the abstract, you have dealt with it in a way specific to the scenario, making it much less abstract and avoiding having first to state the law and then restate the same issues in the application of it.

[6] Again, you are showing good awareness of context and practical matters here, as well as demonstrating a clear understanding of the legal procedure.

[7] This may be a very good reason why Poland would want to take action directly and, although you are speculating, it is useful to give examples of what those reasons might be. It shows good contextual knowledge and awareness which examiners will be looking for.

[8] You do not need to say anything about the case but a well-placed case reference just reassures the examiner that you are not simply making it up.

opinion within three months, Poland can refer the matter to the Court of Justice. Once a judgment has been made, the UK must comply. If it does not, Article 260 TFEU proceedings can be brought.

Poland should again be aware that it can take a significant amount of time for an Article 259 action to be resolved. If compliance by the UK can be achieved early on, this is not problematic, but, if the UK refuses to comply, matters can take years to conclude, leaving Polish citizens in a difficult position. The Polish government may want to consider supporting individuals to bring their cases in the UK courts to challenge deportation or refusal of entry as this may be a quicker way to resolve the issue. Alternatively, Poland may want to try and approach the UK informally to try and ensure compliance with EU law.[9] It may be that the problems here are resolved more easily on a political level without the need to make use of the formal legal framework for enforcement. If recourse to the legal framework is necessary, Poland should consider whether it would prefer to avoid the politically contentious and very public act of taking another Member State to court. If so, it should be advised to report the breach of EU law obligations on the part of the UK to the Commission. If it is not concerned about the publicity and political effect, it can also bring an action direct.[10]

[9] Don't underestimate how powerful political pressure can be, and, by mentioning that here, you show the examiners that you have fully considered the position and have not jumped to the conclusion that legal provisions are always the best answer.

[10] Nice summary of your advice at the end which brings your essay to a logical conclusion and shows that you were indeed finished and did not simply run out of time.

✓ Make your answer stand out

- Consider interim measures and suspensory orders which reduce the impact of the length of the process (Article 278 and 279 TFEU).
- Comment on the level of fines that can be imposed under Article 260 TFEU.
- You could consider Article 273 TFEU relating to Member States' referrals of disputes to the ECJ but in practice this never seems to be used.
- If you have time, you could add one or two sentences about the cases you cite in order to highlight similarities and differences with the current situation. Keep it relevant, though.

❗ Don't be tempted to . . .

- Focus purely on Article 259 TFEU – you must acknowledge that the more likely route is for Poland to refer the breach to the Commission.

- Explain the procedures in the abstract and then say 'therefore Poland should do this'. You need to engage with the scenario throughout.

- Ignore the potential for an informal or political resolution. This is quite unlikely ever to get to the ECJ.

- Write about enforcement generally. Focus on the scenario.

🔖 Question 3

Enforcement actions against Member States under Articles 258 and 259 TFEU are ineffective and need significant revision to be of any practical use. Evaluate this statement.

Diagram plan

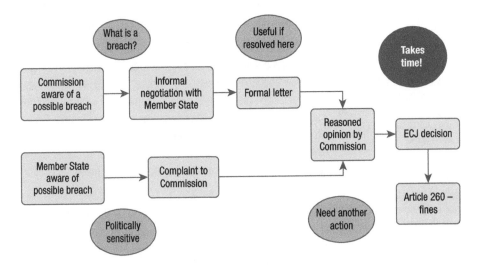

A printable version of this diagram plan is available from **www.pearsoned.co.uk/lawexpressqa**

Answer plan

➡️ Introduce Articles 258 and 259 TFEU.

➡️ Explain the usefulness of the enforcement procedure.

➡️ Discuss the issues with the process, for example:

- What is a breach?
- Notification of breach
- Informal process
- Judicial stage
- Time.

Answer

This essay considers actions brought against Member States by either the European Commission under Article 258 TFEU or by other Member States under Article 259 TFEU. It argues that, while enforcement mechanisms such as these are useful and provide the EU with a control mechanism ensuring compliance with EU law, they are nonetheless ineffective mainly because of the time it can take for proceedings to be brought to a conclusion and because of the limited enforcement powers available to the institutions and Member States.[1]

Article 258 TFEU provides that the Commission should issue a reasoned opinion where it considers a Member State to be in breach of EU law obligations. Where the Member State does not comply, the Commission may bring the matter before the European Court of Justice. Article 259 TFEU affords similar power to Member States where they consider another Member State to be in breach of EU Law obligations.[2] Here a Member State may refer a matter to the European Court of Justice after having sought a reasoned opinion from the Commission.

Clearly, it is useful for the European Union to be able to ensure compliance with EU law.[3] It adds weight and credibility to the idea of supremacy of EU law as well as to the requirements of good faith on the part of the Member States laid out in Article 4(3) TFEU.[4] It also sets the EU apart from international organisations which generally do not have the power to enforce compliance with legal rules. Without a legal mechanism by which Member States could be forced to comply, reliance would have to be placed on political avenues or public

[1] You have set out your stall right from the start; the rest of the essay is now about proving that statement. You show the examiner that you understand the question and have a clear academic opinion on it.

[2] If you have the use of a statute book in an exam, you could quote from the provisions here, but paraphrasing is fine especially if you are not allowed to use a statute book.

[3] When making a statement such as this one which is really just your opinion, make sure you back it up and justify it – this comes next.

[4] It's always useful to state why we might want to have the provisions under consideration in the first place; it makes it easier to assess their effectiveness.

pressure which in some cases may, of course, encourage Member States to do the opposite of what EU law requires. Examples of such instances might include matters relating to free movement of people and national fears of 'swamped labour markets'.

In order to assess how effective the provisions are, a detailed consideration of a number of elements of the provisions is required.[5] This essay will therefore first consider what sort of matters can be dealt with under Articles 258 and 259 TFEU; it will then briefly consider the procedure which leads to the judicial action, before considering the judicial phase of proceedings as well as the enforcement of actions in more detail.[6]

Neither Articles 258 nor 259 TFEU define what constitutes a breach of EU law that is actionable using these procedures. European Court of Justice jurisprudence, however, suggests that actions as well as inactions are covered. Cases brought in relation to inactions generally relate to the non-implementation or the incorrect implementation of directives and other secondary legislation. In *Commission v France* (1974) the court even confirmed that not removing inconsistent legislation even where it was no longer applied still constituted a breach.[7] *Commission v France* (1997)[8] further illustrates the inclusive interpretation of breach in this context. The court held that doing nothing to prevent persons from restricting free movement of goods where action could and should have been taken amounted to an actionable breach under Article 258 TFEU. A wide interpretation of what constitutes a breach is important if the EU is to use enforcement actions to ensure compliance.[9] If the term 'breach' was restricted, to positive acts for example, there would be no way to compel Member States to implement directives correctly and on time, as not doing so would not be a positive act. A related point is that, although Member States are the defendants in these actions, 'Member States' is defined broadly and includes the legislative, executive and the judiciary as well as regional and local authorities (*Commission v Belgium* (1970)). If this were not the case, it would simply allow Member States to shift blame to those administrative bodies and thus avoid implementation.

Under Article 258 TFEU, the Commission may issue a reasoned opinion where it is satisfied that a Member State has breached its obligations under EU law. The Commission can investigate of its own volition or as a result of reported breaches. It is worth noting here, though,

[5] This is a helpful statement telling the examiner what it is you are now going to consider in the essay.

[6] A really useful signpost through the rest of the answer, setting out the structure clearly and making it as easy as possible to follow your argument.

[7] Citing examples such as this one not only sets out the limits of the provisions clearly but also makes your answer less abstract by showing how the area of law has been dealt with by the court. It also highlights that you have quite detailed knowledge.

[8] In this area of law you see a lot of the same case names and remembering case numbers in exams can be tricky. Check with your course leader what exactly is required of you.

[9] In order to avoid becoming too descriptive, it is useful to think about the implications of the law or interpretation of it in every paragraph and include a sentence like this.

that the Commission cannot be forced to take any further action once it has been informed (***Star Fruit Company v Commission*** (1989)). A process whereby the Commission must at least make an initial investigation and respond to the complainant may be more effective in ensuring breaches are taken seriously.[10] The resource implications, however, make this practically impossible.[11]

[10] Do include any ideas you may have for improving the law and explain them clearly.

[11] It is fine to include an idea that works theoretically and legally but also think about practical implications.

Following receipt of a complaint, the Commission may investigate and correspond informally with the Member State(s) concerned. If the Commission comes to the conclusion that there has been a breach, the Member State in question will be informed and given the chance either to put their case or to correct its action/inaction. Should this not happen, the Commission will issue a reasoned opinion setting a time limit for compliance. If the Member State does not comply, the matter comes before the Court of Justice. Under Article 259 TFEU, a Member State may issue proceedings against another Member State for a breach. This must, however, first be brought to the Commission's attention. After hearing from both States, the Commission will issue a reasoned opinion on the matter. The complaining Member State may refer the matter to the Court of Justice once the time limit for compliance or, indeed, the time limit of three months for the reasoned opinion to be issued has elapsed.

The informal discussions with Member States are a useful part of the procedure because they are likely to result in Member State compliance without the need for anything more formal. The 2008 Monitoring report suggests that 68 per cent of actions are settled before the formal process begins.[12] An enforced informal negotiating phase may also prove useful in relation to Article 259 actions.

[12] It's useful to show off your wider reading and contextual knowledge.

The judicial phase can take around 18 months to complete and the judgment is simply declaratory. If the Member State in question does not comply, further proceedings need to be brought under Article 260 TFEU which give the ECJ the power to impose lump sum or penalty payment fines for non-compliance.

The key problem relating to the effectiveness of enforcement actions is the time it takes to investigate suspected breaches and take action in relation to them. The judicial phase alone takes over a year and the informal negotiating phase can add years to the process, potentially causing considerable hardship for those affected by the breach. In order to minder the effects slightly, suspensory orders and interim measures are possible under Articles 278 and 279 TFEU.[13]

[13] At this point you are probably beginning to run out of time, but you should still mention the interim measures even if you do not have time to say much about them.

In summary, the possibility of taking enforcement actions is welcomed and statistics show that the process is a useful one, with most actions being settled before they get to the judicial phase. However, problems remain because of the time the enforcement actions take, and actions taken by individuals to enforce their directly effective rights under EU law are likely to continue to have a bigger impact on Member State compliance.

 Make your answer stand out

- There is some academic commentary you can draw on. Consider Rawlings, R. (2000) Engaged Elites Citizen Action and Institutional Attitudes in Commission Enforcement, *European Law Journal*, 6(1).
- Use additional case examples to illustrate your points, drawing attention to the fact that Article 259 actions are rare.
- Consider interim measures and suspensory orders in more detail.
- You could speculate on what sort of reform might be needed to make the provisions more effective.

! Don't be tempted to . . .

- Only talk about Article 258 TFEU; you need to deal with both Articles 258 and 259, but avoid overlap.
- Ignore Article 260 TFEU. It plays a significant role in making the other two Articles effective because it provides sanctions for non-compliance.
- Outline the actions without commenting on the process.
- Give facts of the cases you use. Mostly you are just citing legal authority, and, where you are illustrating a point, you only need to give as much information as absolutely necessary to make your point.

www.pearsoned.co.uk/lawexpressqa

 Go online to access more revision support including additional essay and problem questions with diagram plans, You be the marker questions, and download all diagrams from the book.

Direct actions before the European Court of Justice

7

How this topic may come up in exams

This topic is often examined by way of problem questions. They allow you to show that you have understood this area of law and can apply it. Essay questions are possible but much rarer because they tend to lend themselves to overly descriptive answers. So, where you do encounter essays, pay particular attention to your assessment or evaluation of the issues and be really careful to avoid pure description.

◼ Before you begin

It's a good idea to consider the following key themes of direct actions before the European Court of Justice before tackling a question on this topic.

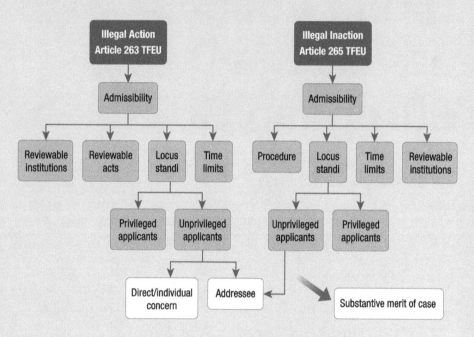

A printable version of this diagram is available from **www.pearsoned.co.uk/lawexpressqa**

❓ Question 1

Whernside Whisky Company Ltd (WWco) has signalled intent to challenge a fictitious Commission decision requiring Member States to impose a maximum alcohol content limit of 33 per cent volume per litre in relation to spirits produced in the European Union. WWco has produced whisky at its distillery in Scotland for the last 250 years and is the largest whisky distiller in the EU market. Its best-selling whisky 'Knockout' is produced with an alcoholic proof above the maximum level allowed by the decision. As a result of the Commission decision, WWco will lose 55 per cent of its annual turnover. This will result in reduced profits which cannot be replaced by the other products it sells. WWco now wishes to challenge the Commission decision.

Advise WWco as to whether it is entitled to locus standi so that it could maintain an action under Article 263 TFEU to annul the Commission decision with respect to the imposition of a maximum alcohol content limit on spirits.

Diagram plan

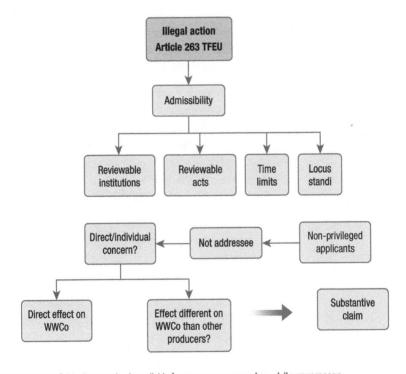

A printable version of this diagram plan is available from **www.pearsoned.co.uk/lawexpressqa**

Answer plan

→ Introduce Article 263 TFEU.

→ Consider whether or not WWco has locus standi as a non-privileged applicant:
  - Is the decision addressed to WWco?
  - Is the issue of direct and individual concern?

→ Consider the substantive merit of the claim.

Answer

[1] This is a useful introductory sentence because it tells the reader what the legal issue is but keeps the focus on the problem question given.

This question concerns action for annulment under Article 263 TFEU of a Commission decision requiring Member States to impose a maximum alcohol content limit of 33 per cent per litre in relation to spirits produced in the European Union.[1]

[2] If you can remember the legal provision, now is a good time to set it out. Paraphrasing or summarising will do; there is generally no need to quote exactly.

Article 263 provides 'The Court of Justice of the European Union shall review the legality of . . . acts . . . of the Commission'. The provision further provides that 'Any . . . legal person may, . . . institute proceedings against an act addressed to that person or which is of direct and individual concern to them'.[2]

As a company, WWco is a 'legal person'. The Commission decision in question has been addressed, not to WWco, but, to Member States. Whether or not WWco can bring an action under Article 263 for an annulment of the Commission decision will depend upon WWco establishing that the Decision is of 'direct and individual concern' to it.[3] If such can be established, WWco will have 'locus standi' to pursue an action for annulment of the decision.

[3] This is a really succinct way of summarising what you need to establish in your answer.

For the purposes of proving 'locus standi', under Article 263, WWco falls into the category of 'non-privileged applicant'. Article 263(4) in this context provides:

> Any natural or legal person may, . . . institute proceedings against an act addressed to that person or which is of direct and individual concern to them, and against a regulatory act which is of direct concern to them.

[4] It is fine to say that there is no clear definition. You must then, however, say how you think the scenario would be viewed and why, which is what the rest of this sentence does.

The terminology of 'act' was introduced by Article 263(4) TFEU. The jurisprudence of the General Court (formerly Court of First Instance) is yet to determine the precise meaning of this term;[4] arguably, however,

5 If you have to make an assumption in an answer, make it explicit such as here: otherwise you are asking the examiner to guess at what your assumption might have been.

it would include a decision, as a form of secondary legislation, taken by the Commission. This answer proceeds on the basis that such interpretation is correct.[5]

For the applicant to establish direct concern in relation to a Community measure, it was held in **Koninklijke** (2009) that the measure must directly affect the legal situation of the individual and leave no discretion to its addressees entrusted with the task of implementing it.[6]

6 So this is the definition WWco must satisfy and it has been summarised from case law, showing you know the law as well as the authority for that provision.

Whether or not WWco can establish direct concern will depend upon whether the action affecting the applicant was within the area of the Member State's discretion.[7] In **Eridania v Commission** (1969) 'direct concern' was not established. The Commission had authorised the decision regarding the allocation of aid and it had been taken by the Italian government and was therefore within its discretion. A broad interpretation of discretion could relate to where the Commission merely permits or authorises a Member State to act: the state still retains a discretion whether or not to act. Alternatively, a narrow interpretation would mean that, where the implementation of a Commission decision is automatic or a foregone conclusion, the state has no real discretion and the measure will be of 'direct concern' to the applicant. In order to establish 'direct concern' in the present case, the detail of the Commission decision would have to be examined to establish whether or not Member States had any say in its implementation.[8]

7 This is quite abstract, so the examples which follow should help show that you really do understand this.

8 This is sitting on the fence a little, but you don't really have the detail to say anything more definitive.

If there is no discretion in the implementation of the decision by the Commission, then direct concern could be established. In these circumstances, WWco would need then to show an individual concern. The concept of 'individual concern' has been interpreted narrowly. It has been held in **Plaumann** (1963) that 'individual concern' will be established where

9 This is too long a case law quote to remember for an exam, so you should just paraphrase, unless you have a particularly good memory for quotes.

> Persons other than those to whom a decision is addressed may only claim to be individually concerned if that decision affects them by reason of certain attributes which are peculiar to them or by reason of circumstances in which they are differentiated from all other persons and by virtue of these factors distinguishes them individually just as in the case of the person addressed.[9]

In **Plauman** the applicant failed because it did not belong to a *closed class of persons* that was engaged in the importation of clementines, 'a commercial activity which may at any time be practised by any person'. The **Plauman** test was applied in **Piraiki-Patraiki** (1985), the effect of which was to deny the Greek applicant yarn exporters the opportunity to challenge a Commission decision to impose a quota system which limited the amount of yarn that could be imported from France to Greece. The business of exporting yarn was clearly a commercial activity which could be carried on at any time by any undertaking.

The **Plauman** test, difficult to satisfy, was confirmed in **Unión de Pequeños Agricultores (UPA)** (2002). The measure must refer to the applicant's situation and affect a closed class. The judgment overruled the Court of First Instance (now the General Court) in which the CFI had relaxed the extremely strict approach that had been taken by the Court of Justice in jurisprudence with respect to the establishment of 'individual concern'.

[10] The preceding paragraphs have set out the legal test for individual concern, but on their own will not get you many marks: you must now consider the application of that test to the scenario.

Whether or not WWco could show that it is part of a closed class, that no one else could engage in this activity in the future in the circumstances may arguably be difficult.[10] It is a distillery; the applicant is producing whisky. In theory at least it could be possible that another distillery could be established, if not in Scotland, somewhere else within the European Union. Whether or not that would transpire in practice would be difficult to determine; distilling is a highly specialised business activity requiring expertise that would make it difficult for new entrants to the market to acquire. With the highly specific business conditions prevailing, it seems that the reality is that new players to the market would arguably be rare or non-existent.[11] If the court were to accept this argument, then WWco may have a chance of successfully arguing that it was part of a closed class.

[11] This paragraph is the application of the law. Sometimes it is easier to outline the law first and then apply it rather than try to do it all in one – that's fine just as long as you do not miss out this step!

It is noted that Article 263 provides that: 'The proceedings provided for in this Article shall be instituted within two months of the publication of the measure.' It is thus necessary to check the date of the publication of the Commission decision to ensure that any action taken is commenced within the time limits imposed under Union law.

✓ Make your answer stand out

■ Consider the substantive claim in more detail.

■ Comment briefly on the other criteria for admissibility – the institution concerned and the act concerned.

■ Summarise your advice at the end to show that you have fully answered the question and are finished and have not just run out of time.

■ Consider alternative actions for WWco: for example, a reference under Article 267 TFEU.

! Don't be tempted to . . .

■ Ignore issues of admissibility and focus just on the substantive claim – the problem is usually admissibility.

■ Go into detail of the case law. You have given sufficient information to make your point.

■ Ignore the substantive claim completely – although the problem is usually admissibility, you must also comment on substantive issues to show that you have recognised them.

■ Set out the law generally without applying it. You need to focus your answer on the scenario given.

 # Question 2

To what extent are Articles 263 and 265 TFEU effective in providing an avenue to challenge illegal actions or inactions by EU institutions.

Answer plan

→ Introduce Articles 263 and 265 TFEU.

→ Outline Article 263 TFEU, going into more detail, for example:

- Reviewable institutions
- Reviewable acts
- Time limits
- Locus standi
- Substantive merit.

➡️ Compare by outlining the differences with Article 265 TFEU.

➡️ Summarise your argument.

Diagram plan

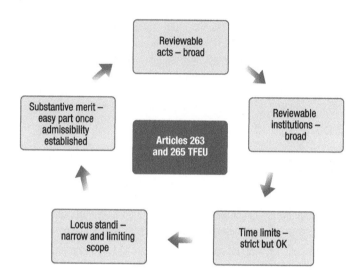

A printable version of this diagram plan is available from **www.pearsoned.co.uk/lawexpressqa**

Answer

This essay considers direct actions before the European Court of Justice and, in particular, deals with actions to annul an act performed by an EU institution and actions challenging the inaction of an EU institution. Taken together, these two types of actions should provide Member States and other institutions as well as individuals in certain circumstances with an effective challenge to EU illegality. However, this essay will argue that problems remain in relation to both actions and that they are therefore not as effective as they could be.[1]

[1] This introduction shows that you understand the area of law and that you have an opinion on it. Good start.

In order to consider whether or not actions for annulment and actions for failure to act provide sufficient scope to challenge the potential illegality of EU institutions, this essay outlines both types of action in turn, commenting on them throughout. It begins with an examination of Article 263 TFEU.[2]

[2] Setting out how you intend to structure your answer helps the examiner follow your argument but also helps you because you can keep referring back to it as you write.

[3] This sentence along with the ones before set out clearly and succinctly what needs to be established under Article 263 TFEU and show that you are logically considering each step of the process.

[4] The cases here are examples of the point you have just made, so there is no need to say anything about them; you have already made your point and knowing more about the cases does not advance your argument in this instance.

[5] If you can, try to make a comment relating directly back to the question in most paragraphs. It avoids description and makes sure that you really do answer the question.

[6] No need to say anything about the cases: you're just citing your authority.

[7] A comment like this shows that your understanding is detailed enough to appreciate how the provisions might apply or operate in practice. Examiners are looking for in-depth knowledge and ability to apply the law, so this should help you to get marks.

[8] You are already commenting on it here, not just describing, which is good.

Article 263 TFEU provides that the Court of Justice shall review the legality of acts of Union institutions intended to produce legal effects in relation to third parties. First, the admissibility of actions must be considered. Admissibility depends on four elements and all four must be satisfied.[3] Acts of the Commission and the Council were originally the only acts which could be challenged, but the ECJ soon included the European Parliament too (see *Luxembourg* v *European Parliament* (1983); *Parti Ecologiste Les Verts* v *European Parliament* (1986) and *Council* v *European Parliament* (1986)).[4] The Lisbon Treaty now clarifies that all Union institutions which enact measures intended to produce legal effects are included. The scope of institutions subject to review has therefore increased significantly to ensure that the EU cannot act illegally whichever of its institutions is making rules.[5]

Which acts are reviewable was given a wide interpretation by the ECJ and extended well beyond the regulations, directives and decisions mentioned in the treaty pre-Lisbon (see *Noordwijks Cement Accord* (1967); *French Republic* v *Commission* (1997)).[6] The Lisbon Treaty amended Article 263 TFEU to take account of the case law and it is now clear that all acts creating a legal effect are caught. The scope has therefore once again been extended, ensuring that illegal measures cannot be 'hidden' in provisions which would not be subject to review.

Article 263 TFEU provides relatively strict time limits to bring an action. An applicant has two months from the date of publication of the measure or the date of notification, or, where there is no publication or notification, from the date it came to the notice of the applicant. Although the time limits are relatively strict, they should give applicants sufficient time.[7] The time limit starts running 15 days after publication, an anomaly left from when publications had to be shipped across the EU. In addition, time limits have been held not to apply where the defects of a measure are so serious that it can be regarded as non-existent (*BASF* v *Commission* (1991)).

The most controversial admissibility requirement[8] is that of locus standi. Privileged applicants include the Member States, the Council, the Commission and the European Parliament. Privileged applicants have unlimited rights to bring an action. Semi-privileged applicants include other Union institutions such as the European Central Bank and the Court of Auditors. They have a more limited right to challenge measures where their interests are clearly affected. All others are non-privileged applicants who must fulfil certain conditions before being able to bring an action. A non-privileged application may challenge a provision addressed to them or which is of direct and individual concern to them. The rights for individual applicants are therefore much more limited than for privileged ones. Decisions directly addressing the individual are relatively easy to understand; more difficult are situations where one is required to establish direct and individual concern. Direct concern refers to the fact that the act must be of concern directly to the individual seeking to annul it; Member State discretion will therefore negate direct concern in most cases (***Bock* v *Commission*** (1971)). Individual concern must also be established and this refers to the applicant being able to distinguish themselves somehow from others potentially affected by the measure (***Plaumann* v *Commission*** (1963)).

[9] Always try to think back to the question. 'Scope' was the word used in the question set so use it too when making your arguments.

The limitations placed on individual applicants to bring an action arguably limit the scope to challenge illegal actions quite considerably.[9] While it is true that the Lisbon Treaty has simplified matters a little and has opened the possibility of individuals challenging acts other than decisions, by broadening the application of direct and individual concern to all acts, showing individual concern in particular remains difficult. This reduces the effectiveness of Article 263 TFEU actions considerably because it is likely to be individual applicants who are keen to have EU acts reviewed and who symbolically at least should benefit most from the rule of law and the associated right to judicial review of legal provisions.

[10] So action is covered, and it is useful to conclude that point explicitly before you move on to inaction. It signals that you have finished with that point and are now moving on. This helps keep the structure clear in the reader's mind.

[11] And because it is so similar, you do not need to spend a lot of time going over the provisions in detail.

Once admissibility has been established, the Court of Justice can turn to a consideration of the merits of the case. Acts can be annulled on the basis that the institution adopting the measure lacked competence to do so (***France* v *Commission*** (1994)); where there was an infringement of a procedural requirement (***Germany* v *Commission*** (1963)); where there has been an infringement of the treaty rules or its applications such as equality or respect for fundamental rights (***Töpfer*** (1978)) or where an EU institution has misused its power. It therefore seems that the grounds of illegal action are covered.[10]

Inaction, however, is not covered and this is dealt with by Article 265 TFEU, which in many ways is very similar to Article 263.[11] In order for an action to be admissible, an EU institution must have been under a duty to act, must have been called upon to act and must have failed to do so. Locus standi requirements are equally restrictive for non-privileged applicants as they are under Article 263 TFEU, although perhaps a little more clearly defined because, instead of a requirement of direct and individual concern, there is a requirement to be the potential addressee of the provision. Therefore, individuals can only request decisions, as directives and regulations cannot be addressed to them.

[12] The conclusion addresses the question directly, which is helpful to the examiners. It also acknowledges that the provisions do not exist in isolation, and this is an important point to remember whenever assessing specific provisions. Think about how they fit in with other processes, procedures and principles.

The provisions give some scope for challenging illegal action and inaction by the EU institutions but that scope is concentrated on the other institutions and Member States. Individuals are more limited and likely to face lengthy and complex legal proceedings to establish admissibility and in particular locus standi before the matter can even be fully heard. Taken in isolation, therefore, the scope of Articles 263 and 265 TFEU is insufficient. However, given that it is a requirement of national courts to make a preliminary reference on the validity of EU law under Article 267 TFEU in cases coming before them, individuals do have other avenues to challenge potentially illegal action.[12]

✓ Make your answer stand out

- Consider briefly EU non-contractual liability as a further way to ensure EU compliance.
- Explain pleas of illegality under Article 277 TFEU.
- Describe in more detail the rationale for the locus standi rules.
- Include academic commentary such as Usher, J. (2003) Direct and Individual Concern – an Effective Remedy or a Conventional Solution, *EL Rev*, 28, 575.

! Don't be tempted to . . .

- Simply explain the process – comment on it in every paragraph.
- Give lengthy case examples.
- Ignore Article 265 TFEU – you are asked to consider actions and inactions.
- Repeat yourself. Where the issues are similar for actions and inactions, refer back to your earlier discussion rather than saying the same thing again.

❓ Question 3

The (fictitious) Regulation 311/2012 on the sale of chocolate and sweets has come into force. It prohibits the sale of chocolate and other sweets to children under the age of 12. It does so on the basis that consuming excessive amounts of chocolate and sweets is detrimental to children's health. Convenient Sweets is a chain of small convenience stores which are well known for having their stores close to schools and sports clubs. As a result of the Regulation, Convenient Sweets' direct sales have declined by 65 per cent and it is facing serious financial difficulties. An action for annulment of the Regulation has failed. Advise Convenient Sweets whether it can seek damages for its losses from the EU.

Answer plan

➜ Introduce Article 268 TFEU relating to EU non-contractual liability.

➜ Consider the admissibility of the claim:

   – Locus standi.

➜ Discuss the relationship of action with Article 263 TFEU proceedings.

➜ Liability for legislative acts:

   – Apply *Zuckerfabrik Schöppenstedt* v *Council* (1971).

   – Apply *Bergaderm* v *Commission* (2000).

➜ Conclude by asking whether it is likely to be able to establish liability.

Diagram plan

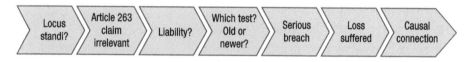

Locus standi? ❭ Article 263 claim irrelevant ❭ Liability? ❭ Which test? Old or newer? ❭ Serious breach ❭ Loss suffered ❭ Causal connection

A printable version of this diagram plan is available from **www.pearsoned.co.uk/lawexpressqa**

Answer

¹ This is helpful because you show that you clearly understand the legal provisions and how they work.

This problem question concerns the possible non-contractual liability of the European Union (EU) under Articles 268 and 340 TFEU. The first consideration is whether or not Convenient Sweets has a claim which is admissible; the second consideration relates to the merit of the action brought.¹

In order to bring a claim, Convenient Sweets must first establish that it has locus standi. The requirement under Article 268 TFEU is not difficult to satisfy. Convenient Sweets must simply show that it is affected by the Regulation in question and has suffered damage in a tangible and provable way. Clearly Convenient Sweets can show that the Regulation has had an effect[2] and will be able to quantify that loss to some extent even if more detailed calculations as to loss are not actually required until the substantive case is heard.

Convenient Sweets must then bring its claim within five years from the coming into force of the Regulation (Article 46 Statute of the Court of Justice, *Zuckerfabrik Schöppenstedt* v *Council* (1971))[3] and in bringing the action must identify the relevant EU institution as the defendant. In this case the defendants are likely to be the Council and the European Parliament who have joint legislative power and are thus likely to be responsible for enacting the Regulation.

The fact that an action for annulment has previously failed does not prevent Convenient Sweets from bringing an action for damages here.[4] The ECJ has held that such an action is an autonomous and independent action and that previous actions are irrelevant. In *Lütticke* (1971), for example, the ECJ rejected the argument that the applicant should not be allowed to bring an action because it effectively circumvented the strict locus standi requirements applicable for bringing actions for a failure to act.[5] The same argument was made in *Zuckerfabrik Schöppentedt* in relation to damages arising from a regulation. Admissibility is therefore not likely to be an issue for Convenient Sweets.

It is clear that liability can be imposed for damages resulting from legislative acts.[6] *Zuckerfabrik Schöppenstedt* was for a long time the leading case and established strict rules for imposing liability on the Union. Convenient Sweets would have had to satisfy a very strict test which would have to show a violation of a superior law; this superior law must exist to protect the rights of natural or legal persons and the violation must have been sufficiently serious.[7] These superior laws would cover principles such as proportionality, legal certainty or equality as in *Zuckerfabrik Schöppenstedt* itself.

However, the Court of Justice reviewed this strict test in *Bergaderm* v *Commission* (2000). In this case it took the opportunity to bring the rules relating to Union liability in line with those applicable in cases

---

[2] If the application of the law to a point in the scenario is fairly obvious like here, don't spend a long time on it. Make the point and move on.

[3] Citing your authority in brackets like this is often a quick and easy way to show you know the law well.

[4] This is important. The scenario mentions that other proceedings had been attempted, so you should engage with that point.

[5] Controversial or difficult points are often best illustrated with a quick case example: it makes the answer less abstract, shows you know the law and are aware of relevant case law.

[6] You do not need to consider the other options: it is clear that you are looking at a legislative act here.

[7] Usually this would be followed by you applying the test to the scenario, but in this case there is a possible alternative test and we have chosen to set that out first before then doing the application.

[8] You are showing off wider knowledge of EU law here.

[9] Don't forget the application of the tests to the scenario: the more explicit the application, the better.

[10] You could explain in more detail here why Convenient Sweets may argue breach of proportionality or sufficient seriousness to really show your analytical skills off.

[11] In this scenario the fact that there are two different tests is not that important because Convenient Sweets is likely to satisfy both. You must still show how both would apply, though: otherwise the examiner will not know that you have recognised that.

[12] Don't forget this: without damage suffered, a claim is pointless.

of state liability.[8] Under this case Convenient Sweets must therefore show that there was a sufficiently serious breach of a rule of law intended to confer rights on individuals. The court will also consider whether there has been a disregard of the limits of discretion by the institution involved. Convenient Sweets may argue that the Regulation does not adhere to the proportionality principle as it is an excessively draconian measure to achieve the reduction of a health risk.[9] The breach also seems serious and the ECJ would consider factors such as the manner of the breach, whether there is a public interest relevant and the number of people affected.[10]

Zuckerfabrik Schöppensted has, however, never been explicitly overruled and there is no authority to suggest that the more complex approach will not be followed in the future. However, even if this were to be the case, Convenient Sweets is likely still to be successful as there has been a breach of a superior rule of law which exists to protect natural or legal persons (proportionality) and that breach has also been of sufficient seriousness.[11]

Convenient Sweets must then prove the damage suffered.[12] In this case it is likely to be purely economic damage and it must be actual damage not speculative. Convenient Sweets must, however, show that the loss suffered must be over and above the risk of loss in normal business (*Dumortier Freres v Council* (1979)). Convenient Sweets must also prove that there is a causal link between the Union Regulation and the loss suffered which should be possible by comparing orders and sales records prior to the coming into force of the Regulation with records from when the Regulation was in force.

To summarise, Convenient Sweets's claim for damages is admissible and it seems likely that Convenient Sweets would be successful even if the older and stricter criteria for liability under *Zuckerfabrik Schöppenstedt* are applied. The damages payable would include lost profits and could include imminent foreseeable damage.

Make your answer stand out

■ Set out the provisions of Articles 268 and 340 TFEU at the start.

■ Address your advice directly to Convenient Sweets in the form of a letter or email. It adds interest to your answer and makes it a bit different.

■ Consider which court would be likely to have jurisdiction over the matter.

■ Apply the scenario to the facts in a more detailed way by examining, for example, the causation argument or the loss over and above normal business risk in more detail.

 Don't be tempted to . . .

■ Outline the law without reference to Convenient Sweets.

■ Go into detail in relation to liability for administrative acts or employees.

■ Ignore the older more complex test: it has not been overruled.

■ Provide lots of factual detail on cases cited. You give enough information for your argument to make sense and that is all you need.

www.pearsoned.co.uk/lawexpressqa

Go online to access more revision support including additional essay and problem questions with diagram plans, You be the marker questions, and download all diagrams from the book.

Customs duties and internal taxation

How this topic may come up in exams

Customs duties and internal taxation are sometimes dealt with separately and sometimes, particularly in problem questions, the two are examined together. Problem questions are popular in this area and tend to focus on the legality of particular measures. If you do get an essay question, it is likely to focus on the importance of the provisions in this area to the internal market. Students sometimes struggle to keep the law on customs duties and internal taxation separate and you should therefore take particular care to identify the relevant provisions. Occasionally examiners will set questions which will overlap with free movement of goods questions, so it is always worth remembering that the law on customs duties, internal taxation and free movement of goods form one coherent framework for the internal market.

■ Before you begin

It's a good idea to consider the following key themes of customs duties and internal taxation before tackling a question on this topic.

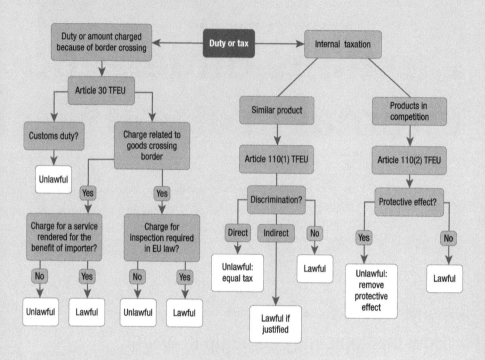

A printable version of this diagram is available from **www.pearsoned.co.uk/lawexpressqa**

Question 1

Critically assess the ECJ's jurisprudence in relation to customs duties and charges having equivalent effect.

Answer plan

→ Set out the Treaty provisions relating to customs duties and 'charges having equivalent effect' (CHEEs).

→ Trace the jurisprudence of the ECJ in relation to duties and CHEEs:

  – Definitions

  – Application

  – Exceptions.

→ Comment on the reasoning for the ECJ's fairly strict approach: Customs Union as vital to the internal market.

Diagram plan

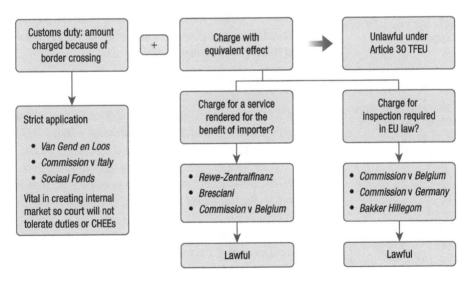

A printable version of this diagram plan is available from **www.pearsoned.co.uk/lawexpressqa**

Answer

[1] Setting the introduction in context like this shows that you fully appreciate the single market and the laws relating to it. You have also clearly signalled that you have recognised this as a customs duty rather than a general question.

The free movement of goods can be impeded through the imposition of customs duties. The duty will increase the price of the goods, rendering the export/import more expensive by comparison to the domestic good. This runs counter to the EU's aim of achieving a single market.[1]

The Customs Union is one of the foundations of the EU. It seeks to combat the protectionism of the customs duty. The Customs Union is established by Article 28 TFEU. It covers 'all trade in goods'. The mechanism whereby the Customs Union is achieved is imposed by Article 30 TFEU. That provision provides 'Customs duties on imports and exports and charges having equivalent effect [CHEE] shall be prohibited between Member States.'[2]

[2] You should start by setting out why the abolition of customs duties is important and what the relevant legal provisions are so that the examiner knows you know the law.

Because the abolition of the customs duty and the CHEE occupies the central single market position, the provisions relating to Article 30 have been interpreted strictly by the court.[3]

[3] This sentence sets out your point – you must then go on to prove that point and show how it has been strictly interpreted.

Identification of a customs duty is unproblematic; the duty of 8 per cent on the import of ureaformaldehyde by the Netherlands in **Van Gend en Loos** (1963) provides a ready example.

The intolerance to customs duties was apparent in early jurisprudence. The Court of Justice made clear that it is the effect of the customs duty that would be crucial; the stated purpose for which the tax was levied would be irrelevant.[4] In **Commission v Italy** (1969), for example, a charge on the export of art and cultural items identified as to protect 'artistic, historic and archaeological heritage' was held unlawful. The effect of that charge was to increase the price of the export. In **Sociaal Fonds** (1969), Belgium raised a charge on imported diamonds to be paid into a social fund for workers in that industry. The charge was unlawful; it had been levied by reason of the diamonds crossing a frontier between Member States. It was irrelevant that the diamond fund was neither to raise money for the government, nor the industry.[5]

[4] This is part of the strict interpretation and using examples will help highlight this.

[5] You need to give a little bit of information on the facts of these cases for the discussion to make sense and to help illustrate your point. Do not go overboard, though.

The prohibition of Article 30 is extended beyond customs duties per se. It includes 'charges having equivalent effect' (CHEEs) to the customs duties. The CHEE targets protectionist measures, charges which are not strictly customs duties in the conventional sense, but whose

[6] You have made this point in relation to customs duties already but it is worth making it again in relation to CHEEs.

[7] This is quite a well-known quote that is often cited but usually you would still not be expected to remember it and paraphrasing would be fine.

imposition on imports/exports has the same effect as a customs duty. The court has strictly applied this part of the prohibition.[6] The attributes of a CHEE have been identified; they are all embracing. In **Commission v Italy** (1969), a CHEE was defined as 'any pecuniary charge however small and whatever its designation and mode of application, which is imposed unilaterally on domestic or foreign goods by reason of the fact that they cross a frontier'.[7]

The definition of a CHEE in **Commission v Italy** presents a signal from the Court of Justice that the provisions of Article 30 will not be circumvented by Member States. The prohibition of CHEEs will apply to national measures presented under other names or where they have been introduced by the indirect means of other procedures. These are measures which would lead to the same discriminatory or protective results as customs duties.[8] A charge fulfilling the above criteria will remain a CHEE despite the nomenclature assigned to it by the Member State. In **Commission v Luxembourg** (1962), for example, a charge on imported gingerbread redesignated by the state as a 'special duty', nonetheless retained the attributes of a CHEE and was in consequence held unlawful.

[8] Try to explain key concepts such as CHEEs in one simple clear sentence such as here. It shows that you fully understand the concept.

[9] You have set out your definitions and should now consider exceptions when CHEEs might be lawful.

A charge presented by the host state as a 'service' to the goods will only be lawful where the benefit of that service to the importer is tangible.[9] If imposed in the general interest only, as in **Rewe-Zentralfinanz** (1975), no service is given and the charge will be unlawful. Neither was the benefit tangible in **Bresciani** (1976) where there was a compulsory public health inspection of raw hides by Italy, or where in **Commission v Italy**, the same state collected general statistical data which benefitted the whole Italian economy.[10]

[10] These brief examples should help clarify the point you are making.

For the charge in respect of the service provided by the host state to be lawful, the strict criteria imposed by EU law must be met. In **Commission v Belgium** (1983), it was held that the placing of goods in special storage in public warehouses would represent a service to the trader: a 'consideration for a service actually rendered to the importer and [be] of an amount commensurate with that service'. By contrast no service would be given where the goods were merely warehoused pre-customs clearance.

The strictness of the approach to the operation of Article 30 is exemplified in the jurisprudence relating to charging for inspection of goods where the inspection is undertaken by the Member State with the

[11] Moving on to the next exception and reiterating that the court takes a strict view in relation to what sort of charges are allowed and which are not reinforces the point made earlier on and keeps your argument flowing logically.

authority of Community legislation.[11] Where that authority merely permits the inspection, following **Commission v Belgium**, no fees can be recovered by the state. Health checks carried out by Belgium on imported poultry were unlawful. Although permitted by Community law, the health checks imposed did not represent a service rendered to the importer; no charge was justified. By contrast, where the service is mandatory as part of a Community regime and it promotes the free movement of goods, the cost of provision can be recovered by the state. In **Commission v Germany** (1988), it was held that a charge may be made where:

(a) the actual costs of the inspections are not exceeded;

(b) the inspections are uniformly applied to all the products concerned in the Community;

(c) they are prescribed by Community law in the general interest of the Community;

(d) they promote the free movement of goods.[12]

[12] A list such as this one should be acceptable to most examiners. If you have been told otherwise, please check with your examiner and, if needs be, write this out in prose.

In **Commission v Germany**, the charges with respect to the transport of live animals satisfied these requirements and were held lawful. The same principles applied in **Bakker Hillegom** (1990) where the ECJ held that fees charged related to the actual cost of plant inspection under an international convention intended to encourage the free importation of plants. Charges for plant inspections only in relation to exported products would, however, constitute charges having an effect equivalent to customs duties on exports.

[13] Here you are reminding the reader of the point you made earlier and which you have now demonstrated. It helps bring your argument home.

Overall, therefore, it can be seen that the ECJ has interpreted the law relating to Article 30 and the prohibition of customs duties and CHEEs strictly,[13] thus rendering unlawful as many situations as possible where charges may be made simply because goods cross a border. The aims of the EU are inextricably linked to the idea of an internal market, and fundamental to that internal market is a customs union. The ECJ's strict interpretation of the rules is therefore unsurprising. Its jurisprudence has, however, no doubt helped shape the Customs Union and sent a clear signal that any charges which are levied simply because goods are crossing a border will not be tolerated.

Make your answer stand out

- Add additional academic commentary. See, for example, Ward, I. (2009) *A Critical Introduction to EU Law*, 3rd edn, Cambridge: Cambridge University Press, Chapter 5.
- Give examples of possible CHEEs to make your analysis less abstract and easier to relate to in practical terms.
- Add further discussion on how the prohibition on customs duties and CHEEs fits into the larger free movement of goods puzzle.
- Consider customs duties in a little more detail at the beginning. You don't need to say much about them but point out that they are prohibited and explain why you now rarely see examples.

! Don't be tempted to . . .

- Simply list relevant case law in chronological order; it's the commentary that is important.
- Go overboard on the facts of cases. You only need to give the facts where they are relevant and only give enough so that the discussion makes sense.
- Write about quantitative restrictions and MEEs instead.
- Bring in questions of taxation; you must keep the areas of law separate.

❓ Question 2

The German government wants to introduce the following measures and seeks your advice as to their legality in EU Law:

(a) Inspection of all live pigs imported to or exported from Germany. A charge is made for this inspection and the inspections are carried out because of a new EU directive requiring health inspections of pigs in transit.

(b) A charge of €50 per 24 hours for lorry parking at certain border crossings. The lorry parks have security patrols and CCTV and facilities such as toilets, showers and a TV room from the drivers.

(c) A charge of €30 per lorry for crossing the border between 11pm and 6am. The charge covers the cost of opening the border at a time when it would normally be shut.

Answer plan

→ Identify the legal issues to be dealt with: customs duties and CHEEs.

→ Set out briefly the law relating to the issue: Article 30 TFEU and case law definition.

→ Go through each of the scenarios:

    – Is it a duty or CHEE?

    – Is it a charge for a service rendered?

    – Is it a charge allowed under EU law?

→ Conclude whether it is lawful or not.

Diagram plan

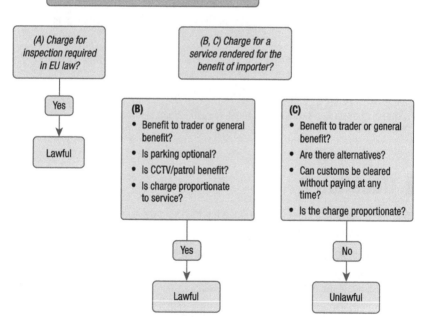

A printable version of this diagram plan is available from **www.pearsoned.co.uk/lawexpressqa**

Answer

¹ Restating the question and stating the legal base is a good way to get going with a problem question and it shows you are clear what the question is about.

The question concerns the free movement of goods in European Union law and in particular where charges are imposed at the frontier on imported goods. Would the charges imposed by Germany in relation to parking, border crossing and the inspection be lawful if introduced? Article 30 TFEU provides 'Customs duties on imports and exports and charges having equivalent effect (CHEE) shall be prohibited between Member States'.[1]

² By stating straight away that you are not dealing with customs duties, you are free to move on to the problem at hand and think about whether you are dealing with CHEEs.

The charges in question are not customs duties in the traditional sense, so can the German provisions be regarded as 'CHEEs'?[2] If so, they will be unlawful. A CHEE has been defined in ***Sociaal Fonds voor de Diamantarbeiders v SA Ch Brachfeld & Sons*** (1969) as:

³ If you can remember quotes like this, great, but do not spend ages learning them. You can paraphrase or use a statute book if allowed.

> any pecuniary charge, however small and whatever its designation and mode of application, which is imposed unilaterally on domestic or foreign goods by reason of the fact that they cross a frontier, and which is not a customs duty in the strict sense, constitutes a charge having equivalent effect.[3]

The charges of €30, €50 and those for the inspections of the pigs are clearly 'pecuniary charges' as identified in ***Sociaal Fonds***. In addition, that judgment makes clear that it is essential to the operation of Article 30 that the goods must 'cross a frontier'. The charges here relate to the import or export of the goods; the health checks imposed by Germany apply in general pigs crossing a border so that requirement is satisfied.[4]

⁴ At this stage now, you have introduced your answer by identifying the relevant area of law. The next stage is to examine each of the proposed charges in the context of the law outlined in your introduction and to give a rationale of whether you would regard each of them as lawful or not.

The question now requires a consideration of whether each of the proposed charges will be unlawful for the purposes of Article 30.

(a) Where a health inspection on animals is required by Community law, ***Commission v Germany*** (1988) provides the criteria to be applied in the assessment of the lawfulness of the national charge. The fees charged cannot be classed as CHEEs where:

   (a) 'they do not exceed the actual costs of the inspections in connection with which they are charged

   (b) the inspections . . . are obligatory and uniform for all the products concerned in the Community

[5]This sets out the legal
criteria relating to inspections
which you can then simply
apply in the next paragraph.
Remember it is OK to
paraphrase this.

(c) they are prescribed by Community law in the general interest of the Community

(d) they promote the free movement of goods.'[5]

The health inspections appear to fall within the criteria set out in **Commission v Germany.** They are uniformly applied to all pigs, whether or not imported or exported. The inspections are required by EU law and are obligatory. The charge imposed must represent the actual cost to Germany for the inspections; we have no information on this so do not know whether that is the case.[6] The health check must promote the free movement of goods which may be proved, for example, if the existence of the health check could be associated with an increased level of consumer confidence in buying pig products.

[6] It is better to say you do not have the information than it is to make something up which is not supported by the information from the scenario.

(b) The payment for customs clearance between 11pm and 6am would be considered as a CHEE for the purpose of Article 30 and, in consequence, its imposition would be unlawful. However, we need to consider whether the payment is made in consideration of a 'genuine service' received. In **Commission v Italy** (1991), for example, customs formalities were completed outside the customs area or outside normal office hours. In that instance, the services were rendered simultaneously to several undertakings in connection with the completion of customs formalities; the amount charged by Italy to the importer/exporter was held disproportionate. In **Commission v Italy** (1989), Italian customs houses charged for the cost of customs clearance completed outside normal civil service hours but within the opening hours for customs houses as stipulated by national law. It was held that no specific benefit was received by a haulier who attended at a customs office during normal business hours; the Italian charge was a CHEE.[7]

[7] Using a couple of examples is often a good way to illustrate how the legal provisions work in practice and thus highlights how they should be applied here.

Whether the charge for customs clearance in this instance is lawful or not will depend on whether the importer/exporter receives a specific benefit from obtaining customs clearance between those times. The benefit to the importer of receiving customs clearance during the time customs offices are normally closed can arguably be measured in terms of both time and money. The charge must be proportionate; it must represent the actual cost of administration incurred by Germany of administering the clearance in these circumstances. An assessment of the cost to Germany of carrying out the clearance in such circumstances must be made. If, for example, Germany has recouped more than the actual cost of providing the clearance, the amount charged will be disproportionate and illegal.[8]

[8] You just have to weigh up whether you think there is a genuine benefit and come to your own conclusison.

It seems that in this case the charge would be lawful as long as it is proportionate because the importers/exporters have a choice to complete formalities in office hours or to pay and take advantage of clearance at other times.[9]

[9] You could come to the opposite conclusion if you do not think that the benefit of the service is specific enough to the importer/exporter.

(c) The imposition of a charge of €50 per 24 hours for the use of lorry parking facilities at specified borders is a pecuniary charge. It is imposed by reason of importation or goods crossing a border and therefore, on the face of it, Article 30 renders the lorry park fee unlawful.[10]

[10] Try to set out the relevant law in the context of the scenario such as here.

[11] This is a clear statement of the relevant law showing your detailed understanding, which is then quickly followed by the application to the scenario. This way, you should not miss anything and would pick up marks easily.

If the charge, however, represents a 'consideration for a service actually rendered to the importer and is of an amount commensurate with that service, when the charge concerned . . . is payable exclusively on imported products' then **Commission v Belgium** (1983) dictates that it would not be regarded as a CHEE.[11]

Do importers/exporters receive a benefit from the parking facilities for which they are charged? It is arguable that the patrols by security guards together with the CCTV monitoring would make up a genuine service to the importers if, for example, their existence contributes to the security of the vehicles which leads to an increased level of protection for the imported goods. By contrast, if provision of the CCTV together with the patrols is deemed only to be of general benefit to importers/exporters, it will be held to be a CHEE within Article 30 and will thus be unlawful.[12] A statistical levy on goods exported to the other Member States, for example in **Commission v Italy** (1969),[13] was held to be an unlawful CHEE; the information in that instance was deemed to be 'beneficial to the economy as a whole'. No specific benefit to exporters incurring the charge was identified. Presuming that parking in this car park is not compulsory but an option open to drivers who wish to leave their lorries in a secure place, and further presuming that the charge reflects the actual cost of the security provisions and maintaining facilities for drivers, the

[12] Set out the factors suggesting a genuine service and those against, and then conclude – that comes next.

[13] Use an example to show the sorts of things that might or might not be a service: it adds credibility to your argument and allows you to draw a conclusion by analogy.

[14] The conclusion is open to interpretation, and in this case it is easy to make the argument the other way, too. You could argue that the parking facilities represent a general benefit.

[15] You should summarise your conclusion at the end to signal clearly that you have finished rather than just run out of time.

charge is lawful because it represents a charge for a genuine service for the benefit of the drivers.[14]

In conclusion, then, it seems that all three charges are lawful. The first two are services rendered to the importer and the third is an inspection imposed by EU law.[15]

✓ Make your answer stand out

- Include more discussion on the application of the law to each of the issues raised. Consider what additional factors might help you to decide more definitively if there is genuine service provision.

- Conclude each section fully with the advice you would give on that particular issue.

- Set out advice direct to the client. This adds interest for examiners reading multiple answers to the same question and also shows you have confidence in your ability to explain the law.

- Add a little more case law to illustrate. Remember, though, that you do not need to say much about the cases for your points to make sense.

! Don't be tempted to . . .

- State the law and jump straight to the conclusion. You must apply the law to each of the scenarios.

- Write a general answer about customs duties and free movement of goods; stick with the scenario and focus on what is relevant.

- Repeat the detail of the legal provisions for each section; you will run out of time if you do that.

- Base your answer on just the treaty provisions; you need to highlight how they have been interpreted with reference to case law.

🅚 Question 3

You are to advise the Danish government on whether any of its proposed changes to the system of indirect taxation will contravene EU law. The intention is:

(a) To impose VAT on chocolate but not on liquorice.

(b) To tax carbonated drinks more heavily than pure fruit juice.

(c) To reduce the rate of VAT on triple glazed doors, most of which are made in Denmark; the VAT on single and double glazed doors, which are mostly imported, will stay the same.

Write a memorandum to the relevant government minister detailing your advice.

Answer plan

→ Identify the relevant legal provision – here Article 110 TFEU and its two subparagraphs.

→ Explain the application of Article 110(1) to similar products and Article 110(2) to products in competition.

→ For each scenario consider whether the products in question are similar or in competition.

→ Conclude, stating whether the tax is lawful, unlawful and must be equalised (similar products) or unlawful and must have the protective effect removed (products in competition).

Diagram plan

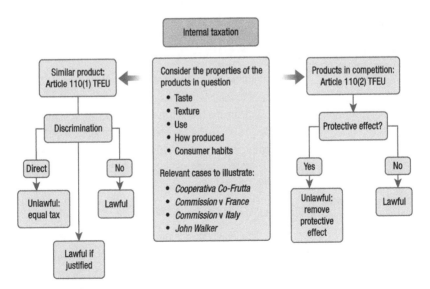

A printable version of this diagram plan is available from **www.pearsoned.co.uk/lawexpressqa**

Answer

¹ Always identify the legal issue to deal with – if you do this right at the start, the examiner can be sure you are on the right track.

² Once you know the legal issue, the next logical step is stating the legal provisions which apply and then define them.

³ If you are allowed to use a statute book, you can set the provisions out like this. If not, it is probably easier just to state the law in your own words.

⁴ You have now set out the legal provisions and should then think about their application. As the same provisions apply to each of the sub-scenarios, it makes sense to set the law out once and then apply it in relation to each of the products mentioned.

⁵ When starting your application of the law, it can be useful to restate the issue at hand in the context of the scenario. It shows the examiner you know how to apply the law and can also help you to focus your answer and structure your argument.

The question concerns the regulation by the EU of the internal taxation of Member States.[1] The legalities of proposed changes with respect to rates of VAT on chocolate, and liquorice and doors, and rates of duty on carbonated drinks and juice, fall for consideration within the scope of Article 110 Treaty on the Functioning of the European Union (TFEU).[2] This provides that:

1 No Member State shall impose, directly or indirectly, on the products of other Member States any internal taxation of any kind in excess of that imposed directly or indirectly on similar domestic products.

2 Furthermore, no Member State shall impose on the products of other Member States any internal taxation of such a nature as to afford indirect protection to other products.[3]

Article 110 applies where the charges are levied as part of a general system of internal dues applied systematically to categories of products. Both VAT and duty levied in Denmark fall into general system of taxation of that Member State.

Where the goods are held to be 'similar' products, the tax system of the Member State must treat the domestic and imported products in the same way. If the products are found to be in competition with each other, then any protective effect in the system of taxation must be removed.[4]

In consideration of whether the proposed changes by the Danish government to the internal taxation system are lawful, the enquiry is twofold. First, are the goods to be compared 'similar' for the purposes of Article 110(1) TFEU? Secondly, in the context of Article 110(2) TFEU, are those goods in competition with each other? This two-stage enquiry is made in each instance in which the application of Article 110 to the national charge is in issue.

(a) VAT on chocolate and liquorice:

(i) The initial consideration then must be whether chocolate and liquirice can be considered to be 'similar' for the purposes of Article 110(1).[5] It does not matter that Denmark does not produce chocolate. In ***Cooperativa Co-Frutta***

(1987), in consideration of the lawfulness of the Italian tax regime, the court considered the 'similarity' of bananas and 'other kinds of fruit', Italy did not produce bananas.

The court will assess the 'similarity' of the products, objectively. It was held in **Commission v France** (1980) that similarity will depend on the products having 'similar characteristics and meet the same needs from the point of view of consumers'.[6] It is an assessment 'on the basis not of the criterion of the strictly identical nature of the products but on that of their similar and comparable use'.

An appraisal of the various characteristics of the products will be undertaken together with an analysis of consumer habits. The imposition of VAT on chocolate but not liquorice may, for example, crystallise consumer habits. Liquorice may be bought at the expense of purchasing chocolate. If this is so, the products may be deemed 'similar'. The analysis of the product characteristics is an objective assessment. In **Commission v Italy** (1987) an assessment of bananas and table fruit typically produced in Italy was made[7] on the basis of their organoleptic characteristics and their water content, and consumer needs. Chocolate and liquorice, though both possibly classed as treats or sweets, are made in different ways, from very different ingredients and are likely to be consumed on different occasions by different groups of people. Therefore, it seems unlikely that they will be held to be similar, given that they fulfil different needs.[8]

(ii) Is there a competitive relationship in the Danish market between chocolate and liquorice?[9] In **Commission v Italy**, for example, there was competition in the Italian market between bananas and other fruit. Does chocolate afford an alternative choice to liquorice in the UK? This is a question of fact. Could the tax imposed on chocolate result in the potential reduction in the purchase by consumers of the imported product (**FG Roders** (1995)). Given **Commission v Italy**, it seems likely a competitive relationship exists.

[6] You should mention how similarity has been assessed in previous cases and then assess similarity in this case.

[7] This is the most cited example in this area, but in this case it is particularly useful because the facts are similar – both concern fruit. The closer the example to the scenario, the more convincingly you can argue by analogy.

[8] You should have a go at stating your conclusion on this, even if it is the court that would ultimately decide based on all the evidence before it.

[9] Once you have dealt with similarity and decided the products are not similar, you must think about whether there is competition.

(b)   Tax on carbonated drinks and fruit juice:

(i)   Are they 'similar' products? The question would involve, for example, an analysis of the content and the method of production as can be seen from cases involving alcoholic drinks. In **John Walker** (1986), in holding that liqueur fruit wine was not similar to scotch whisky, the court considered the alcohol content, methods of production and the consumer perception relating to both products.[10] The contention that scotch whisky may be consumed in the same way as fruit wine of the liqueur type, as an aperitif diluted with water or with fruit juice, even if it were established, would not be sufficient to render scotch whisky similar to fruit wine of the liqueur type, whose intrinsic characteristics are funda-mentally different.

With respect to the similarity of carbonated drinks and fruit juice, consideration may be made, for instance, with respect to the intrinsic characteristics and organoleptic properties of those two products. Could these be considered to be the same? Have the products a similar and comparable usage? The court would make an objective assessment. Arguably, the two products are similar having a similar use and being for consumption in similar ways.[11]

(ii)   Are the products in competition? An assessment of the market-place would be conducted. In **Commission v UK** (1980), for example, wine and beer were found to be in competition at the cheaper end of the market. The two beverages were capable of meeting identical needs; there was a degree of substitution. While it is arguable that carbonated drinks and fruit juice are not 'interchangeable drinks', actual analysis of the drinks market in the UK may be undertaken to establish whether this is true. They are very likely to be in competition.

(c)   Doors:

(i)   Are single/double glazed doors and triple glazed doors 'similar' products? As far as the consumer is concerned, they have 'similar characteristics and meet the same needs' (**Commission v France**). It seems likely that these products are classed as sufficiently similar because they

[10] Again, you can show your broad knowledge of this area of law by using a case as an authority which dealt with similar issues as those under consideration here.

[11] You should conclude here and either conclusion is fine as long as you explain how you have come to it. If, as we have here, you conclude that the products are similar, you actually do not need to continue to the second consideration, but, as this is open to interpretation, we have provided a possible answer for you.

[12] Do not provide a consideration of competition between products if not relevant because you have established clearly that they are similar.

meet the same need and are mostly interchangeable and therefore the tax on them must be equalised under Article 110(1), and no further consideration of whether they are in competition is necessary.[12]

✓ Make your answer stand out

- Include more discussion on whether you think the products are similar or in competition and why.
- Use additional case law examples to help your analysis of similarity or competitive relationships. Consult your lecture notes or textbook for examples you have covered.
- Conclude at the end stating what should happen to the tax in relation to each problem. Should it be equalised or the protective effect be removed?
- You could state the law first and then consider the similarity/competitive relationship of each of the products in the scenario, and then conclude for all rather than treating the sections as separate mini-problems.

! Don't be tempted to . . .

- Write a general answer about internal taxation.
- Repeat the law for each section of the scenario; refer back to it instead.
- Give the facts of the cases cited unless the point you are making does not make sense without them; then be brief.
- Discuss other elements of free movement of goods law or customs duties. The question is just about taxation.

? Question 4

Kinderland (a fictitious EU Member State) is reviewing its laws on taxation in order to raise more money for healthy school dinners and to discourage the consumption of sweets high in fat. It therefore wants to increase the taxation on chocolate and other high fat sweets. The tax it currently levies on wine gum type sweets with low fat content will stay the same. Kinderland is the EU's main producer of wine gums and similar sweets but it imports nearly all of its chocolate. Advise Kinderland whether the proposed measures would be lawful in EU law.

Answer plan

→ Identify the relevant legal provision – here Article 110 TFEU and its two subparagraphs.

→ Explain the application of Article 110(1) to similar products and Article 110(2) to products in competition.

→ Consider whether or not wine gums and chocolate are similar products or products in competition.

→ Conclude, stating whether the tax is lawful, unlawful and must be equalised (similar product) or unlawful and must have the protective effect removed (products in competition).

Diagram plan

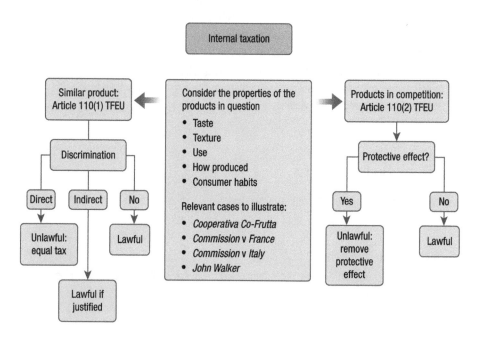

A printable version of this diagram plan is available from **www.pearsoned.co.uk/lawexpressqa**

Answer

The question concerns the regulation by the EU of the internal taxation of Member States. The legalities of proposed changes with respect to rates of tax on chocolate/high fat sweets and wine gums/low fat sweets fall for consideration within the scope of Article 110 Treaty

[1] First identify the problem and then state the relevant legal provisions.

[2] By setting out what law applies here, you can then go on to apply it to the scenario directly and you are not being descriptive at all.

[3] Set out that you understand the consequences of a breach of the provisions. What must the Member State do if it is found to be in breach? If you do not know this, then knowing there has been a breach is not much use to your client.

[4] This paragraph sets out the considerations you must go through. You now have to apply them.

[5] This paragraph will be very familiar if you have read the previous answer. That is because you are going through exactly the same issues, just in respect of different products.

on the Functioning of the European Union (TFEU).[1] This provides that Member States shall not impose taxes on products of other Member States which exceed the tax imposed on similar domestic products (Article 110(1) TFEU) and that Member States should not protect the domestic product through internal taxation (Article 110(2) TFEU). Article 110 TFEU applies to any charges made as part of an internal system of taxation, so the taxes levied here appear to fall within this definition.[2]

Where the goods are held to be 'similar' products, the tax system of the Member State must treat the domestic and imported products in the same way. If the products are found to be in competition with each other, then any protective effect in the system of taxation must be removed.[3]

In consideration of whether the Kinderland's taxation system is lawful, the enquiry is twofold. First, are the goods to be compared 'similar' for the purposes of Article 110(1) TFEU? Secondly, if they are not similar, are those goods in competition with each other, in the context of Article 110(2) TFEU? This two-stage enquiry is made in each instance in which the application of Article 110 to the national charge is in issue.[4]

The initial consideration then must be whether wine gums and chocolate can be considered to be 'similar' for the purposes of Article 110(1). It does not matter that Kinderland does not produce chocolate in any great quantity. In **Cooperativa Co-Frutta** (1987), in consideration of the lawfulness of the Italian tax regime, the court considered the 'similarity' of bananas and 'other kinds of fruit', Italy did not produce bananas.

The court will assess the 'similarity' of the sweets objectively. It was held in **Commission v France** (1980) that similarity will depend on the products having similar characteristics and meet the same needs from the point of view of consumers. It is an assessment of similarity and comparable use rather than of whether the products are identical.

An appraisal of the various characteristics of the products will be undertaken together with an analysis of consumer habits. The imposition of higher taxes on chocolate but not wine gums may, for example, crystallise consumer habits, with wine gums being bought at the expense of purchasing chocolate. If this is so, the products may be deemed 'similar'.[5] In **Commission v Italy** (1987) an assessment of bananas and 'table fruit typically produced in Italy' was made on the basis of their organoleptic characteristics and their water content, and consumer needs. Whether or not the organoleptic characteristics etc. of wine gums and chocolate are 'similar' will be objectively decided by the court based on evidence provided. However, it seems unlikely that the court will consider them to be similar, given that they are very different types of sweets. They are made differently, used differently and have different tastes and textures.[6]

[6] Be as detailed as you can in listing characteristics to show that you really are applying the law and thinking critically about this.

The second question to address is whether there is a competitive relationship in the market between wine gums on the one hand and chocolate on the other. In **Commission v Italy**, for example, there was competition in the Italian market between bananas and other fruit. Does chocolate afford an alternative choice to wine gums in Kinderland?[7] This is a question of fact. Could the tax imposed on chocolate result in the potential reduction in the purchase by consumers of the imported product? These questions will need careful examination by the court and evidence will need to be brought showing the competitive relationship between the sweets. It seems, however, that consumers, faced with a shortage of chocolate, might instead buy wine gums.

[7] A clear statement of the question that needs answering helps build your argument logically and also highlights that you have correctly identified the issues.

In conclusion, it seems that it is unlikely that the court would consider the two types of sweets to be sufficiently similar to come within Article 110(1). However, they might, following **Commission v Italy**, be found to be in a competitive relationship and, as such, any protective effect of the taxation system which favours wine gums to the detriment of chocolate must be removed.[8]

[8] In stating your conclusion, you should make clear what the implications of that conclusion are: what needs to happen to the tax for there not to be a breach.

✓ Make your answer stand out

- Add more detail on your assessment of the similarities and competitive relationship between the products.
- Integrate the analysis more with the law – only do this if you feel confident, though: otherwise, it can end up quite chaotic.
- You could consider the possible justification of the taxation based on health but this would only apply if the products are similar.
- Give more case law examples to highlight how the legal provisions have been interpreted and how they therefore should be applied here.

❗ Don't be tempted to . . .

- Write a general answer about internal taxation.

- Get drawn into your preference for chocolate or wine gums; it is an objective assessment of the products' properties.

- Just say that the court would decide if the products are similar/in competition. You need to explain how it would decide.

- Give the facts of the cases cited unless the point you are making does not make sense without them; then be brief.

---

www.pearsoned.co.uk/lawexpressqa

Go online to access more revision support including additional essay and problem questions with diagram plans, You be the marker questions, and download all diagrams from the book.

The free movement of goods

How this topic may come up in exams

Free movement of goods is a very popular examination topic. Problem questions are common and focus on the application of the law to situations where it appears that the movement of goods is being obstructed in some way. Essay questions tend to focus on the development of the law by the ECJ and those areas which remain problematic, such as the scope of 'selling arrangement' and the post-*Keck* case law. The trick to answering both types of question successfully is to be really systematic in the application and analysis of the law. There is quite a lot to remember and it appears complicated but the principles are actually very simple, so focus on learning principles rather than specifics about cases and then use cases as illustrations of the principles.

■ Before you begin

It's a good idea to consider the following key themes of the free movement of goods before tackling a question on this topic.

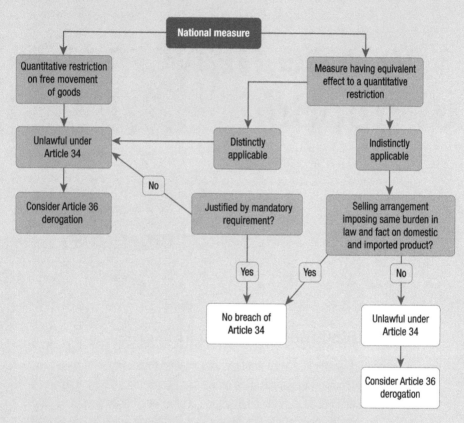

A printable version of this diagram is available from **www.pearsoned.co.uk/lawexpressqa**

❓ Question 1

The furniture importer and dealer 'PinesRUs' has approached you for advice on a number of issues:

(a) PinesRUs imports a line of high-end Italian wooden furniture. In a recent delivery a parasite was found to have infected the wood in a number of pieces in this line. The parasite can also infect live trees and has been controlled carefully in the UK since 2000.

As a consequence of the discovery of the parasite, the customs authorities are now insisting that every imported batch of Italian wood furniture is inspected fully. The inspection takes time, meaning that PinesRUs are unable to fulfil orders. In addition, the inspectors need to cut into the wood to test for the parasites. This damages the furniture, which as a result becomes unsaleable.

(b) The government have recently implemented a law which only allows one sale event per year. This sale must take place after Christmas. However, PinesRUs holds three big sale events per year and makes a significant amount of money during them all. Their autumn event is, however, their most successful.

(c) The government has been concerned for some time about the differing packaging for the different types of handles. It therefore specifies that different types of cabinet and door handles must be packaged differently. It is argued this will reduce consumer confusion.

Answer plan

→ Identify the legal issue – free movement of goods under Article 34 TFEU.

→ Scenario (a) relates to a distinctly applicable measure so is unlawful unless it comes within an Article 36 TFEU derogation.

→ Scenario (b) relates to an indistinctly applicable measure. Consider whether it is a selling arrangement and conclude accordingly.

→ Scenario (c) is an indistinctly applicable measure which is not a selling arrangement. Is it justified under a mandatory requirement? If not, does it fall within Article 36 derogations?

Diagram plan

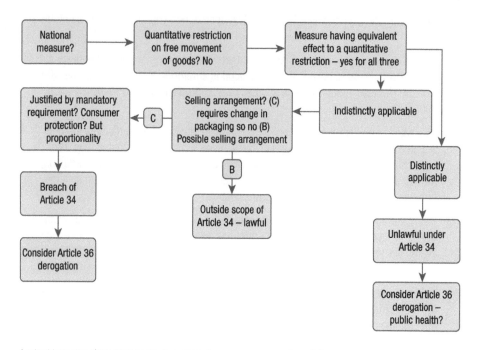

A printable version of this diagram plan is available from **www.pearsoned.co.uk/lawexpressqa**

[1] This is such a well-known and well-used quotation you can probably manage to remember this one, but if not paraphrase or use a statute book if you are allowed one.

[2] The *Dassonville* definition of the MHEE is crucial to each answer that considers the application of Article 34 and the MHEE, and this is worth learning because, if you can set it out in full, you can refer back to it, making sure you don't miss anything, and build a logical argument.

Answer

The question concerns the free movement of goods in Union law and in particular the application of Article 34 TFEU. Article 34 provides: 'Quantitative restrictions on imports and all measures having equivalent effect shall be prohibited between Member States'.[1] Measures having equivalent effect (MHEEs) have been defined by ***Procureur du Roi v Dassonville*** (1974) in the following way: 'All trading rules enacted by Member States which are capable of hindering, directly or indirectly, actually or potentially, intra-Community trade are to be considered measures having an effect equivalent to quantitative restrictions.'[2]

(a) The customs inspection has impeded imports by delaying the Italian furniture and rendering some of it unsaleable. It is thus

[3] Setting out your conclusion at the beginning can help focus your answer but make sure it is obvious or you go on to justify it.

[4] Consider whether the MHEE can be justified. By setting out the law and immediately applying it, you are highlighting both your knowledge and your analytical skills in applying the law.

[5] While this statement is true, put yourself in the position of your client: what would you want to know? Using an example to highlight this will help clarify this point.

[6] On its own, this is quite abstract. What does 'proportionate' really mean? Use an example or two to illustrate your point.

a MHEE within the *Dassonville* definition of Article 34 and is unlawful.[3]

A MHEE may be justified. Article 36 TFEU provides that 'the provisions of Article [34] . . . shall not preclude . . . restrictions on imports . . . or goods in transit justified on grounds of . . . the protection of health and life of humans'. The UK therefore may seek to justify the inspection by the customs authorities of the furniture on the grounds of 'the protection of health and life of humans'.[4] A measure which is merely a disguised restriction on trade is not justifiable; the UK will have to prove that the grounds claimed are genuine.[5] In criminal proceedings against *Sandoz BV* (1983), the Netherlands claimed that the addition of vitamin supplements to foods would be harmful to public health. The risk to health, however, was not general; it existed only where consumption was excessive. In consequence, the Netherlands could not justify its general prohibition on vitamin additives in food.

Where a health risk does exist, the response of the state must be proportionate.[6] In *Commission v UK* (1984), for example, the establishment of a licensing system to protect the health of domestic poultry in Northern Ireland was proportionate. The additional administrative and financial burdens imposed by the licensing system in the circumstances were justified, given the need to protect the health of that poultry flock. However, extending the licensing system to the rest of the UK other than Northern Ireland would be disproportionate; the poultry was not of the same high standard as the poultry in Northern Ireland. In *Commission v UK* (1983), the systematic checking of sealed cartons of UHT milk rendering the contents unusable, thereby increasing the costs to the importer, was held unlawful. In the context of the protection of the health of humans, this was disproportionate; the UK could put in place safeguards equivalent to those which it has prescribed for its domestic production of UHT milk. Certificates of compliance from authorities in the home state could have been required from the importer.

In the present instance, is the action taken by the UK government proportionate? It would seem to be difficult for the government to argue successfully that its action in examining every batch of

[7] You must consider what the law you have just set out means for the present scenario: otherwise, you will not pick up marks for the application of the law.

[8] Consider the measure in light of the *Dassonville* formula, then consider whether there is anything that takes it outside the scope of the provisions or justifies it – in this case, selling arrangements. That way, your argument builds up logically and you cover everything you need to.

[9] If you have already managed to learn the *Dassonville* formula, you might as well use the exact wording as done here to highlight your understanding and skill in using legal authority.

[10] You must now apply the law to the scenario given, otherwise the preceding discussion is meaningless for this answer. To get the marks, you have to show what the law means in this case.

[11] Use the facts given in the scenario and your general knowledge to explain how the scenario fits with the law highlighted earlier.

furniture and having to cut into the wood is a proportionate response to the perceived problem posed by the existence of the parasite.[7]

(b) The government restriction on sales would appear to be a restriction on trade between Member States. As such, it would fall within *Dassonville* as a MHEE. The restriction is a trading rule; its imposition by the United Kingdom governs the conditions under which alcohol is sold in the United Kingdom. It is 'capable of hindering, directly or indirectly, actually or potentially, intra-Community trade' in furniture products.[8]

However, Article 34 may not apply if the national measure here can be considered to be a 'selling arrangement' which relates to when, where or how goods are sold. The concept was introduced in *Keck and Daniel Mithouard* (1993). *Keck* held that a national measure regarded as a selling arrangement would 'not be such as to hinder directly or indirectly, actually or potentially, trade between Member States within the meaning of the *Dassonville* judgment'.[9] The national measures must apply to all relevant traders operating within the national territory and the effect must be the same in law and fact. Where regarded as a 'selling arrangement', the national measure is not classed as a MHEE; in consequence it would be lawful.

The trading rule in this instance, the restriction on sales events, may be regarded as a selling arrangement.[10] In *Tankstation* (1994) and *Hünermund* (1993), Dutch rules providing for the compulsory closure of petrol stations and German rules prohibiting advertising outside pharmacies were held to be selling arrangements. The national rules applied without distinction as to the origin of the products and did not affect the marketing of the import any differently from that of the domestic products.

The restriction on sales events exhibits no discrimination between UK and foreign-owned businesses; it applies equally to all products, domestic or imported. In addition, the effect of the restriction is the same in fact; no retailer can have more than one sale event.[11]

(c) The UK law standardising packaging is a MHEE within the meaning of *Dassonville.* In *Commission v Ireland* (1988) for example, the Irish requirement that cement pressure pipes in public tenders comply with national standards was restrictive of imports. The UK law directing the standardised packaging of

[12] If you have an example which is similar, it can make the application of the law much easier. You have set out the law at the beginning and then give an example from case law. Then, basically say 'the present case is essentially similar, so is likely to be decided in the same way'.

handles is likewise restrictive of trade.[12] The measure breaches the principle of mutual recognition imposed on the host state by ***Rewe-Zentral*** (1975). This provides that where a product has been lawfully marketed in another Member State, the host state has to recognise the standards in that state.

In this instance, the UK law would not be regarded as a 'selling arrangement' because, although concerned with the sale of products, in requiring repackaging it discriminates against the import. In ***Mars*** (1995), for example, measures related to packaging of the product nonetheless required repackaging of the import before it could go on sale in the German market. As a result the requirements regarding packaging would be unlawful and it seems unlikely that it can be justified as contributing to consumer protection (see, for example, ***Rau*** (1982)). There also does not seem to be an Article 36 derogation which would apply here.

[13] Remember to sum up at the end to show you have finished your answer.

In conclusion, then, the inspections and the requirements regarding packaging are unlawful MHEEs which cannot be justified. The restriction on sales events, however, can be considered a selling arrangement and therefore falls outside the scope of Article 34.[13]

 Make your answer stand out

- Add details of how your client could enforce their EU law rights.
- Integrate your application of the law more closely with the application if you are confident you can do this without getting confused.
- Expand your discussion relating to the application of the law in each case.
- Expand your consideration of possible justification for different packaging sizes.

! Don't be tempted to . . .

- Give too many case examples: you do not need to mention every case you can remember; just back up your analysis.
- Write a general answer on free movement of goods.
- Give any more detail than you have to on the cases; you only need enough detail to allow you to illustrate the point you are making.
- Forget to mention Article 36 derogations – you need to highlight you are aware even if they do not apply. Just say that.

❓ Question 2

UK sheep farmers are suffering from competition with cheaper imported animals from elsewhere in the European Union. Consider the following:

(a) Last week sheep farmers started a blockade of the cold storage facilities at each UK port used to import lamb from France. The blockade has been allowed to continue, the police claiming that there would be a potential danger of civil unrest and injuries to the lorry drivers and farmers if they intervened in the dispute.

(b) A UK government instruction has dictated that lambs reared in the United Kingdom can be served in National Health Service canteens. The claim is that only British lamb is free from a strain of viral infection which affects lambs reared in other Member States.

(c) An advertising campaign has been run recently by 'British lamb producers'. It is funded by the UK government. It has promoted British lamb produced in England as 'tasty and succulent and superior to French lamb'.

Answer plan

➜ Identify the legal issue – free movement of goods.

➜ Consider whether each measure is, in fact, a state measure:

– Inaction can be a 'state measure' – see *Angry farmers* case

– Government instruction

– State action – see *Buy Irish Campaign* case.

➜ Consider whether the measures are discriminatory.

Diagram plan

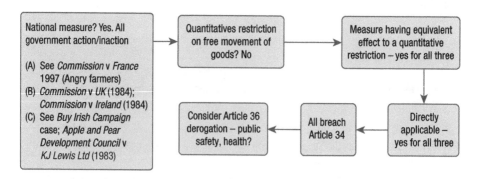

A printable version of this diagram plan is available from **www.pearsoned.co.uk/lawexpressqa**

Answer

This question concerns the free movement of goods in Union law. Article 34 TFEU must be applied to assess the legality of the physical hindrances to trade that have been identified.[1]

Article 34 provides: 'Quantitative restrictions on imports and all measures having equivalent effect shall be prohibited between Member States'. Measures having equivalent effect (MHEEs) are defined in **Procureur du Roi v Dassonville** (1974) in the following way: 'All trading rules enacted by Member States which are capable of hindering, directly or indirectly, actually or potentially, intra-Community trade are to be considered measures having an effect equivalent to quantitative restrictions.'[2]

(a) The blockade of storage facilities in the United Kingdom by farmers is a restriction on imports from France.[3] It is the purpose of Article 34 to eliminate all barriers to trade; this includes the restriction on the imports of lamb from France caused by the blockade imposed by the sheep farmers. Article 34 places a positive duty on the UK government to adopt measures upholding the principle of the free movement of goods. In this instance, the blockage must be removed. In **Commission v France** (1997) (the *Angry farmers* case) a failure by the French authorities to prevent a blockade by French farmers of Spanish fruit and vegetables was held unlawful.[4] Article 4(3) TEU provides 'Member States shall . . . ensure fulfilment of the obligations arising out of [the] Treaty'. Article 34, when read in conjunction with Article 4(3), imposes more than a negative duty, to abstain from adopting measures, or engaging in conduct liable to constitute an obstacle to trade. It seems there is a positive duty on Member States to take all necessary and appropriate measures to ensure that this fundamental freedom is respected on their territory.

In this question the United Kingdom has failed to prevent a blockade of the cold storage facilities at each port. This has resulted in a direct hindrance to intra-Community trade in lamb. That the hindrance to Community trade has been allowed to continue by the UK represents a failure to uphold the positive duty imposed by Article 34 to act to ensure that the free movement of goods is respected.[5]

[6] Here we have first explained the scenario in relation to the law and then stated the conclusion. It is as effective and makes your point, as well as doing it the other way round. Which way you do it is a matter of personal preference.

[7] Students often forget to consider derogations, so always try to give them a thought once you have established that you have a MHEE. Even if you conclude that none apply, at least you have shown the examiner that your knowledge is comprehensive.

(b) The government instruction relates only to lamb that has been raised in the UK. It is directly discriminatory of imported lamb: in this instance lamb from France cannot be served in National Health Service canteens. For the purpose of Article 34, the Government instruction would be regarded as a MHEE.[6] In *Commission v UK* (1984), for example, measures preventing the import into Northern Ireland of poultry products were held to be a MHEE.

A national measure which has been held to be a MHEE for the purposes of Article 34 may be justified.[7] Where the measure has been directly discriminatory in relation to the imported product, justification may be made on the grounds given in Article 36 TFEU. The applicable ground here is that of the protection of 'health [of] animals'. However, Article 36 is strictly interpreted by the ECJ. In *Commission v UK*, for example, the national restriction on imported poultry meat on the grounds of protection of the poultry flock in Northern Ireland against avian diseases was not made out by the UK. There was veterinary evidence which showed that, although avian diseases were present within the Community poultry flock and that it was not possible to eradicate infection from that source, infection was not normally spread by poultry meat. By contrast, however, in *Commission v Ireland* (1984) it was accepted that the exceptionally high standard of the Irish poultry flock rendered it highly vulnerable to infection and, in consequence, national measures taken to protect the flock might in such circumstances be justified.

[8] If you are aware of a case with similar facts, mention it early on and draw out the analogy. It makes it easy to apply the law and strengthen your argument.

(c) It appears that the campaign run by British Lamb Producers (BLP) gives preference to domestic lamb at the expense of the imported French product. The BLP is funded by the British government. In *Commission v Ireland* (1982) a 'Buy Irish' campaign was run by the Irish Goods Council (IGC), a body funded by the Irish government.[8] The campaign aimed to achieve a switch in spending from the imported product in favour of Irish goods. It was held that the funding arrangements of the Irish Goods Council meant that the state could not dissociate itself from the activities of the IGC. Similar funding arrangements now exist between the BLP and the British government. The advertising campaign and the use of a 'guaranteed Irish' symbol, which promoted Irish goods on account of origin in *Commission v Ireland* had the potential to affect the volume of trade between Member States.

It is arguable that to promote British lamb produced in England as 'superior to French lamb' would similarly have the potential to affect the volume of lamb imports by the United Kingdom. As a campaign based on the origin of the product, it would be caught by Article 34 and would be regarded as unlawful.

[9] Again, a useful example, and throughout the answer you have used different case examples illustrating similar issues in free movement of goods but relating most closely to the given facts. This shows a broad understanding of the case law in this area.

The advertising claim that UK lamb is 'tasty and succulent' may well be lawful. In ***Apple and Pear Development Council v KJ Lewis Ltd*** (1983) it was held that Article 34 does not prevent the promotion of specific qualities of particular products.[9] Such promotion may not, however, discourage the purchase of the imported product. If UK lamb is in reality 'tasty and succulent', and the effect of the campaign has not been to discourage the purchase of imported lamb, then the advertising campaign in this respect will be lawful.

 Make your answer stand out

- Add further discussion on whether or not the state inaction in (a) is a 'state measure' and what factors might influence whether it is or not.
- Consider potential justifications for the measures.
- If you have time, expand your application of the law and explain in more detail how the law applies to the facts. You can do this in the context of existing case law.

! Don't be tempted to . . .

- Include a discussion of those areas of free movement of goods which are not relevant here.
- Add a lot of detail about the cases you use.
- Ignore derogations; many students forget to deal with Article 36.

 Question 3

Critically assess the current state of the law relating to the free movement of goods under Article 34 TFEU. Where do you see its strengths and weaknesses and how could it be developed in the future?

Answer plan

→ Set out the law, referring to Article 34 and the cases of *Dassonville*, *Cassis* and *Keck*.
→ Set out the strengths and weaknesses for each.
→ Consider possible future developments.
→ Conclude.

Diagram plan

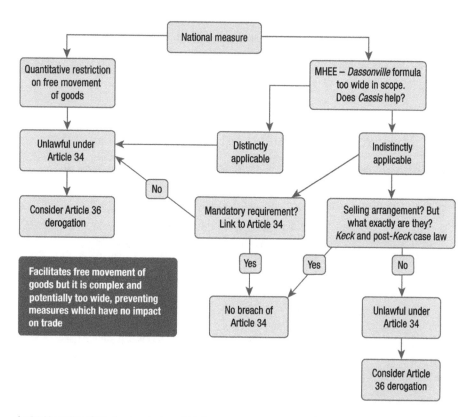

A printable version of this diagram plan is available from **www.pearsoned.co.uk/lawexpressqa**

Answer

'Since **Keck** . . . the Court has laboured to try and fix with precision the necessary extra element pertaining to damage to the internal market with which the challenged national measure must be infected

1 Starting with a quote can show you have really grasped the topic in question but they are also difficult to learn. If this is not how your memory works, then don't worry about it. This might be something to save for coursework essays.

2 This effectively is your conclusion and answer to the question – the rest of the essay should justify it.

3 If you do not say that it is now repealed, the examiner will not know that you know this and is likely to question why you are citing old law.

4 This bit sets out the law but, by referring to 'generous provisions', you are also already commenting on the provisions, which makes the piece less descriptive.

5 Wherever possible, show awareness of political and contextual issues. It shows you have fully engaged with the study of this subject.

for article [34] to bite' (Weatherill, 2009).[1] In this essay it will be submitted that Article 34 TFEU has provided a broad framework for the creation of a free market. However, the judicial decisions have struggled to create a clear path to the formalisation of the legal framework.[2]

The aim of Article 34 TFEU was to ensure that any national measure which restricts or prohibits trade between states is not allowed. The Article states: 'Quantitative restrictions on imports and all measures having equivalent effect shall be prohibited between Member States'. To aid interpretation, this has further been defined by secondary legislation, Directive 70/50, now repealed but nonetheless useful guidance,[3] and by judicial decisions. Therefore, Article 34 TFEU in itself provides the framework, with Directive 70/50 and the court's decisions, providing practical guidance on what is caught by Article 34 TFEU.

It is worth noting at this stage that 'quantitative restrictions' was interpreted by the court as measures which 'amount to a total or partial restraint of . . ., imports, exports or goods in transit', and the measures having equivalent effect (MHEEs) have been interpreted widely. The generous interpretation by the court includes distinctly applicable measures which are overtly protective against imports and also indistinctly applicable measures which are applicable to both imported and domestically produced goods.[4]

At first glance, Article 34 TFEU looks relatively straightforward. However, in practice the story has been much more complicated. Much of the complication has come from the desire of Member States to push the boundaries of interpretation and also from the court trying to simplify its purpose. The irony for the Member States is that they all want to benefit from a common market, yet remain protective of their own national markets often through pressure from the business community.[5]

Reviewing the strengths of Article 34 TFEU, it can be argued that the broad definitions are a way of pre-empting unusual or innovative ways to counteract national interests protecting their own internal marketplaces. One can also argue that Article 34 TFEU provides a catalyst to the underlying move to a free market for goods, a move much greater than merely a customs union. A further strength has been that it has been designed to cover measures which have the effect of restricting trade, even if that was never the intention. There can be no doubt that

[6] This paragraph summarises the strengths, and it makes sense to start with either strengths or weaknesses and deal with them in turn. That way, you make sure that your answer is well structured and easy to read.

[7] Now for the downsides, and you are not only highlighting that you are now moving on but also setting out how you are exploring the weaknesses. This is helpful because the approach is slightly different to the one taken in relation to strengths.

[8] Do not worry too much about remembering quotes from academics; if you've got the gist of it, your own words will do just fine.

[9] In this question you need to highlight that the law has developed and that these developments have often sought to simplify matters but have actually made things more complicated. The next paragraph continues along these lines.

[10] Potentially difficult concepts such as selling arrangements are often best illustrated with case examples. They get the point across more clearly than trying to explain the concept in the abstract.

Article 34 TFEU has caught many non-fiscal barriers to trade such as statutory levies, restricting national procurement contracts and even the lack of police protection against demonstrations. In doing this, Article 34 TFEU has helped, in conjunction with Article 110 TFEU and Article 30 TFEU, achieve the aims for the free movement of goods, which a mere customs union would not have achieved.[6]

In looking at the current situation the strengths are still evident; however, to understand the weaknesses, a short review of the evolution of case law is necessary, as the desire for clarity has often had an opposite effect.[7]

Dassonville (1974) attempted to define measures having equivalent effect as 'all trading rules . . . hindering, directly or indirectly, actually or potentially, intra-Community trade'. As Barnard (2013) points out, these types of measures allowed individuals to 'participate on the market on whatever terms they choose . . . to challenge any national rule'.[8] Clearly, this was not a workable situation as the Member States had to be in a position to have some commercial freedom within their own markets to meet economic, social or cultural issues.

The strength of the broad framework had become a weakness overnight and required the court to develop the ***Dassonville*** formula. The case of ***Cassis*** (1975) brought two new principles to the arena: the idea of protecting mandatory requirements, known as the 'Rule of Reason' and also the idea that if a product is marketed in one country then it should be able to be marketed in another Member State. Once again, these two principles, far from clarifying the situation, led to many more justifications from Member States around mandatory requirements. For instance, evidence of the World Health Organization was used to look at the effect on health of additives in beer in ***Commission v Germany*** (1987).[9]

Keck (1993) once again tried to re-establish a working position, balancing national requirements with the concept of an internal market. The court identified that 'certain selling arrangements' would not breach Article 34 TFEU if they affected all traders and did not prohibit commercial freedom. Therefore in ***Belgapom*** (1995) laws were allowed restricting the sales of products at a loss, and in ***Tankstation*** (1994) the restriction on times and places for petrol sale were not seen as a breach of Article 34 TFEU.[10]

This development at least reduced the emphasis on justifying many commercial decisions through mandatory requirements. However, **Keck** has led to further confusion, with Weatherill (2009) concluding that 'national courts are understandably baffled as to exactly what is expected of them'. The problem lies once again with an unclear definition of certain selling arrangements. This has led to hunting bans not being seen as a breach of Article 34 TFEU, yet the banning of trailers with motorcycles was in breach.[11]

[11] Using examples from both sides of the line is a good way of illustrating the difficulties with the provisions.

Perhaps one could argue that the evolution since **Keck** has stalled much in the same way that the move towards a unified constitution did in 2005.[12] National interest and autonomy have resurfaced and these will potentially provide more pressure during recessionary times. Protectionism contravenes Article 34 TFEU, yet protects fragile economies in the current economic climate.

[12] This is one possible way of showing you have wider knowledge of the EU; do not get drawn into irrelevant material, though.

In conclusion, the evolution of Article 34 TFEU has been central to the emergence of Europe as a single market. However, the court has a fine balance to achieve between a unified free market on one hand and the respect for national autonomy on the other. The evolution from **Dassonville** to **Keck** has in some ways helped this process, but maybe the answer lies less in defining what or what doesn't breach Article 34 TFEU and more in the general area of derogation under Article 36 TFEU. In a fast-moving world it is almost impossible for the law to keep pace with different and changing trading and selling techniques. It may therefore be easier to give clarity around justification rather than refining Article 34 TFEU which has proved difficult in the past and no doubt will be as challenging in the future.[13]

[13] The conclusion sets out clearly what you think but is based on what you have argued before. It is the logical end to the essay and refers back to the question in sufficient detail to show you have really answered it.

✓ Make your answer stand out

- Consider the future of free movement of goods provisions in more detail.
- Consider strengths and weaknesses from various perspectives more explicitly rather than just from one perspective.
- Add some additional case law examples.
- Add academic commentary. Consider, for example, Craig, P. and De Burca, G. (2011) *EU Law. Text Cases and Materials*, 5th edn, Oxford: Oxford University Press, Chapter 18, or Ward (2009) *A Critical Introduction to EU Law*, 3rd edn, Cambridge: Cambridge University Press, Chapter 5.

! Don't be tempted to . . .

- Write a general answer on free movement of goods.
- Focus just on the post-*Keck* case law: the question is broader than this.
- Cite too many cases: pick ones which highlight your point.
- Ignore the advantages or disadvantages. You need to deal with both, although it is OK to make an assessment overall.

Question 4

To what extent has the decision in *Keck* clarified the law relating to selling arrangement?

Diagram plan

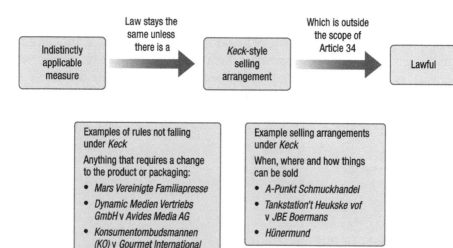

A printable version of this diagram plan is available from **www.pearsoned.co.uk/lawexpressqa**

Answer plan

→ Set out the basic legal provisions that form the background to *Keck*.

→ Set out the *Keck* principle.

→ Consider the post-*Keck* case law.

→ Conclude as to the extent of *Keck*'s impact.

Answer

The distinctions drawn in early free movement of goods case law between quantitative restriction and measures having equivalent effect (MHEE) and indistinctly applicable MHEE and distinctly applicable MHEE were fine for the early case law, but proved rather a blunt instrument when considering issues around what has been termed market circumstances or selling arrangements.[1] These sorts of rules essentially cover who does the selling, where and how. They generally do not protect the home market and usually apply equally to domestic and imported products both in law and fact. Market rules also generally affect the retailer rather than the producer or importer. On the face of it, therefore, you could argue that these rules do not fall within Article 34 Treaty on the Functioning of the European Union (TFEU) at all. However, the ***Dassonville*** (1974) formula was so wide that these sorts of rules seem to be covered (they might potentially have an indirect effect on inter-state trade).[2] The ECJ jurisprudence was less than helpful: some cases indicating that these 'equal burden rules' fall outside Article 34 TFEU (e.g. ***Oebel*** (1981); ***Quietlynn Ltd v Southend on Sea Borough Council*** (1990)) and other cases indicating that Article 34 TFEU applied (for example, ***Cinetheque SA v Federation Nationale de cinemas Français*** (1985); ***Torfaen Borough Council v B&Q plc*** (1989)).[3]

These issues came to a head in **Keck**. The facts are straightforward.[4] Keck sold goods at a loss; this was illegal in France and he was prosecuted. In his defence, he stated that the French law prevented him using his chosen method of sales promotion, thus restricting the volume of sales of imported goods thus breaching Article 34 TFEU. The ECJ disagreed and made its displeasure at traders increasingly using this Euro-defence clear. In its judgment, the court drew a distinction between product requirements and certain selling arrangements, holding the latter to be outside the scope of Article 34 TFEU: 'Contrary to what has previously been decided, the application to products from other Member States of national provisions restricting or prohibiting certain selling arrangements is not such as to hinder

5 This is a key quote and, if you are going to learn any quotes, it should be the *Dassonville* formula and this one. Most examiners, however, will be happy with you stating this in your own words.

6 This might seem like you are just repeating the point, but by restating it in this way you are showing that you understand this and you are also giving examples as you go.

7 Where you can illustrate a legal principle with a case or example, it brings it to life and shows you have understood it.

8 This paragraph starts taking you through the post-*Keck* case law and some of the problems those cases have thrown up.

9 You do need to give a little bit of case detail here because you are illustrating the application of the principle.

10 Here you have the example first and the principle which was established follows it. Which way round you present your argument does not really matter. Both ways build a logical argument.

11 You need to build up your argument logically. You have finished showing the difference between dual and single burden rules and are now going on to show how even single burden rules are not without problems.

directly or indirectly, actually or potentially, trade between Member States within the meaning of the *Dassonville* judgment'.[5] *Keck* thus established a general rule to be applied in the context of equal burden rules. It distinguished between rules that lay down requirements to be met by goods (such as those relating to designation, form, size, weight, composition, presentation, labelling, packaging) which continue to fall within the *Cassis* doctrine and 'selling arrangements' which might include times and places goods can be sold.[6] A recent example is the case *A-Punkt Schmuckhandel* (2006), in which an Austrian rule restricting the sale of certain goods at private homes was held to be a selling arrangement.[7]

The *Keck* doctrine has been applied in a large number of cases and it has not been unproblematic.[8] In *Tankstation 't Heukske vof* v *JBE Boermans* (1994) national rules provided for the compulsory closure of petrol stations. *Keck* applied and the rules did not fall within Article 34 TFEU because they related to 'selling arrangements' which applied equally to all traders without distinguishing between origin. It was an equal-burden rule, affecting domestic traders and importers equally. Similarly, in *Hünermund* (1993) a restriction on pharmacists advertising was a selling arrangement within the meaning of *Keck*.[9] However, it is in relation to advertising that the principle first ran into difficulty. In *Mars* (1995), the manufacturers challenged a national law in Germany which prohibited the selling of Mars Bars marked '110 per cent' (as part of a Europe-wide selling campaign). The Court of Justice held that these requirements related to the presentation, labelling and packaging of the product lawfully manufactured and marketed in another Member State. The prohibition imposed a dual burden on the manufacturer and was therefore, prima facie, in breach of Article 34 TFEU.[10] The same reasoning was applied in *Vereinigte Familiapresse* (1997) where a prohibition on the inclusion of games with prizes in newspapers was held to be more than a mere selling arrangement because it required a change to the product itself. The same issue arose more recently in *Dynamic Medien Vertriebs GmbH* v *Avides Media AG* (2008), where the ECJ again held that the need to alter a product (in this case relating to the labelling of DVDs) precluded the measure in question from being a selling arrangement under the *Keck* principle.

However, even where no product alteration is necessary, some advertising measures can still find themselves within Article 34 TFEU.[11] *Konsumentombudsmannen (KO)* v *Gourmet International*

Products AB (GIP) (2001) is a useful example. Restrictions on the advertising of alcoholic beverages in periodicals were at issue in this case. The ECJ concluded that if national provisions restricting or prohibiting certain selling arrangements are to avoid being caught by Article 34 TFEU, they must not be of such a kind as to prevent access to the market by products from another Member State, or to impede access any more than they impede the access of domestic products. In this case, not being allowed to advertise made access to the market almost impossible for the imported product. Similar reasoning is evident in *Deutscher Apothekerverband* (2003) relating to the retail sale of medicinal products over the internet and by mail order. However, the Court has recently confirmed that equal burden rules which apply equally in law and in fact to domestic and imported products do all outside the scope of the Treaty (*Pelckmans* (2014)).

[12] By commenting on the judicial and academic criticism, you are adding credibility to your own argument and showing your wider reading. You do not have to cite many cases: one or two selected examples will make the point just as well.

The *Keck* doctrine has received considerable critical comment both judicially and academically.[12] Judicial concern was voiced when Advocate General Jacobs in *Leclerc-Siplec* (1995) insisted selling arrangements such as advertising were crucial in breaking down barriers to inter-state trade, therefore should not be excluded from Article 34 TFEU in all circumstances. He preferred all undertakings engaged in legitimate economic activity to possess unfettered access to the market, which if posed with a substantial restriction should fall within the scope of Article 34. Although his approach was rejected by the ECJ in *Leclerc-Siplec*, it proved influential in subsequent cases.

[13] You do not have to use exact quotes, and your time in exam preparation is better spent learning principles, but you should try to remember one or two key arguments put forward by academics and then you can draw on that to back up your own analysis.

Weatherill (1996) argued that 'focusing on factual and legal equality . . . to the exclusion of questions of market access' led to the 'notion that there might be an individual right "to trade" . . .'. Barnard (2013) reinforced such an argument by stating the courts ought to recognise 'national restrictions on the opening hours of shops do not substantially hinder access to the market . . . [however] extreme limits may . . . substantially hinder access to the market and so should breach Article [34] and need to be justified'.[13]

[14] This little part of the sentence shows that you understand that the ECJ has to wait for an appropriate case to come along so the examiner knows you appreciate the practicalities of how the ECJ works.

In spite of the concerns raised, it is undoubtedly true that *Keck* moved the law forward in relation to indistinctly applicable measures. It is a shame, however, that the ECJ did not take the trouble to clarify the scope and limits of the principle and it is perhaps high time that, should an opportunity arise,[14] it revisits the *Keck* principle and clarifies the clarification.

✓ **Make your answer stand out**

- There is additional academic commentary you could draw on. See Craig, P. and De Burca (2011) *EU Law. Text Cases and Materials*, 5th edn, Oxford: Oxford University Press, Chapter 19.
- Provide a slightly more gentle introduction to the topic at hand.
- Explain in more detail the 'market access approach' and how this might provide a more useful way of addressing issues in free movement of goods.
- Add comments about future developments based on your assessment of the case law to date.

! **Don't be tempted to . . .**

- Go through the detailed facts of all the cases; you merely need to illustrate your point, so select those details that are relevant.
- List all cases you can think of relating to selling arrangements.
- Spend too much time on the pre-*Keck* case law; focus on the case itself and the development of the principles since then.
- Describe in detail the facts of *Keck*. You need to focus on the relevant principles.

❓ Question 5

The UK government seeks your advice on the introduction of the following measures:

(a) £10 a day fee for the use of lorry parking facilities at Dover; each lorry park is patrolled by security guards and monitored by CCTV.

(b) To reduce the rate of VAT on folding bicycles, most of which are made in the UK, with a view to encouraging their use by commuters. All racing bicycles are imported and the rate of VAT on them will not be changed.

(c) Paying for an advertising campaign backed by celebrity chef Jamie Oliver, under the slogan 'British Pork is Better Pork'.

Write a memo detailing your advice.

Answer plan

➜ Set out the answer in memo style with header information.

➜ Deal with each scenario in turn:

- Outline the law relating to customs duties and explain why the charge may be lawful as a genuine service
- Explain whether the two types of bike are similar products or merely in competition and apply Article 110 TFEU to your conclusion
- Consider the *Buy Irish Campaign* case and its application to this free movement of goods scenario.

➜ Sign off the memo.

Diagram plan

```
○ ○ ○ ○ ○ ○ ○ ○ ○ ○ ○ ○ ○ ○

           MEMO

1 Customs duties: genuine service
  provision

2 Internal taxation under Article 110
  TFEU – products in competition

3 Free movement of goods under
  Article 45. Buy Irish Campaign
  case is almost the same
```

A printable version of this diagram plan is available from **www.pearsoned.co.uk/lawexpressqa**

Answer

From: Legal Department

To: Minister for Trade

Date:

Re: Advice on the introduction of three measures

[1] Even in a memo, you need a general introduction which signals to the examiner that you have understood the question, and identifies the structure of your answer.

You recently requested European Union law advice on three measures to be implemented in the UK. All measures relate to the free movement of goods in the broadest sense. As each of the measures falls within a different area of free movement law, the measures have been dealt with separately and in turn.[1]

2 Although you are setting out advice in a memo style, you still need to set out the legal provisions clearly. You can do that quite informally, as shown here.

3 Remember that the government wants to implement these measures, so your advice should be based around how they can do so. This shows a real understanding of the law and should pick up marks accordingly.

4 At the end, summarise what the legal position is so your client (examiner) is in no doubt about what you mean.

5 This point is often missed by students who refer to uniform taxation in the EU. Recognising this point shows you fully understand the law.

1 Charging fees of any kind at border crossings is always a difficult issue because customs duties and any measures which have the equivalent effect to customs duties are unlawful under Article 30 TFEU.[2] As the EU operates as an internal market, customs duties cannot be charged and any charge made at a border has the potential to be interpreted as a measure which has the same effect as a duty. It is therefore imperative to establish that the proposed charge of £10 is, in fact, a charge which is made for a genuine service provision.[3] If this can be shown, the measure will be lawful as it is not a fee charged because goods are crossing a border. A number of issues are relevant here. First, the car park must be one which can be used by lorry drivers wishing to leave their vehicles there. It must not be a car park which is used as part of the customs clearance process or which is compulsory. If this was to be the case, it could not be described as a genuine service provision. In addition, the cost of the car parking must not exceed the cost of the service provision. You must therefore carefully consider the actual cost of providing the car park including the provision of security guards and CCTV. If £10 is a charge which reflects the actual cost, the charge will be lawful.[4]

2 The second measure you propose concerns VAT which forms part of the UK's internal taxation system. VAT rates are for the government to set and the EU does not interfere in matters of internal taxation.[5] However, Article 110 TFEU does render unlawful any taxation system which has a protective effect on the domestic product thus disadvantaging imported products. The Article is split into two parts: firstly dealing with products which are similar and then dealing with products which are merely in competition. The first question to determine is therefore whether or not folding bikes and racing bikes are similar products. While they are both bikes and arguably both modes of transport, I would suggest that they are not sufficiently similar to fall within the category of similar products for the purposes of EU law. It seems to me that they fulfil different needs for consumers. Folding bikes are being used mainly by commuters who are using their bikes to get from A to B, perhaps as part of their commute. Racing bikes on the other hand are likely to be used for sport and are more likely to be purchased by cycling enthusiasts rather than the population generally. I would therefore suggest that the two are considered products which are not similar but between which there may be a degree of competition. For example, a cycling enthusiast who also wants to use a bike for a daily commute may want to buy only one bike and will have to decide what sort of bike

6 You need to apply the law here. Just saying that you must decide whether the products are similar is not enough. You actually have to make and justify that decision.

7 Here you are stating the law but you are doing so in the context of the scenario, which should pick up marks for both legal knowledge and application and saves you having to say the same thing twice.

8 This should gain some marks for originality and contextual knowledge because it suggests a practical way 'protective effect' might be assessed. It also gets you off the hook because you do not have to come to a decision on this issue.

9 The scenario is so obviously similar to the *Buy Irish Campaign* case that you really do have to mention the case. If you don't, the examiner can only presume you don't know it.

10 Giving practical advice such as this shows you have a good grasp of the law and have engaged with how it works in practice.

to buy.[6] Equally, someone who uses a bike to get from A to B may also want a racing bike because that is their personal preference but may be persuaded to buy a folding bike if there is a significant difference in price. If it is accepted that folding bikes and racing bikes are not similar, having different taxes on them is legitimate as long as there is no protective effect.[7] In other words, the higher tax on racing bikes must not be such as to deter people from buying a racing bike and encourage them to buy a folding bike instead. If there is such a protective effect as a result of the difference in tax, it will breach Article 110(2). However, it may be possible to justify the difference on the basis that it is a proportionate way of achieving a legitimate aim. The legitimate aim here is to encourage the use of bikes and reduce traffic and use of cars. Reducing tax on folding bikes may well be a legitimate aim of achieving that. However, there seems no logical or proportionate reason why racing bikes fall outside the scope of that aim and therefore the measure would, in my opinion be unlawful if it produces a protective effect. This is something that could perhaps be determined using some carefully designed market research.[8]

3   Your third measure concerns the marketing campaign for British pork. The free movement of goods is ensured by treaty provisions as well as settled case law which makes it unlawful to introduce any measure which may hinder trade between Member States. Taking action, such as funding a campaign suggesting British pork is better pork, would be a Member State action which is directly designed to interfere with trade and promote the national product over others. This is clearly unlawful under EU law. The measure is reminiscent of the *Buy Irish Campaign* case which you may be aware of, which was backed by the Irish government (see ***Commission v Ireland*** (1982)).[9] Although the campaign had no appreciable effect on the sale of Irish products, it was still held to breach EU law because it had the potential to impact on trade and make it more difficult for imported products. The measure as it stands cannot therefore be implemented. However, there is nothing to prevent you from labelling British pork as British (although, note that you cannot insist on origin labelling) and you can employ other marketing tools. For example, you may want to draw out the particular qualities of British pork, and, as long as it is the characteristics rather than the origin that you are marketing, the measure should not fall foul of EU law. This is a very fine line to tread, though, so be sure to take detailed advice on any proposed marketing or advertising before it goes live.[10]

[11] Sign off your memo. If your institution uses anonymous marking, please do not sign your name here – make one up or use 'Legal Department', as we have here.

I hope the advice answers your questions but if there is anything else you need, please just email me.

Legal Department[11]

 Make your answer stand out

- Add an example or two from the case law for each scenario. Pick a relevant case from your lecture notes. It will ensure you place a similar emphasis on the topic as your lecturer/examiner.
- Suggest possible alternatives for the measures in 1 and 2 as you have done for 3.
- Give your opinion as to whether the VAT reduction would produce a protective effect.
- Set out the legal provisions in more detail – if you have a statute book, you could set out the provision. Alternatively, provide details as to where additional information can be found.

! **Don't be tempted to . . .**

- Ignore the instructions to write a memo. If your examiner has asked you to do this, there will be some marks attached to doing it correctly.
- Spend lots of time on one scenario and neglect the others. Unless you are told otherwise, the three parts are likely to carry equal marks, so you must spend roughly the same amount of time on each.
- Presume all scenarios are free movement of goods, customs duties or taxation issues because you immediately recognise one. Carefully analyse the situation and expect overlap such as there is here. Part of the legal skill tested here is the ability to identify the right area of law.

www.pearsoned.co.uk/lawexpressqa

 Go online to access more revision support including additional essay and problem questions with diagram plans, You be the marker questions, and download all diagrams from the book.

10

The free movement of workers

How this topic may come up in exams

The free movement of workers is a popular question in exams and both problem and essay questions are common. Essay questions often ask about the development of workers' rights over time or an assessment of the rights available. Problem questions are likely to ask about whether someone falls within the definition of worker; what rights they have in relation to access to the labour market and what other social rights they may have access to. In some cases questions will also extend to the rights of workers' families. The trick to doing well is to apply the law in a very systematic and logical way.

■ Before you begin

It's a good idea to consider the following key themes of the free movement of workers before tackling a question on this topic.

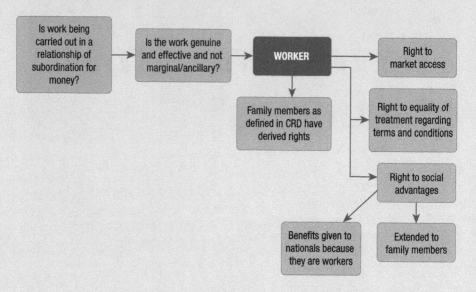

A printable version of this diagram is available from **www.pearsoned.co.uk/lawexpressqa**

 # Question 1

How effective is Article 7(2) of Regulation 492/2011 in ensuring EU migrant workers can access rights in their host state?

Answer plan

→ Introduction: EU workers have right to social advantages under secondary legislation and this is also extended to families.

→ Provide examples of social advantages for workers.

→ Provide examples of extension to family members.

→ Discuss examples of the limitations.

→ Conclude by discussing the generous and broad interpretation and the effect it has to ensure equality.

Diagram plan

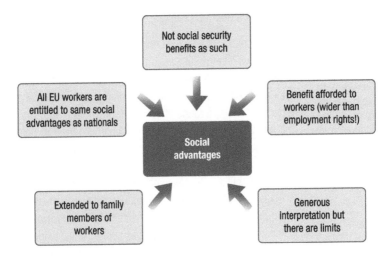

A printable version of this diagram plan is available from **www.pearsoned.co.uk/lawexpressqa**

Answer

Article 45 TFEU establishes the concept of the worker. It provides 'Freedom of movement for workers shall be secured within the Union'. Secondary legislation, Article 7(2) Regulation 492/2011 plainly states

¹ Your first sentence introduces all the main sources of legal rights you will need to consider and thus shows that you have correctly identified the issues.

² You are clearly stating how you see social advantages here; now you need to go on to prove your point to show the examiner that your conclusion is one that can logically be made.

³ Telling the reader what comes next clarifies your structure and guides the reader through your essay, making it easier to follow your arguments.

⁴ This is the first point that proves the wide interpretation. Do not worry about quoting this in an exam: paraphrasing or summarising is fine.

⁵ Here's the second point proving social advantages are interpreted widely, so you are building up your evidence to prove the wide interpretation. Once you have proved that, you can consider the implications of that wide interpretation and that will help you fully answer the question.

⁶ Examples really help with this area of law because social advantages are not clearly defined. You therefore need to consider past cases to get a sense of what might constitute social advantages. To do so, you must give a bit of background to the cases. You are also showing you have a detailed knowledge of this area.

that an EU worker is entitled to 'the same social . . . advantages as national workers'.[1]

The Regulation does not provide further detail. However, the jurisprudence of the Court of Justice has interpreted the concept of 'social advantages' widely.[2] It is jurisprudence that has used that concept as a vehicle for the acquisition of rights, not only by the worker, but by members of the worker's family. This essay will consider that jurisprudence and attempt to show that a generous and effective interpretation has been given to the concept of 'social advantages'.[3]

It is important in the first instance to note that the concept of 'social advantages' is not confined merely to the employment situation. It was held in criminal proceedings against *Gilbert Even* (1979) that 'social advantages' 'whether or not linked to a contract of employment, are generally granted to national workers primarily because of their objective status as workers or by virtue of the mere fact of their residence on the national territory'.[4] The judgment accords with the previous decision of *Fiorini v SNCF* (1975). Such interpretation presents a very wide platform as the source of the worker's rights.

In the context of *Even*, the Court of Justice has presented an interpretation that 'seems suitable to facilitate [the worker's] mobility within the Community'. It is an interpretation of the concept of 'social advantages' which views the worker not merely as a unit of labour but as part of the social fabric of society. In *Mutsch* (1985), for example, it was held that a Luxembourg national who lived in Belgium, had the right to have proceedings against him conducted in German on account of the fact that German-speaking Belgian nationals were similarly so entitled. On the same basis, it would seem that the right to 'social advantages' has been extended not only to the worker per se, but also to members of the worker's family.[5] In *Fiorini v SNCF* the concept of 'social advantages' was applied to the worker's family to claim an entitlement to the fares reduction cards that were issued by a national railway authority to large families of host nationals. Such entitlement applied even after the death of the worker.

Other examples exist in which the right to 'social advantages' has been extended to the worker.[6] In *Reina* (1982), for example, an Italian worker in Germany was entitled to a special childbirth loan that had under German law been payable only to Germans living in Germany. The loan was deemed a 'social advantage'; it had been payable by virtue of either an 'objective status as workers or by virtue of the mere fact of their residence on the national territory'. Further, in **Castelli** (1984), an Italian mother living in Belgium with her retired son, who had been a worker in that state was entitled to the guaranteed income for old persons payable to all persons living in Belgium. Such entitlement was on the basis of the son's entitlement to 'social advantages', which in this instance had operated to prevent discrimination of equal treatment against the worker's dependent relatives. In **Deak** (1985), a third country national was held entitled, on the basis of 'social advantages', to the special unemployment benefits provided by Belgian legislation for young people who were unable to find employment after completing their studies or finishing their apprenticeships. The entitlement was by virtue of Deak's mother, an Italian national who possessed worker status in Belgium and also the fact of Deak's residence in Belgium which was held to be 'on the same basis as the nationals of that state'.

Deak is a clear example of the broad application of free movement and associated rights in ECJ jurisprudence. The rationale for the application in **Deak**, as in the other cases discussed, was the principle that if dependants of migrant workers do not have access to the 'social advantages', then this may act as a barrier to workers exercising the free movement rights of Article 45.[7]

[7] Here you are offering a reason for the broad interpretation and are also signalling that you are now moving on to the next point.

There are, however, limits to the development of the concept of 'social advantages' and in some circumstances there is legitimacy in the difference of treatment between the migrant worker and host state national.[8] In **Kaba (No. 2)** (2004), for example, there was confirmation that entitlement to 'social advantages' continues only in so far as the migrant remains a worker in the host state. This point was made again in **Leclere** (2001), in which, on the grounds that Leclere was no longer a worker, it was held that there was no entitlement to the child allowance of the host state. As Leclere was not now working, he could not claim rights that were not linked to the former employment.

[8] You need to explore the limits too, even if you are saying the concept is very broad, to show that you understand how the concept works in practice.

There are limits too on the ability to use the concept of 'social advantages', aside from the issue of social security benefits. Migrants seeking work in the host state are not entitled to 'social advantages'. The distinction between the work seeker and the worker, the latter entitled to 'social advantages', the former not, was made in **Lebon** (1987), and confirmed in the later case of **Collins** (2004).[9]

[9] Here you are using the cases as authority for the examples you are making rather than as examples themselves, so you do not need to go into as much detail as you have done previously.

Where the 'benefit' claimed by the worker is not available to the host national, there is no inequality of treatment as between host national and migrant worker. In these circumstances, as in **Taghavi** (1992), the worker cannot then use the conduit of 'social advantages' to pursue the claim for equal treatment.

[10] Although this is a new point and therefore shouldn't really be in the conclusion, it does follow logically from the examples given, so keeps your argument flowing.

In conclusion, the jurisprudence of the Court of Justice appears to have developed the principle of 'social advantages' in an extremely practical manner,[10] one which ensures that there can be no hindrance placed on the worker's ability to exercise the right of free movement in the host state. Behind the application of the concept of 'social advantages' lies the desire of the Court of Justice to place the migrant and family on an equal footing with the host nationals with respect to living conditions enjoyed by the latter in the host state. It is an application of the principle of equal treatment which is designed to support the free movement rights afforded to workers and encourage intra-EU migration and it seems to be effective.

✓ Make your answer stand out

- Clarify the difference between social advantages and social security benefits in more detail with reference to work seekers and cases such as *Collins*.
- Introduce the idea of social advantages as supporting equal treatment earlier when discussing the case law.
- Discuss the extent to which the motivation of providing social advantages is social or economic.
- Add some academic commentary: for example, Barnard, C. (2013) *The Substantive Law of the EU: The Four Freedoms*, 4th edn, Oxford: Oxford University Press, Chapter 9.

! Don't be tempted to . . .

- List the cases without commenting on them: you need to use them to illustrate your argument.
- Get drawn into a lengthy discussion of who is classed as a worker – that is a different question.
- Do not consider family members' rights in detail; keep the focus on social advantages.
- Do not go into a huge amount of detail about the case facts. You need to give a little information to make your argument, but do not go over the top.

 Question 2

The concept of EU migrant worker has been broadly defined by the Court of Justice. To what extent to you agree with that assessment of the jurisprudence in this area?

Answer plan

➡ Brief introduction outlining that EU workers have the most generous free movement rights when compared to other EU citizens.

➡ Explain how 'worker' is an EU concept which cannot be defined at Member State level.

➡ Refer to the *Lawrie-Blum* definition of a worker, including the key ideas of subordination and remuneration.

➡ Expand the consideration of who is a worker by referring to the concept of genuine and effective work which is not marginal and ancillary.

➡ Conclude by weighing up the evidence for a generous and broad interpretation to ensure maximum numbers are included in provisions.

Diagram plan

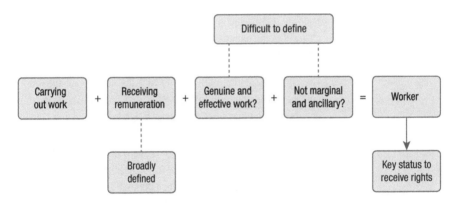

A printable version of this diagram plan is available from **www.pearsoned.co.uk/lawexpressqa**

¹ Restating the question can be a useful way to start an answer, especially if you are struggling to get going. It shows you understand the question and can give you a minute or two to gather your thoughts.

Answer

This question concerns the concept of the worker in European Union law. It charts the European Court of Justice's (ECJ) development of the concept of worker and assesses its scope.[1] Article 45 provides

[2] This introduction gives you a quick overview of what a worker is and why it might be important to know that. The rest of the answer is then concerned with expanding on that. You can therefore summarise your argument to show your own academic opinion, and the rest of the essay then follows logically and proves your point.

'Freedom of movement for workers shall be secured within the Union'. The worker is the migrant EU national who is employed in the host state. According to *Lawrie-Blum* (1986), for Union law purposes, the definition of worker was expressed thus: 'The essential feature of an employment relationship is that a person performs services of some economic value for and under the direction of another person in return for which he receives remuneration'.[2]

Article 45 merely states that the worker is to be given the right of free movement; it does not indicate which EU nationals are to be the beneficiaries of such status. The task of defining the concept of a worker has therefore fallen to the Court of Justice. Its judgments have generally given an expansive interpretation to the definition of the worker.

[3] This is a really important point because it explains why the ECJ has been able to develop this concept and take control of it.

In early case law, *Hoekstra* (1964), the court determined that the term 'worker' was to be a Community concept, and was to be defined by EU law.[3] The statement in *Hoekstra* is important; the alternative, handing to national courts the power to develop the concept of the worker, could have had the consequences that a restrictive interpretation of the concept may have subsequently been allowed to develop. Such an interpretation would in turn impact detrimentally upon the ability of Union nationals to take employment in other Member States under the protection of Article 45.

[4] In an essay such as this one, it is easy just to go through the case law chronologically, but this becomes descriptive, so try to make your point first and then use case law to illustrate it.

The Court of Justice has ensured that the concept of the worker applies to the migrant national who is in full-time and part-time employment in the state of migration.[4] In *Levin* (1982) it was held that a UK national, working as a part-time chambermaid in Holland and receiving a wage below the minimum legal wage level prevailing at the time in that state, was nonetheless to be considered to be a worker for European Union law purposes. The judgment further established that the award of worker status would depend upon whether the migrant's employment in the host state could be considered to be 'effective and genuine activit[y] . . ., to the exclusion of activities on such a small scale as to be regarded as purely marginal and ancillary'.[5]

[5] Genuine and effective, and not marginal and ancillary, are the key points here and you should remember those even if you do not remember the rest of the quote.

The term 'effective and genuine activity' in application has been liberally construed by the Court of Justice. As if to reinforce the assertion that it is a concept in EU law, rather than for determination by the Member State, it has been held in *Trojani* (2004) that the enquiry as to 'effective and genuine' is one that is to be conducted on the basis of objective criteria, including an overall assessment of all the circumstances relating to the activities concerned and the employment relationship. In the context of promoting the wide application of Article 45 TFEU, this statement is arguably significant. The imposition of 'objective criteria' conspires to remove from the national court any temptation to impose subjective assessments relating to the nature of the particular employment record of the migrant EU national under scrutiny.[6]

[6] Explain how the ECJ ensures it keeps control of the concept of worker to make sure your argument is made strongly and follows logically.

Jurisprudence has applied the concept of 'effective and genuine' to particular circumstances.[7] In **Kempf** (1986), for example, a German national working part-time as a music teacher in Holland, giving 12 lessons a week from 26 October 1981 to 14 July 1982,[8] was held a worker on the basis that this amounted to an 'effective and genuine activity'. An even more generous interpretation was given in **Raulin** (1992) in relation to an on-call waitress who had a record of irregular employment, working only from 5 to 21 March 1986 inclusive as a waitress for 12 days, 5 hours a day, a total time of 60 hours. That activity was deemed 'effective and genuine'. Likewise, in **Ninni-Orasche** (2003) it was held that employment of an Italian national as a waitress/cashier in Austria for a temporary period of two and a half months could amount to an 'effective and genuine' activity. **Ninni-Orasche** distinguished the judgment in **Bettray** (1989), wherein the worker status was not given to a German national who was employed in the Netherlands on a drug rehabilitation programme. Refusal to accord worker status was on account of particular characteristics in the Dutch programme. It was confirmed in **Athanasios Vatsouras** (2009) that the fact that employment is of short duration cannot, in itself, exclude that employment from the scope of Article 45.

[7] Indicate at the beginning of the paragraph what the cases you are dealing with show and why you have grouped them together. It tells the reader what to expect and makes your argument really easy to follow, and that in turn makes it easy to award marks.

[8] It isn't really necessary to give these dates; when revising, concentrate on remembering the important issues relating to legal principles rather than facts that do not add anything. Here, there's no harm in setting them out if you know them, though: they form part of a useful illustration.

As further evidence, however, of a broad intent of the Court of Justice to broaden the scope of the beneficiaries of Article 45 status as workers, the judgment of **Levin** (1982) extended the concept not only to migrant nationals in full- and part-time employment, but also to migrants who 'wish . . . to pursue an activity' in another Member State.[9] In **Antonissen** (1991), for example, the court confirmed that job seekers come within the scope of the worker. A broad reading in **Antonissen** of Article 45 by the court in this instance allowed a

[9] The third issue of interpretation is dealt with here and brings work seekers within the definition. You are trying to establish how wide the category of worker is, so this is the next logical argument and you are building a picture of the worker category and guiding the reader through it.

Belgian migrant national imprisoned for drug related offences entry and residence to the UK. The opportunity to seek employment would arise where there is a genuine chance of the migrant being engaged in the host state. To deny the migrant such an opportunity would otherwise negate the purpose of the treaty.

The extension of the concept of the worker to encompass migrants not only working in but also seeking work in another Member State is significant. While it is noted that Directive 2004/38, Article 7(3) now gives to the migrant national a statutory right in certain circumstances to look for work within the state of migration, it is clear that the jurisprudence of the Court of Justice had addressed these issues some time earlier.

[10] This is the point suggested in your introduction which you have now proved and can confidently state as your conclusion. It answers the question fully and directly and is based on the examples given, so there is no jump in logic, which is great.

In conclusion, it appears that the jurisprudence of the Court of Justice has given the widest possible meaning to the concept of worker,[10] indicating that the ECJ was trying to include as many EU citizens as possible within the scope of Article 45 TFEU.

✓ **Make your answer stand out**

- Consider the category of workers in the context of other categories such as students, volunteers or even the self-employed. Use this as context, though; your essay must focus on workers.

- Consider some of the limits placed on the rights of work seekers to illustrate that differences do remain.

- Include a paragraph towards the beginning which explicitly sets out why gaining worker status might be important and why therefore the ECJ has interpreted it widely. Consider the extent to which encouraging free movement is important to the EU's core aims and show that you understand the context in which these rights operate.

- Comment a little more on whether you think the interpretation of worker is appropriate. Consider, for instance, the examples provided by Barnard, C. (2013) *The Substantive Law of the EU: The Four Freedoms*, 4th edn, Oxford: Oxford University Press, in Chapter 9.

Don't be tempted to . . .

- Go through the facts of the cases in too much detail; you just need to give enough information to illustrate your point. The facts are not really important here; it is the principles that you need to focus on.

- Ignore the limitations of worker status; to define who is a worker, you need to consider where the line is drawn. Consider, for example, the position of work seekers or areas where work is considered marginal as in student cases such as *Brown* (1988).

- Write about worker rights in great detail. This is mainly a definitional essay.

❓ Question 3

Amélie is a French national who has recently started full-time employment with a travel company based in London. She is now living in the UK with her French partner, Pierre. Amélie and Pierre's only child, Jacqueline, is four years old. Next year, Jacqueline will attend primary school and at that time, Pierre intends to look for work in the UK. Amélie and Pierre have made enquiries as regards to schooling next year with respect to Jacqueline and have been told that she will be placed in the school within the authority that is the least subscribed. Amélie knows from conducting enquiries that the normal policies of the local authority are that school places are allocated on a 'first come, first served' basis. In addition, Amélie, has just discovered that she receives from the travel company, one week's holiday less than other employees engaged on the same grade as she is.

Advise Amélie and Pierre as to their rights in European Union law.

Diagram plan

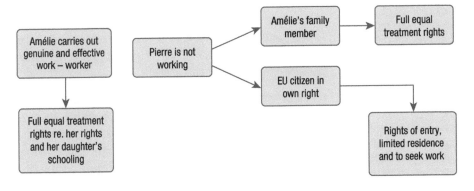

A printable version of this diagram plan is available from **www.pearsoned.co.uk/lawexpressqa**

Answer plan

➜ Introduction: EU workers have the most generous free movement rights, so this is a useful EU status to have.

➜ Are Pierre and Amélie workers? Apply *Lawrie-Blum* and *Levin*.

➜ Is Pierre a family member?

➜ Conclusions: summarise advice.

Answer

In a question of this nature, it is first necessary to establish whether or not Pierre and Amélie are workers for the purposes of European Union law. If they are, they would fall under the protection of Article 45 Treaty on the Functioning of the European Union (TFEU) and would be entitled to the right of free movement within the Union.[1] To assess whether Amélie is a worker, recourse must be had to the jurisprudence of the Court of Justice. In **Levin** (1982), the ECJ held that workers had to pursue 'effective and genuine' activities that would not be considered to be purely 'marginal and ancillary'. Full-time employment with the travel company in London is an 'effective and genuine' activity and, on this basis, Amélie would be regarded as a worker within Article 45. It appears that Pierre is not currently employed and is therefore not an EU worker.[2]

Pierre as partner of Amélie falls within the definition of Amélie's 'family' for the purpose of European Union law. Directive 2004/38/EC's definition of family member includes a partner with whom the EU national is in a durable relationship. As a family member, the right of free movement is parasitic upon the worker status accorded to Amélie. Pierre does, however, have the right to enter and reside in the UK for three months in his own right and will acquire worker status when (next year) he seeks work in the UK.[3]

For the purpose of working or seeking work on his own account, both Amélie and Pierre enjoy the right of residence in the UK. Article 7, Directive 2004/38/EC provides that: 'All Union citizens shall have the right of residence on the territory of another Member State . . . if they (a) are workers . . . in the host Member State.'[4] **Levin** extended the concept of the worker to the migrant looking for work in the host state. Pierre's right of residence in the UK originating from this status,

[1] Here, you start by simply saying what needs to be established and therefore indicate to the examiner that you have correctly identified the legal issues.

[2] Amélie can be dealt with fairly quickly here because she appears to fall within the worker category fairly easily, so don't waste time on this when the outcome is clear: you are better off spending your time on controversial issues.

[3] Pierre's status is not particularly complicated either, but you need to say clearly where his rights come from: otherwise, the examiner will not know that you know.

[4] You could use a statute book here to get the wording right, but, before you start revising, check that you are allowed to take a statute book into the exam with you.

technically is limited to the time given to him to find work in this state. However, in this instance, this is practically of little importance as, if he does not find work on his own account, he could still remain as part of Amélie's family.[5] His residence rights in the UK would still then flow from his status, under Article 7(1)(d) Directive 2004/38/EC as a 'family member . . . accompanying . . . a Union citizen' who is a worker in the host state. Jacqueline is also regarded by Article 2(2)(c) Directive 2004/38/EC as a member of Amélie's family, and on that basis she is entitled to residence in the UK.

The right of equality of treatment is extended to the worker and family by European Union law. In this context, the principle of equality of treatment is given by Article 45(2) with respect to the worker and fleshed out by Regulation 492/2011. Article 45(2) accords to the worker the 'abolition of any discrimination on the grounds of nationality'. With respect to the receipt of fewer holidays, this is clearly discriminatory and is unlawful. This is reinforced by the further provision in Article 7(1) Regulation 492/2011 that the worker 'may not, . . . be treated differently from national workers by reason of his nationality in respect of any conditions of employment and work'. To give the migrant less holiday than employees at the same level in the company is discriminatory and therefore on this account is unlawful as well.[6] In *Ugliola* (1969) ECJ, German law stipulated that military service carried out in Germany counted towards length for the purposes of pay and other benefits. This gave rise to indirect discrimination against non-Germans who were in reality more likely to have done military service in their home state. In addition, *Sotgui* (1974) made it clear that all conditions of employment with respect to migrant and host nationals must be equal once the worker is engaged.

The offering by the local authority of the school place to Jacqueline on a different basis to that offered to other children living in that area is prohibited under European Union law. Jacqueline has been identified as part of the worker's family. To treat her differently from other local children with respect to the allocation of school places is actionable discrimination by virtue of Amélie's status as a worker and in consequence to her entitlement to the 'same social advantages as national workers'.

The worker is entitled to the concept of 'social advantages' by virtue of mere residence in the host state. In *Even* (1979), the Court of Justice held that 'social advantages' are 'those which, whether or not linked to a contract of employment, are generally granted to national workers primarily because of their objective status as workers or by virtue of the mere fact of their residence on national territory'. Importantly, however, in the context, the court has given a very wide interpretation to the term 'social advantages', extending that entitlement, not only to the worker as such, but also to family members of the worker. In **_Fiorini v SNCF_** (1975), the concept of 'social advantages' was expansively treated, the ECJ holding that it applied not only to the worker but also to family members if it provided an indirect advantage to the worker. On this basis, therefore, the right of equality of treatment with respect to the allocation of school places means that Jacqueline must be offered a school place on the same basis as the children of nationals of the host state. For the authority to attempt to do otherwise would be unlawful.

 Make your answer stand out

- Consider the rights of migrant children to education in more detail with reference to relevant cases such as _Casagrande_ (1974) or recently _Ibrahim_ (2010) and _Teixeira_ (2010) which really illustrate the children's EU status in their own right.

- Discuss Pierre's right to social advantages as an EU citizen and as Amélie's family member to show you appreciate that Pierre's rights come from his own status as well as Amélie's.

- Question Pierre's family member status: what does 'partner' actually include? This shows you have an awareness of the wider issues too.

- You could draw on European Union Agency for Fundamental Rights (2010) Homophobia, transphobia and discrimination on grounds of sexual orientation and gender identity, _2010 Update Comparative Legal Analysis_, Luxembourg: Publication Office of the European Union, which provides a useful consideration of the meaning of 'partner'.

! Don't be tempted to . . .

- Ignore Pierre's rights as an EU citizen generally and presume he can only rely on derived rights.
- Go through the case law on social advantages. They are relevant but you do not need to go through them all. Keep the focus on the question.
- Explain equal treatment under Regulation 492/2011 in general terms. You need to establish the law but then apply it just to the scenario.
- Forget to deal with the rights of all three. You need to advise on all the issues raised, and students sometimes forget to or run out of time to deal with the children's rights.

? Question 4

Ilias, a Greek national, has been offered a part-time job in Sweden. He will be working 20 hours per week as a technician. He will move to Sweden with his wife Sonia (a Pakistani national) and their two youngest children Hannah (18) and Eleni (22). Their eldest child Georgia (25) already works in Sweden as a personal assistant. Sonia would also like her mother, Alyah (also a Pakistani national), to move with them as she is dependent on Sonia both financially and for care.

The Swedish authorities have indicated that Hannah will not be allowed entry into Sweden as she was arrested for a minor drug offence last time the family visited Sweden.

Explain the rights and obligations under European Union law given in respect of Ilias and his family.

Answer plan

→ Identify the relevant law: free movement of workers and their families.

→ Establish the status of the family in EU law.

→ Consider Ilias's right to entry, residence and work.

→ Consider Sonia's status as third-country national.

→ Consider Hannah's arrest.

Diagram plan

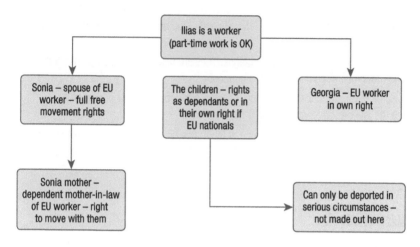

A printable version of this diagram plan is available from **www.pearsoned.co.uk/lawexpressqa**

Answer

[1] This short sentence quickly outlines the main issue that the question concerns. This clearly shows the examiner you have identified the key area of law and sets the parameters for the rest of your answer.

The question concerns the status and the rights accorded to the migrant European Union national who is employed in the host state. It concerns the status of worker and family under European Union law together with the application of the principle of non-discrimination.[1]

Ilias is a Greek national. Under Article 45 TFEU, he has the right to work in another Member State. Article 45 provides that 'Freedom of movement for workers shall be secured within the Union'. The right to work in the host state on a part-time basis was extended to migrant Union nationals by **Levin** (1982) in circumstances wherein the work could be considered to be 'effective and genuine'. Work of 30 hours a week is 'effective and genuine' work; in **Raulin** (1992), work as an 'on call' waitress for 12 days in duration and totalling 60 hours in total, formed the basis of 'effective and genuine' work.[2]

[2] You do not need to go into any more detail than this regarding Ilias's status – just give enough law to make your point and then move on.

For the purposes of working in Sweden, Ilias has the right of entry to the host state by virtue of his worker status and by Article 5 Directive 2004/38/EC.

The family of the worker derives rights from the worker status enjoyed by Ilias. By Article 2(2) Directive 2004/38/EC, family of the worker is defined as '(a) the spouse; . . . (c) the direct descendants who are under the age of 21 or are dependants . . . (d) the dependent direct relatives in the ascending line and those of the spouse'. Clearly, Sonia as spouse falls within the category of family member, as does Hannah. Eleni is over 21, so will only derive rights if she is dependent on her parents (or more accurately, her father as the EU national). Aliyah, as a dependent relative staying with the family also falls within the definition.[3]

Article 5(1) Directive 2004/38/EC gives to family members the right to enter a Member State 'with a valid identity card or passport'. However, Sonia's mother is a Pakistani national and, as a non-EU national, Article 5(1) directs that she must have an 'entry visa'.

By virtue of Article 6 Directive 2004/38/EC, EU citizens have the right of residence in the host state. Article 7 provides that the right will extend for more than three months as long as Ilias remains a worker; Ilias's family will also enjoy such a right, including the family member accompanying who is not herself an EU national.

Georgia is already working in Sweden. As she has taken employment and now resides in that state on her own account, she will be regarded as a worker under Article 45; her free movement rights in Sweden will stem from that status.[4] At 25 years old, Georgia falls outside the definition of Ilias's family for European Union law purposes, and she would in consequence not have any free movement rights from that source.

[4] It is useful here to clarify that you understand that Georgia's rights come from her own status and are not derived rights, because otherwise the examiner will presume you do not fully grasp how EU citizenship works and you will lose marks.

The matter of Hannah's criminal record may give rise to concern in so far as it might affect her right to enter Sweden and to continue to exercise her free movement rights there as the family member of a worker. The right of residence is given to the worker by Article 7 Directive 2004/38. The right of the worker and his or her family to free movement is, however, not absolute. It may be denied to migrant Union nationals, but only on grounds specified in Article 45(3). The provision provides that the right of free movement shall be 'subject to limitations justified on grounds of public policy'. The public policy limitation is repeated with respect to the Union citizen by Article 27 Directive 2004/38. In addition, Article 27(2) provides that 'Measures taken by the host state on grounds of public policy shall comply with the principle of proportionality and shall be based exclusively on the personal conduct of the individual concerned'. With respect to

[5] You have a little bit of information in the scenario, so make use of it and be as specific as you can in your application. It shows you are engaging with the question set rather than reproducing a generic answer on the topic. It also helps you check you are not missing anything. Usually all facts are given for a reason.

[6] It is OK not to have a definitive conclusion here, given that you have little information. You should, however, avoid sitting on the fence completely, and give an indication of your view based on the information you do have. It shows confidence in your critical analysis skills.

Hannah's arrest record, the drug offence must of itself amount to 'personal conduct' upon which Sweden could then deny her the right to enter into that state. In this context, it is relevant that it is stated that the drug offence is stated to be minor.[5] According to **Orfanopoulous** (2004), the concept of public policy demands 'a particularly restrictive' interpretation of the derogation. The court held in both **Régina v Pierre Bouchereau** (1977) and in **Donatella Calfa** (1999) that the public policy exception could be invoked to justify restrictions on the free movement of workers only if 'there was a genuine and sufficiently serious threat affecting one of the fundamental interests of society'. The right of Sweden to deny free movement rights to Hannah will be restrictively applied; Sweden's response must be proportionate to the seriousness of the offence committed. Whether the refusal of entry is lawful would depend on whether the drug offence of which she was guilty could be regarded as a 'genuine and sufficiently serious threat' to Sweden. This seems unlikely as the offence has already been described as minor.[6]

It is, however, noted that Article 27(2) Directive 2004/38 provides that 'previous criminal convictions shall not in themselves constitute grounds for taking such measures'. It was held in **Régina v Pierre Bouchereau** that the circumstances giving rise to the personal conduct must evidence a 'present threat to the requirements of public policy'. In addition, in **Orfanopoulous,** the court also emphasised the need for the state to take account of fundamental human rights in deciding on the issue of deportation. Such assessment was to be made on a case-by-case basis, to decide a fair balance between the legitimate interests of compliance with the general principles of Community law on the one hand, as opposed to the protection of fundamental rights such as the right to family life on the other.

 Make your answer stand out

- Add a paragraph at the end summarising all your advice; this is particularly useful where the problem question is quite complex.
- Restructure your answer slightly to deal with all the rights of entry and residence together; it would make the answer more coherent but does require careful writing to articulate all the different rights.

- Establish Ilias's worker status in more detail, applying the case law you cite more directly.
- Examine the position of Sonia and Alyah in more detail; particularly think about the latter and dependence.
- Think about Eleni in more detail. Is she dependent?

❗ Don't be tempted to . . .

- Presume that allowing Hannah to enter is automatically against public policy. This needs careful consideration, without which you will lose marks because you are not applying the law to the scenario properly.
- Ignore the third-country national point in relation to the wife and her mother but simply treat them as any other family member. You need to engage with the point, even if the outcome in terms of practicalities is very similar, in order to show that you fully understand the law.
- Get drawn into a long description of the case law. Give enough information to allow you to apply the law clearly, no more.

www.pearsoned.co.uk/lawexpressqa

Go online to access more revision support including additional essay and problem questions with diagram plans, You be the marker questions, and download all diagrams from the book.

11
Freedom to provide services and freedom of establishment

How this topic may come up in exams

The freedom to provide services and establish oneself in a Member State other than one's own is enshrined in the TFEU and forms part of the 'four freedoms'. This topic is likely to come up in courses on the substantive law of the European Union. While they are sometimes treated as two separate topics, they are closely linked and it makes little sense to deal with them in isolation. This chapter therefore deals with the right to establishment enshrined in Articles 49–54 TFEU and the right to provide services in another Member State (Articles 46–62 TFEU) together. Problem questions are very common in this area of EU law; essay questions are less common but not unheard of and tend to concentrate on the development of the law here, in particular the European Court of Justice's influence.

■ Before you begin

It's a good idea to consider the following key themes of freedom to provide services and freedom of establishment before tackling a question on this topic.

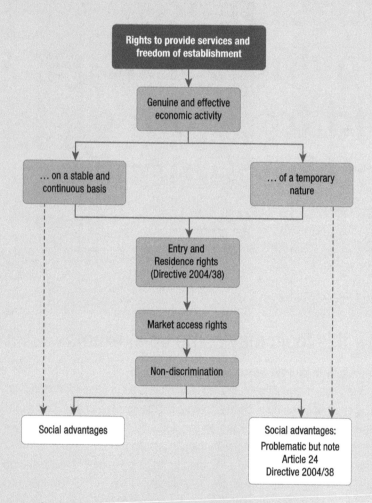

A printable version of this diagram is available from **www.pearsoned.co.uk/lawexpressqa**

 # Question 1

Critically assess the extent to which the European Court of Justice (ECJ) has been instrumental in turning the free movement of the self-employed within the EU from a theoretical right to a practical reality.

Answer plan

➜ The self-employed are those providing services and those established in another Member State.

➜ Rights to provide service and establish oneself.

➜ What were the problems with these rights?

➜ How has ECJ case law addressed those issues?

➜ Impact of ECJ involvement?

Diagram plan

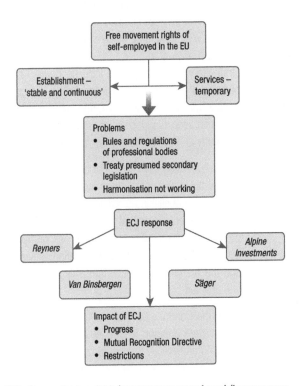

A printable version of this diagram plan is available from **www.pearsoned.co.uk/lawexpressqa**

Answer

[1] This paragraph sets out clearly that you have understood the question. It shows recognition that self-employment can refer to service provision as well as establishment in another Member State. It identifies the relevant treaty provisions and sets out clearly how this question will be answered.

The European Court of Justice (ECJ) has been instrumental in expanding the free movement rights of economically active and inactive EU citizens. This essay considers the court's role in relation to the right to establishment (49–54 TFEU) and the right to provide services in another Member State (Articles 56–62 TFEU). It will first consider the Commission's approach to implementing the rights enshrined in the treaty, highlighting the pitfalls of the approach. It will then consider how the ECJ approach differed and has moved the law forward in this context.[1]

The self-employed are granted free movement rights in two similar but distinct contexts. First, Article 49 prohibits Member States from imposing restrictions on the freedom of establishment and gives the self-employed rights to enter another Member State on a long-term basis and take up and pursue economic activities on a stable and continuous basis (*Gebhard* (1995)). Secondly, the self-employed may provide services in another Member State on a temporary basis (Article 57) and Member States are prohibited from restricting such service provisions (Article 56).[2] Although these treaty rights appear straightforward, putting them into effect was a slow process mainly because of a whole host of national rules and conditions regulating professional activities in their territories. The treaty provisions envisaged that secondary legislation would flesh out the rights granted in the treaty and this is the path taken by the Commission.[3]

[2] This section sets out clearly the legal base for the discussion which follows.

[3] This section introduces the issues raised by the question and shows an awareness of how this area of law has developed.

The Commission initially set out on a harmonisation process which was complex and time-consuming. It sought to implement a series of directives abolishing restrictions to the free movement of people and implementing mutual recognition of qualifications in specific professions. Directives dealing with one profession at a time and setting out specific technical information allowed for little progress and the Architects Directive famously took 18 years to be agreed and enacted.[4]

[4] This paragraph is important as it highlights the Commission approach, using an example to illustrate the point. It sets the context for the next paragraph, thus helping your argument to flow logically.

While the Commission was making no real progress, the self-employed were bringing legal cases because they were finding their treaty rights severely hampered by national rules on membership of professions and recognition of qualifications. The ECJ thus had an opportunity to move the law forward. The first two cases were the vital

5 This paragraph summarises
the early contribution made
by the ECJ, stressing the
importance of direct effect in
creating freestanding rights.
It is beginning to build a
picture of the ECJ as highly
influential.

6 This paragraph moves the
argument on and shows wider
knowledge by referring to the
workers' jurisprudence. This
paragraph could be expanded
if time permitted.

7 The cases are the authority
for the examples given.
Explaining the cases would
not really add anything, so
just citing them is fine.

8 By mentioning the
derogations like this you
show you know about them;
but keep the focus of your
answer on the more difficult,
interesting or controversial
aspects.

9 This paragraph recognises
that free movement rights
for the self-employed are not
absolute and that the ECJ
has also been influential in
defining the limits of those
rights. This is then nicely
illustrated with examples.

10 As the essay has dealt with
services and establishment
together, you need to highlight
that you do appreciate that
there are differences.

step in creating usable free movement rights for the self-employed. **Reyners** (1974), concerning establishment, and **Van Binsbergen** (1974), concerning service provision, established that the treaty rights in this area were directly effective and thus created free-standing rights which Member State nationals could rely on and enforce through their national courts. It was therefore no longer necessary to wait for the enactment of secondary legislation on each profession.[5]

Instead, the ECJ was now in a position to flesh out the rights granted by the treaty and to deal with potential restrictions in the cases before them as it saw fit. The ECJ took a similar approach to the one taken in the free movement of worker jurisprudence.[6] It tackled rules which were directly (**Gouda** (1991)) or indirectly discriminatory (**Commission v Germany** (1986) (insurance cases)) and those which were non-discriminatory but nevertheless prevented market access (**Säger v Dennemeyer** (1991); **Gebhard** (1995)).[7]

While the ECJ has contributed significantly to the realisation of free movement rights for the self-employed, it also recognised that this right is not absolute. The usual derogations on the grounds of public policy, security and health apply.[8] In addition, the ECJ noted that some restrictions on the provision of services and the right to establishment are legitimate. In **Gebhard** it set out to clarify the position and concluded that those national measures which hinder or make less attractive market access for the self-employed may be lawful if they fulfil four conditions. They must be non-discriminatory in law and fact; justified by an imperative reason relating to the public interest; suitable for achieving that public interest objective, and proportionate. An example of a case where national measures were justified is **Alpine Investments** (1995), where consumer protection and safeguarding Dutch financial markets were held to be legitimate reasons. Other measures might include licensing requirements for certain professions.[9]

In this context the difference between establishment and service provision is quite limited. Perhaps obviously, as qualifications do not have a bearing on your ability to carry out your activity on a temporary or permanent basis. However, it is worth noting that rules relating to establishment are generally easier to justify, especially if the profession of the service provider is also regulated in the home state.[10]

¹¹ Conclusion summarising the impact of ECJ intervention in direct answer to the question, showing the examiner that you have answered it properly rather than just reciting any learned answer on services and establishment.

The ECJ's intervention in this area of free movement law had a significant impact. It not only translated the treaty provisions into free-standing rights to be enjoyed by the self-employed wishing to carry on their business in a Member State other than their own: it also changed the Commission's approach to legislating in this area. As soon as the early case law was decided, the Commission changed tactics, realising that legislating for one profession at a time was not likely to achieve any significant results.[11] Instead, the Commission set out to legislate for mutual recognition of qualifications more generally. It did so through the Mutual Recognition of Diplomas Directive in 1989. Directive 2005/36 now deals with the recognition of qualifications, incorporating both the earlier directive and those relating to specific professions.

✓ Make your answer stand out

- Add a little more detail on the problems of national rules relating to professions and why these were so problematic.
- Show awareness that these issues mainly related to professions and have been less prevalent in other areas of economic activities.
- Expand the case law discussion as this should be analytical detail about the principles rather than factual detail.
- Draw parallels with the free movement of workers and goods principles.

! Don't be tempted to . . .

- Simply go through the ECJ case law chronologically. This will be too descriptive.
- Write everything you know about freedom of establishment and services. The question is quite broad but your answer still needs to be specific to it.

❓ Question 2

Anita and George, both UK nationals, are fashion designers running a small business in London. They have private clients based in France and that client base is growing. Anita and George want to set up in business in France next year and have come to you for advice. Currently they work together in London, visiting their clients in France when the occasion demands. Business trips to France are becoming more frequent.

Anita and George are considering buying business premises in Paris so that they can have a base from which to operate in that country.

They both intend to keep their base in London during this year and then set up in business in Paris on a permanent basis in approximately 12 months' time. At that point Anita and George intend to buy a home in France and to take their respective families to France with them.

How will both Anita and George and their respective families be treated in European Union law? Identify the rights to which they will be entitled.

Diagram plan

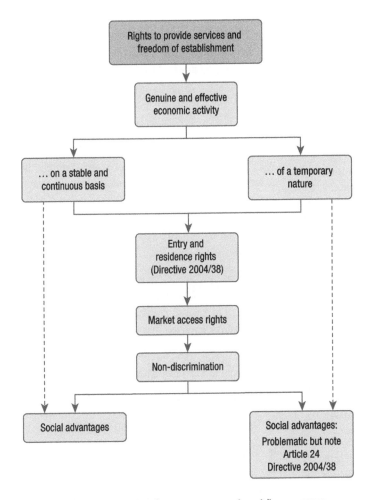

A printable version of this diagram plan is available from **www.pearsoned.co.uk/lawexpressqa**

Answer plan

→ Consider the service provision and establishment.

→ Discuss the right to move to and reside in another Member State.

→ Explain the right to have access to the market.

→ Discuss the right not to be discriminated against.

→ Include any other social and ancillary rights.

Answer

[1] This paragraph highlights that you have identified the key issues of services and establishment and recognise the close relationship between them.

This scenario requires a consideration of Anita and George's position in Union law: in particular, the rights to provide services and the right to establishment need to be considered. As these rights operate on a continuum and give rise to very similar ancillary rights, I will consider them together pointing out differences where relevant.[1]

[2] This paragraph sets out the legal provisions and confirms that Anita and George's activity falls within the scope of the provisions. You are building up a logical argument which is easy to follow.

Anita and George are currently providing services in a Member State other than their own. They are engaged in an economic activity for which they can reasonably expect to get paid, and that activity is genuine and effective. Their service provision therefore satisfies the definition in Article 57 TFEU and the test laid down in **DeLiege** (1985). Once Anita and George have moved and set up their business in France, they will be subject to the rules relating to freedom of establishment set out in Articles 49–54 TFEU.[2]

[3] It can be useful to include a bullet point list like this for clarity and for you to come back to as you are writing. As in other free movement cases, it is useful to think practically about what you would have to be allowed to do to move. Logically, you have to be able to enter the host state and live there; you need access to the market and you need equality of treatment and other social benefits.

Restrictions by Member States on service provision or establishment are prohibited by Articles 56 and 49 respectively. However, for those prohibitions to have any practical effect, it is important that EU citizens have certain other rights. These can be broken down into the following categories:

■ The right to move to and reside in another Member State.

■ The right to have access to the market.

■ The right not to be discriminated against.

■ Other social and ancillary rights.[3]

[4] It is important to recognise that the right to move and reside freely applies to EU citizens in general and where that right comes from.

The right to move and reside freely in the territory of another Member State is laid down in Directive 2004/38. Anita and George and their families have the right to move to France and to reside there.[4] Their

5 It is worth noting that some
restrictions exist, but, as there
is no indication that they apply
in this case, you do not need
to provide detail.

right can only be restricted in very specific circumstances on grounds of 'public policy, public security or public health' as identified in Chapter VI, Directive 2004/38/EC.[5] There is no indication that any of these grounds apply in this case.

They also have the right to market access both in relation to service provision and in relation to establishment (Articles 57 and 49 TFEU), so Anita and George are lawfully providing their service in France now and also have the right to set up their business there on a more permanent basis.[6] The rights afforded to them include not merely access but access on the same terms as would apply to nationals of the host state. This is explicit in Article 57 TFEU but applies equally in relation to establishment, as the provisions must be read in conjunction with the non-discrimination principle enshrined in Article 18 TFEU.[7]

There are certain specific situations in which Anita and George's right to provide services or establish themselves in France might be restricted. First, any restrictions on service provisions may be justifiable if they are non-discriminatory (i.e. they apply to nationals of the host state and other Member State nationals alike) and they can be objectively justified and are proportionate (see **Van Binsbergen** (1974), **Webb** (1981) as well as **Sägar** in relation to the application of Article 56 to non-discriminatory restrictions). In relation to establishment, a test similar to the one found in **Van Binsbergen** and subsequent cases can be found in **Gebhard** (1995), which suggests that restrictions on the freedom of establishment can be lawful if they are applied in a non-discriminatory manner, are justified by an imperative requirement in the general interest and are suitable for securing the attainment of the objective and do not go beyond what is necessary in order to attain it.[8]

There is no indication given in the scenario that Anita and George or, indeed, the services they provide will fall within a category that might be subject to one of these exceptions. We must therefore presume that their rights in this area cannot be restricted.[9]

The last category of rights mentioned concerns social and ancillary rights. The regulation dealing with those types of rights (Regulation 1612/68) only applies to workers and makes no reference to the self-employed. We therefore have to rely on other provisions to ascertain the rights Anita and George, and their family members,

6 Try and link back to the
problem question wherever
possible rather than just
stating the law generally.
Here, saying that there is a
right to establishment and
service provisions means that
what Anita and George are
doing now is lawful, as are
their plans.

7 This is a good opportunity to
pick up extra marks and show
wider knowledge. If you have
more time, you could give a
little more detail on Article
18 TFEU.

8 This paragraph shows
a good understanding of
the law relating to services
and establishment and
summarises quite succinctly
when Member States can
impose some restrictions.

9 It is difficult to say any
more than this as you are not
asked to consider any specific
restriction in this case, but
you should still consider what
your previous discussion in
this paragraph means for
Anita and George.

[10] These two sections show wider understanding of the free movement of people law. It is not strictly necessary to mention Regulation 1612/68 here, but it does set the context and shows that you appreciate the difference in treatment between workers and self-employed.

[11] It is important to make clear that services and establishment are different here and why they are different. The why comes next.

[12] You could add a little more detail on to bring home the point, but do not go overboard with the facts of the case.

[13] The final paragraph essentially summarises the advice to be given to Anita and George not only in terms of their rights but also in relation to how to make the most of their rights.

might have.[10] In certain circumstances Article 18 TFEU on non-discrimination may be invoked to ensure they have the same rights as those afforded to nationals of the host state. This is uncontroversial in relation to establishment. However, the position is much less clear in relation to service provision.[11] There is an argument which suggests that the provision of ancillary rights such as access to benefits and other social advantages should be the responsibility of the state in which the potential beneficiary is established and/or resident rather than the state in which a service is merely provided on a temporary basis. However, Article 24 of Directive 2004/38/EC extends the principle of equal treatment to all migrant EU nationals, subject to some limitations regarding student grants and social assistance during the first three months of residence, so there is a legal basis for arguing that service providers are entitled to the same social advantages as nationals of the host state. Indeed, the scope of ancillary rights for service providers has been extended significantly by the *Carpenter* case (2003), in which Carpenter, who was a service provider, was allowed to rely on EU law rights against his own state in relation to family rights.[12] The scope of exactly what rights are available to service providers and their families is, however, still a little uncertain.

Applying this situation to Anita and George means that, in order for them to have access to the same social advantages as French nationals, they should show that they are established rather than merely providing services. This is not problematic once they have moved to France and set up their business on a permanent basis. However, should they wish to access social advantages sooner, it will be worth ascertaining when service provision stops being service provision and turns into establishment. The case of *Gebhard* gives some guidance as to the difference between the two concepts. The ECJ said that the concept of establishment was broad and should allow a Community national to participate 'on a stable and continuous basis' in the economic life of a Member State other than his/her own Member State. Services are carried out on a temporary basis. The temporary nature has to be defined taking all things into account including the duration but also the regularity, periodicity or continuity. Arguably, therefore, Anita and George could show that they are established in France even before they permanently move there if they have begun to participate in economic life on a 'continuous and stable basis'.[13]

Make your answer stand out

■ A clear structure always helps, so try to deal with the issues logically in turn.

■ You could add extra detail of the types of social rights Anita and George might be entitled to, such as educational rights for partners/spouses and children.

■ More detailed explanation of how social advantages are problematic in service provision, dealing with some of the case law (in addition to *Carpenter*).

■ If you have time, you could expand your discussion about why it matters when service provisions turns to establishment.

Don't be tempted to . . .

■ Add the facts of cases in your answer; they rarely add anything to your argument.

■ Deal with services and establishment separately – there is likely to be significant overlap and you will run out of time.

■ Write everything you know about services and establishment. Your answer must focus on the scenario.

■ Ignore the treaty provisions. You must establish the legal base for your argument.

Question 3

To what extent are those providing services or established in another Member State entitled to social advantages in EU Law?

Answer plan

→ Set out the legal provisions relating to the movement of the self-employed
  – no equivalent to Regulation 1612/68.

→ Consider how the rights to social advantages have been developed by the court:
  – in relation to establishment
  – in relation to service provision.

Diagram plan

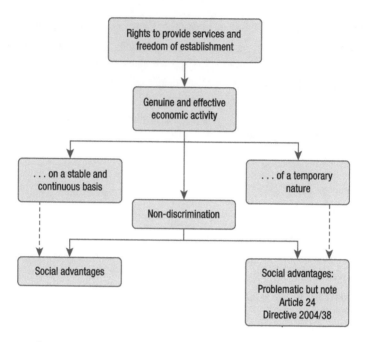

A printable version of this diagram plan is available from **www.pearsoned.co.uk/lawexpressqa**

Answer

The rights of EU citizens to provide services and/or establish themselves in another Member State are uncontroversial. Restrictions by Member States on service provision or establishment are prohibited by Articles 56 and 49 respectively. However, the rights to social advantages and ancillary rights have proved less straightforward in the case of the self-employed.

[1] It is important to remember this and its implications, which comes next.

The regulation dealing with those types of rights (Regulation 1612/68) only applies to workers and makes no reference to the self-employed.[1] We therefore have to rely on other provisions to ascertain the rights. In certain circumstances, the treaty provisions in relation to establishment and services together with Article 18 on non-discrimination may be invoked to ensure they have the same rights as those afforded to nationals of the host state. ***Steinhauser*** (1985) is a useful example.[2]

[2] A few facts here are helpful to make the point.

A German artist was barred from tendering for the use of arts and crafts boutiques in France. The French authorities argued that equal treatment under Article 49 applied only to access to the profession; the ECJ disagreed, stating that Article 49 also covered access to rights more broadly such as, for example, renting business premises. In **Commission v Italy** (1988) the ECJ confirmed that to ensure equality of competition, self-employed migrants had to be able to obtain housing under the same conditions as their national competitors (see also **Commission v Greece** (1986)).

[3] This is a point that is important to make and which many students miss.

This is uncontroversial in relation to establishment and is, in fact, now borne out by Article 24 of Directive 2004/38 which explicitly refers to the principle of equal treatment in relation to migrant EU nationals.[3] However, the position is much less clear in relation to service provision. There is an argument which suggests that the provision of ancillary rights such as access to benefits and other social advantages should be the responsibility of the state in which the potential beneficiary is established and/or resident rather than the state in which a service is merely provided on a temporary basis. However, Article 24 of Directive 2004/38 extends the principle of equal treatment to all migrant EU nationals, subject to some limitations regarding student grants and social assistance during the first three months of residence. So there is a legal basis for arguing that service providers are entitled to the same social advantages as nationals of the host state.

[4] It is useful to make the point that there is less of a rationale to extend social advantages to someone who is only in the host state for a short amount of time. It shows you understand the context in which these rights operate and have done more than just learnt the legal provisions.

In the case of those taking advantage of service provision in another EU Member State, the rationale is perhaps easier to understand.[4] **Cowan** (1987) is a useful example. A British tourist was attacked in Paris and was later refused criminal injuries compensation because he was not French or resident in France. The ECJ held that where EU law gave a person the right to go to another Member State, the individual must be protected from harm in the same way as nationals of the host state. Similar reasoning was used in **Commission v Spain** (1994) to show that a Spanish law providing for free admission to museums for Spanish nationals and foreign residents in Spain but not tourists was contrary to Member States tourists' right to receive services and also in breach of Article 12 relating to non-discrimination. In relation to service provision rather than receipt, the scope of ancillary rights seems to have been extended significantly by the remarkable **Carpenter** case (2003). Carpenter, who was a service provider, was allowed to rely on EU law rights against his own state in relation to family rights. Mr Carpenter was established in the UK and sold advertising space in medical and scientific journals. The journals were based, and much of Mr Carpenter's work was conducted, in other Member States. Mr Carpenter's Filipino wife successfully challenged British immigration rules which would have seen her deported, on the basis that this would be detrimental to the Carpenters' family life and that in turn would be detrimental to the conditions under which Mr Carpenter exercised his right to provide services. The scope of exactly what rights are available to service providers and their families is, however, still a little uncertain. Craig and De Burca (2011) suggest that there will have to be some kind of link between the nature and purpose of the temporary residence for service provision and the nature of the social benefit sought.

Article 24 of Directive 2004/38/EC now provides an umbrella equal treatment clause for EU citizens who are resident in another Member State and therefore there is less uncertainty over whether and how the equal treatment provision in relation to social advantages applies in relation to establishment and service provision. However, the extent to which temporary residence for service provision will give rise to access to the full range of social advantages remains controversial.

 ## Make your answer stand out

- Provide some examples of when service providers might want to access social advantages in the host state rather than rely on the home state and discuss these.
- Consider the situation where EU nationals travel to receive what might in itself be termed a social advantage, for example relating to healthcare.
- Comment on why the provisions are framed in the context of workers but not the self-employed. Why the distinction between the categories?
- Consider some of the academic commentary. See Barnard, C. (2013) *The Substantive Law of the EU: The Four Freedoms*, 4th edn, Oxford: Oxford University Press.

> ! **Don't be tempted to . . .**
>
> ■ Explain the cases used as examples in minute detail. Give sufficient information regarding the facts for the discussion to make sense.
>
> ■ Deal with establishment and services together in this answer. There are differences in the issues that arise even if the law itself is very similar.
>
> ■ Write about Regulation 1612/68 in any detail: this is about workers' rights.
>
> ■ Presume the rights are less developed just because there is no secondary legislation. Explain the rights fully.

❓ Question 4

John is a scientist. He is a UK national and lives and works in London. However, he has contacts in Amsterdam and frequently travels to the Netherlands to carry out work there. Because he has a lot of sensitive technical equipment, he has rented a warehouse which functions as a basic laboratory and storage facility. He also has a small bedsit in Amsterdam where he stays when he is working there. His family continue to live in London, and he continues to do a lot of work in the UK.

The Netherlands passes the (fictitious) Protection of Scientific Expertise Law. This provides, inter alia, that all scientists must be licensed by the Dutch government to carry out their work in the Netherlands. The licensing procedure constitutes a police check and a short interview, to ensure that the scientist is legitimate and uses their scientific knowledge only to help advance Dutch science. No such requirement for a licence exists in the UK.

In order to apply for the licence, John goes to the relevant office in Amsterdam, and is told by a civil servant that he will not be granted a licence. This is because it is a complex and expensive business for the Dutch authorities to run a police check in the UK, and therefore the rule is that licences are only granted to people who have been living in the Netherlands for the past five years.

Advise John as to his position under EU law.

Answer plan

→ Set out the applicable law.

→ Explain whether you think John is established in the Netherlands or providing services.

→ Consider the legitimacy of a licensing requirement.

→ Consider the legitimacy of the residence requirement to get a licence.

→ Summarise your advice.

Diagram plan

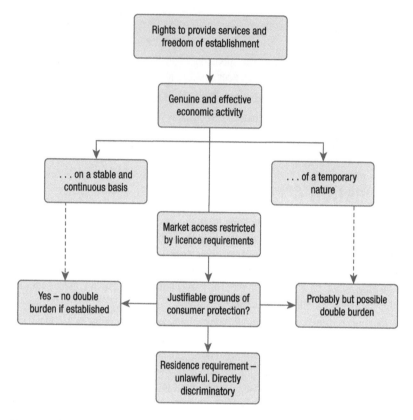

A printable version of this diagram plan is available from **www.pearsoned.co.uk/lawexpressqa**

Answer

[1] By setting out what law applies, you are showing from the start that you have understood the question.

The scenario requires the application of the law relating to the freedom of establishment and freedom to provide services in EU law.[1] As an EU citizen, John has the right to move and reside freely within the territory of the EU for three months without restrictions. Longer residence in a host Member State requires him to fulfil certain requirements, one of which relates to economic activity.

He has the right to establish himself in another Member State and he also has the right to provide services on a more temporary basis. While the rights are similar, there are some differences, and it is therefore important first to establish whether John is providing services under Article 57 TFEU or whether he is established under Article 54 TFEU in the host Member State.[2] The case of **Gebhard** (1995) sets out the test to be applied to determine this question. Does John 'participate on a stable and continuous basis in the economic life of the state'?[3] The scenario given is not entirely clear on this. John seems to do a significant amount of work in the host state, as he has decided it is worth him renting premises in Amsterdam to store his equipment and carry out work. However, the premises alone do not necessarily mean that he operates out of Amsterdam on a permanent basis or that the office is his base. If this was the case, then John would fall within the provisions for establishment. However, in this case it seems that John provides services. His base seems to be in the UK as his family is based there. While he does travel a lot, there is no indication that he intends to move to Amsterdam more permanently or, indeed, run the majority of his business from there. He does keep a bedsit in Amsterdam which might indicate that he does see his business there as more permanent. Overall, however, his business base appears to be in the UK. Having storage facilities in Amsterdam, especially when there are good practical reasons for having such facilities, is not incompatible with the notion of temporary service provision. The bedsit may also simply be a way of avoiding costly hotel bills when working in the host state. While additional enquiries should be made of John to establish the amount and regularity of work done in the Netherlands, on balance it seems that he is providing services.[4] He is not, at this point, participating in the Dutch labour market on a continuous and stable basis and therefore does not satisfy the test for establishment.

On the face of it, a licensing requirement such as the one imposed here would be seen as a barrier to temporary cross-border provision and would therefore be unlawful.[5] This would be the case even where the requirement is imposed indistinctly on nationals of the host state and nationals of other Member States (see, for example, **Webb** (1981); **Gouda** (1991); **Alpine Investments** (1995)). This is because the law intends to ensure the freedom to provide services, and a licence may be more difficult to obtain for a national from another Member State. Even where this is not the case, it makes market access more difficult and must therefore be justified on a public policy ground. In this case there might be legitimate reasons

Margin notes:

[2] Here you are setting out the first issue to deal with, showing the examiner that you are taking a logical step-by-step approach, which should get you a lot of marks.

[3] Where possible, keep your explanation of the law focused on the question to get the maximum marks for application.

[4] It is OK to say you need more information and you would ask John if he was sitting in front of you. Nonetheless, you should use all the information you have been given and come to a conclusion on balance.

[5] This is a clear statement of the law in the context of the scenario and should pick up marks.

[6] This is where you can pick up marks for analysis. You have said the provision can possibly be justified and now you explain how that applies here.

[7] This is something students often forget to mention but it is potentially important. No requirement means no double burden, making it easier to justify the requirement in the host state.

[8] As you have indicated that it is possible John might be established, it is worth pointing this out and it will also show the examiner your grasp of this area of law.

[9] Just citing cases is OK in an exam. If you have time, you could add a little more detail to show you are not just guessing at the cases but fully understand why they are relevant.

[10] Don't forget this. Noting this point shows you really do understand how the law works and what its aims are.

to require a licence in order to protect consumers.[6] It is possible that John and others in his profession will undertake sensitive work and it is important that they can be trusted and are legitimate. We do not have sufficient information about the nature of the work to be certain. It is also essential that they have sufficient and up-to-date technical knowledge to carry out their work competently. Furthermore, there is no licensing requirement in the UK, which suggests that the home state in this case offers no protection for the consumer.[7] It might therefore be legitimate to require a licence here and the principle of proportionality must be considered. In this case the pertinent question is whether or not there is a less restrictive way of ensuring consumer protection. One way might be to have a voluntary scheme such as a kitemark or membership of an association which accredits scientists working in a particular field. However, overall, the licensing requirements do not seem too onerous on John and they arguably fulfil a legitimate aim and do not seem disproportionate. They are thus likely to be lawful.

It is worth noting that if John does, in fact, fall under the establishment provisions, it is even more likely that the licensing requirement is justifiable,[8] as such requirements are generally easier to justify when an activity is being carried out on a more permanent basis. There is some considerable logic behind this in that the home state should take some of the burden and risk in relation to temporary service provision, and those providing services should not be subject to a double burden by having to meet requirements in more than one member state (see **Gullung** (1988) and **Gebhard**).[9]

There is, however, a further issue in relation to the licence and this relates to the process for acquiring one.[10] If we assume that the requirement itself is legitimate, the process for acquiring a licence must still be non-discriminatory. In this case that appears not to be the case. The residence rule is distinctly applicable, and according to **Van Binsbergen** (1974) discrimination on grounds of residence is tantamount to discrimination on grounds of nationality. This must be the case: otherwise, much of the point of Articles 54 and 57 would be lost. It is extremely difficult to justify distinctly applicable measures, especially under Article 57 and there seems no justification in John's case. While the cost may be higher to carry out the relevant police checks, the cost is not likely to be prohibitive, and the rules appear to put nationals at a distinct advantage and treat non-nationals with some suspicion.

[11] Summarising your advice at the end is a useful way of signalling that you have finished and fully answered the question.

To summarise,[11] John is entitled to provide services and establish himself in the Netherlands. In this case, on balance, his activity seems to fall within the rules relating to service provision. While the licensing requirement is likely to make market access more difficult, it also may be justifiable on the grounds of consumer protection; but it is not lawful to grant licences only to those who have resided in the Netherlands for five years or more and John should therefore challenge that decision.

✓ Make your answer stand out

- Add a little more detail of the cases cited to explain the law more clearly.
- Consider the question of consumer protection in more detail, using case examples to illustrate your argument more fully.
- Explain the difference in rights between service provision and establishment a bit more by commenting, for example, on the access to social advantages.
- Add advice on how John would make a complaint. You could mention both an informal complaint to the relevant office in Amsterdam as well as the possibility of challenging the decision not to grant a licence in the Dutch courts.

! Don't be tempted to . . .

- Set out the law without reference to the problem question. Try to focus on the problem as much as possible.
- Sit on the fence here. While it is OK to say you need more information on certain aspects, try to come to a conclusion on balance. As long as you argue it convincingly, you should get the marks.
- Jump to the conclusion that it is establishment because of the office and flat: you need to reason this through logically. Either conclusion is possible, but do not just jump to it. Explain your thought process.

❓ Question 5

Jamie is a UK national who is a highly qualified translator. She moved to Spain three years ago to work for a large law firm in Barcelona. As a result of the recession, Jamie was made redundant. She has been looking for work but is struggling to find employment. She has no savings left and the Spanish authorities are questioning her right to residence in Spain. Jamie now wishes to work freelance as a translator. She has been told she must join the

Guild of Translators and pay a fee of €500 per year to maintain her accreditation as a licensed translator. Without this accreditation, she is unlikely to get much work. The fee for a native speaker of Spanish is €150. Jamie seeks your advice on her rights under EU law.

Answer plan

→ Set out the definition of worker in EU law and apply it to Jamie.

→ Consider whether she retains her worker status.

→ Explain what rights she has as a work seeker.

→ Set out the right of establishment.

→ Consider whether the requirements regarding accreditation are lawful.

Diagram plan

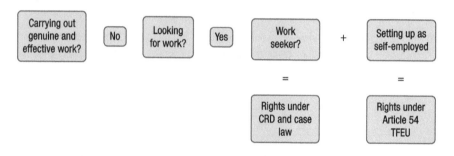

A printable version of this diagram plan is available from **www.pearsoned.co.uk/lawexpressqa**

Answer

[1] A clear introduction setting out the area of law and structure of the answer shows you understand the question.

This scenario requires the application of the law in relation to the free movement of workers and the law relating to the freedom for Jamie to establish herself as a self-employed translator. They will be considered in turn.[1]

The scenario suggests that Jamie exercised her right under Article 45 TFEU as an EU worker to take up an employed position with a law firm in Barcelona. As a result of her redundancy, she is no longer employed and therefore no longer satisfies the definition of 'EU migrant worker' set out in cases such as *Lawrie-Blum* (1986) and *Levin* (1982). The question arising is therefore whether or not Jamie retains her worker status, or, even if she does not, she still has the right to reside in Spain on the basis that she has been a worker and is now a work seeker.[2]

As Jamie is no longer in employment and therefore not engaged in genuine and effective economic activity which is not marginal or ancillary, she cannot, in EU law, be considered a worker. Her rights in EU law are therefore limited to those rights available to EU citizens generally and work seekers more specifically. Jamie has a general right to reside in a Member State other than her own under the Citizens' Rights Directive (2004/38). As long as she is self-sufficient and does not become a burden on the host state, there is no time limit on the residence right. As we are told that she does not have any savings left, it seems likely that she no longer satisfies the criteria of self-sufficiency.[3] However, the citizenship provisions also suggest that the self-sufficiency requirement is proportionality bound (see, for example, **Baumbast** (2002) and **Grzelczyk** (2001)), so the fact that Jamie has been working in Spain for a considerable amount of time would suggest that she should not lose access to all rights immediately but should be given time to secure new employment. This reasoning is borne out by the case law relating to work seekers (see **Antonissen** (1991), **Collins** (2004) or **Ioannidis** (2005), for example) which suggests that where a migrant has a reasonable chance of getting a job, they should be entitled to residence rights and additional help in finding work. In Jamie's case, though, the scenario suggests that there is no reasonable prospect of her getting work as she is struggling to find employment.[4] As such, Spain may legitimately question whether she is still exercising rights or whether her status actually no longer warrants those rights.

However, Jamie has indicated that she now wishes to work freelance. She has the right to establish herself in Spain under Article 54 TFEU.[5] She is entitled to be treated the same way in relation to market access as nationals of the host country. Membership of the Guild of Translators, even if a universal requirement on nationals of the host state as well as nationals of other Member States, potentially hinders market access and is thus a prima facie breach of EU law. However, there is a potential justification which is that it is in the public interest and, in particular, in the interest of protecting consumers, to ensure that translators are properly accredited and competent in their work. Therefore, the requirement to join the guild is likely to be legitimate unless it can be shown that it is disproportionate and the same aim can be achieved in some other way which is less restrictive. However, the fact that Jamie must pay more than a native speaker seems to be clear discrimination on the grounds of nationality. It is therefore unlawful and Jamie should challenge the higher fee.

[6] In problem questions it is really useful to summarise your advice at the end. It allows you to check you've dealt with everything and that your answer is consistent. It also clearly shows that you have actually finished and did not just run out of time.

In summary,[6] while Jamie does not retain worker status, she does have some rights as a work seeker and cannot be asked to leave Spain just because she has not yet been able to find work. Her stronger position is, however, to establish herself as a self-employed translator and make use of the rights then afforded to her under Article 54 TFEU.

✓ Make your answer stand out

- Consider citizenship rights in more detail.
- Set out any differences in rights between the employed and self-employed by, for example, explaining that Regulation 1612/68 relating to social advantages would not apply to Jamie as a self-employed person.
- Set out your advice in the form of a letter or email to Jamie to add interest and make your answer stand out from all the others.
- Add details of possible courses of action and remedies for Jamie.

! Don't be tempted to . . .

- Focus only on workers or only establishment – the question deliberately overlaps these issues so you must deal with both.
- Get drawn into a discussion about service provision. While services and establishment questions often overlap, the overlap here with workers and service provision is not relevant.
- Jump to the conclusion that no work and no savings means her residence is no longer lawful. For that to be the case, Spanish authorities would have to withdraw lawful residence and they can only do so after considering the issues you need to set out, including proportionality.

www.pearsoned.co.uk/lawexpressqa

Go online to access more revision support including additional essay and problem questions with diagram plans, You be the marker questions, and download all diagrams from the book.

The social dimension and EU citizenship

12

How this topic may come up in exams

This topic can cover a fairly broad area. In some cases the focus will be on citizenship rights and the Citizens' Rights Directive; other questions will emphasise the examination of the more social aspects of the European Union and the development of an EU social policy. There is often overlap with the free movement provisions applicable to workers and their families, so watch out for questions that cover both topics. Essay questions are common but problem questions can also come up and will usually focus on the free movement rights of Union citizens who are not workers.

■ Before you begin

It's a good idea to consider the following key themes of the social dimension and EU citizenship before tackling a question on this topic.

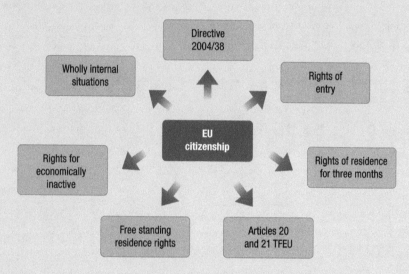

A printable version of this diagram is available from **www.pearsoned.co.uk/lawexpressqa**

 Question 1

To what extent does EU citizenship provide nationals of EU Member States with rights not previously available to them as a result of the free movement provisions?

Answer plan

→ Introduction: outline the origin of EU citizenship.

→ Consider the rights linked to citizenship referring to:
  – Residence rights, family rights
  – Non-economically active
  – Students
  – Job seekers.

→ Conclude: discuss whether it is more than just symbolic.

Diagram plan

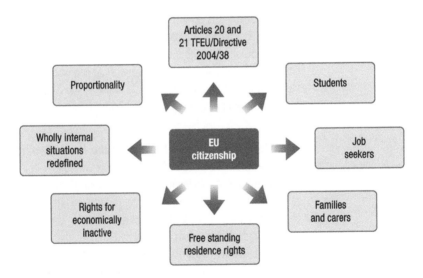

A printable version of this diagram plan is available from **www.pearsoned.co.uk/lawexpressqa**

Answer

Union citizenship was finally formally introduced into the European Union (EU) by the Maastricht Treaty in 1992 in an effort to bring the Union closer to the people. This essay assesses the extent to which the introduction of citizenship into the EU legal framework actually adds concrete rights to EU citizens or whether it is of symbolic importance only.[1]

Article 20 TFEU states that each individual who is a national of a Member State is also automatically an EU citizen. Article 21 grants free movement rights to all EU citizens within the limits of the treaty and secondary legislation. The free movement rights of economically active citizens are well established under Article 45 TFEU and thus the question arises whether EU citizens who are not economically active gain some of the rights previously only afforded to workers.[2]

[2] Effectively, this is a restatement of the question, but it shows that you understand what is being asked of you.

The principle of EU citizenship is often used in conjunction with the principle of equal treatment now enshrined in Article 18 TFEU to ensure that there is no discrimination between nationals of a host state and EU national migrants.[3] The effect of citizenship as a tool to develop concrete rights can be seen in particular in relation to the non-economically active EU citizens, including work seekers and students. First, though, it is useful to consider the extent to which residence rights are extended merely on the basis of citizenship status.

[3] This is an important point and one often ignored by students; it is really the combination of the provisions which gives rise to additional rights.

Baumbast* v *Secretary of State for the Home Department (2002) held that 'a citizen of the Union who no longer enjoys the rights of residence as a migrant worker in the host MS can, as a citizen of the Union, enjoy there a right of residence by direct application of Article 18(1) . . . . Those limitations are applied in compliance with general principles of community law and, in particular, the principle of proportionality'.[4] ***Baumbast*** thus clarifies that citizenship does grant free-standing additional rights. ***Zhu and Chen* v *Secretary of State for the Home Department*** (2004) confirms this by granting residence rights to baby Catherine who was born to a Chinese mother in Northern Ireland and thus obtaining Irish nationality. These cases also illustrate the extension of citizenship rights to families and carers and the ***Carpenter*** case (2003) confirms an expansive approach.

[4] Don't worry about learning a quote like this one unless you happen to have a good memory for that sort of thing. Providing a summary in your own words would be just as acceptable.

[5] First you say there has
been an extension of rights,
then you cite a case which
suggests there shouldn't
really be such an extension.
You now need to deal with the
inconsistency.

[6] If you have a little more
time, just giving a sentence or
two about these cases would
probably clarify the point and
emphasise how they illustrate
your argument.

[7] There are limits to the
extension of rights and
you must recognise this
rather than just listing those
examples where citizenship
has provided additional rights.
It shows you have a balanced
understanding of the law.

[8] Short quotes like this
can add interest to your
writing and make it appear
less abstract. Including the
quote and the reference also
shows you have read more
widely than just the textbook
and lecture notes, which is
important.

Citizenship of the Union was not, however, intended to extend the scope ratione materiae of the treaty also to wholly internal situations (*Garcia Avello* v *Belgium* (2003)).[5] However, it seems that in some cases the interpretation of what might be a wholly internal situation has changed following the introduction of citizenship so as to ensure EU citizens equal treatment, and cases such as *Chen; Schempp* v *Finanzamt München V* (2005) or *Zambrano* (2012) illustrate this.[6]

We must now turn to the development of rights afforded to the non-economically active. The first case to note is *Sala* v *Freistaat Bayern* (1998), which confirms that when an EU national is lawfully resident in another Member State, they can rely on the citizenship provisions to receive equal treatment in all matters that are within the scope of the treaty. In the case of *Trojani* (2004), however, the court had to deal with whether an EU citizen could use Article 21 directly to derive a right of residence. The ECJ held that they could not where the sufficient resource requirement is not met.[7]

Within limits, therefore, citizenship does extend the rights to non-workers – some say it 'exploded the linkages' (see O'Leary, 1999)[8] between economic activity and rights previously thought to be necessary. Students provide a further useful example of citizenship provisions in operation. In fact, it was in *Grzelczyk* v *CPAS* (2001), where the ECJ proclaimed that citizenship would be the fundamental status of EU citizens, and cases such as *R (Bidar)* v *London Borough of Ealing* (2005) confirm that EU citizens lawfully resident should receive equal treatment. However, there are limits, and a real link with the host state can be required before the most generous provisions of social advantages are afforded to migrants. It was, therefore, lawful to impose a residence requirement of three years in the case of *Bidar* or even five years in the case of *Förster* v *Hoofddirectie van de Informatie Beheer Groep* (2009).

Job seekers have also benefitted from citizenship rights. In *D'Hoop* v *Office Nationale de l'Emploi* (2002) a Belgian national in France was refused a tide-over allowance while searching for her first job in Belgium, on the basis that she had completed her secondary education in France. The ECJ held that disadvantaging citizens because they have exercised their right to free movement is incompatible with the treaty. However, *Collins* v *Secretary of State for Work and*

Pensions (2004) shows that there are limits. An Irish and American national sought employment in the Netherlands and applied for job seekers allowance. He was not a Netherlands national or resident but had moved there to seek work. The criteria for job seekers, however, required residence. Collins challenged that residence requirement. The ECJ held that requiring a link between the individual and the host state before any social advantages could be accessed was legitimate but would, of course, depend on proportionality. **Ioannidis** (2005) confirms **Collins** by saying a link to the host state was a legitimate requirement, but in this case it was met, as Ioannidis had studied for a diploma in Belgium already.

EU citizenship is therefore of real benefit to EU citizens and does extend rights particularly to those not previously able to take advantage of the most generous free movement provisions under Article 45 TFEU.

✓ Make your answer stand out

- Consider family rights as a separate category with a focus on cases such as *Chen*, *Zambrano*, and *McCarthy* (2011).
- Consider the implications of citizenship for third-country nationals and, in particular, cases such as *Zambrano* and *McCarthy*.
- Consider other categories such as volunteers or carers further.
- Include academic commentary such as Dougan, M. (2006) The Constitutional Dimension of the Case Law on Union Citizenship, *EL Rev*, 31, 613.

! Don't be tempted to . . .

- Go through the relevant cases in chronological order. Your point is more important than the cases; use them as illustrations.
- Go into detail about the provisions on entry and residence in the Citizens' Rights Directive.
- Ignore seminal cases such as *Baumbast*, *Chen* and *Grzelczyk*.

2 Question 2

John and Fiona are Irish nationals based in the Netherlands. They have two children, Helen and Dermot. John worked in both Ireland and the Netherlands for a while but for the last three years has worked for an American company, spending a significant period of time in the US.

Fiona does not work. She is a qualified legal secretary but has not been able to find work and is no longer looking. Both Dermot and Helen are thinking of starting university next year. Dermot is finishing his education in Ireland and intends to move to the Netherlands to study. Helen has finished her A-levels and has been travelling. She now intends to study in Paris.

Discuss the issues arising, with particular reference to European Union Citizenship.

Diagram plan

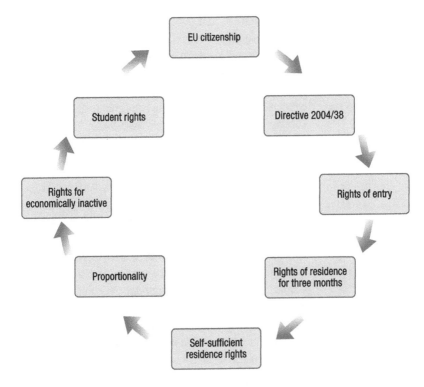

A printable version of this diagram plan is available from **www.pearsoned.co.uk/lawexpressqa**

Answer plan

→ Introduction: outline citizenship rights rather than EU worker rights.

→ Discuss entry and residence rights.

→ Consider longer residence and self-sufficiency.

→ Fiona – discuss whether derived rights for a longer stay.

→ Children: discuss equal treatment regarding access but not maintenance.

Answer

[1] A helpful statement of the law applicable, which immediately confirms you have identified the correct issues to be dealt with.

This problem question requires the consideration of provision under Articles 20–21 TFEU as well as under the Citizens' Rights Directive (Directive 2004/38, CRD).[1] John has not, according to the scenario given, an EU migrant worker status although it seems he did have that status in the past. As he now works for a US company and spends a significant amount of time there, he does not fall within the definition and is therefore not entitled to the most generous free movement rights. However, that does not mean that he and his family are without rights and these rights will be discussed in turn. First, we will consider the family's rights to entry and residence. We will then consider their right to equal treatment with host nationals in relation to social advantages as well as in relation to access to higher education for Helen and Dermot.[2]

[2] There is quite a lot going on in the scenario, so this signposting is useful.

All nationals of a Member State are also European Union (EU) citizens. EU citizenship, though destined to be the fundamental status of EU citizens (see **Grzelczyk** (2001)), is additional to national citizenship and does not replace it. It is clear from the scenario that all four persons concerned here are EU citizens. As such, they have free-standing rights under Article 21 to free movement within the limits of the TFEU and secondary legislation. **Baumbast** (2002) confirmed that this applies to all citizens whether economically active or not, and indeed this interpretation is supported by the Citizens' Rights Directive which gives all citizens the right to enter another Member State and reside there for a period of three months.

[3] The others are in the UK, so entry is not going to concern them, although residence rights might, of course, be an issue. You consider them in context below.

As most of the family is already based in the Netherlands, the right to entry and initial residence is of most interest to Dermot who wishes to come to study in the Netherlands.[3] He has the right to entry and residence in his own rights but, depending on his age and whether or not he is dependent on his parents, he may also have derived rights as a family member. The same applies to Helen in relation to entry and initial residence in France for her studies.

For citizens wishing to reside for longer, they must prove that they will not be a burden on the host state and have sufficient sickness insurance. We are not given much information in relation to the family finances but there is no evidence to suggest that they have needed to have recourse to the welfare system. John is working in the US and is likely to provide a family income, which means that Fiona and her children are not a burden on the host state.[4] Sickness insurance is not mentioned and this may be grounds for further investigation. However, it should be noted from cases such as **Baumbast** and also **Grzelczyk** that the sufficient resources and sickness requirements are proportionality bound. In other words, if the family is lawfully resident in the territory of a Member State, they are supporting themselves and perhaps have sickness insurance in their home state (as was the case in **Baumbast**), they cannot be refused residence purely on that basis.

[4] You are making an educated guess about this really, but there is enough in the scenario to support the conclusion.

Fiona's situation is perhaps the most difficult. While she is an EU citizen and thus has the rights set out in the Citizens' Right Directive, she is not economically active and is no longer a work seeker. If she was looking for work and could show a realistic prospect of securing a position, she would be granted additional protection in EU law. This is not the case and she has to rely on the rights she derives as a family member of a self-sufficient EU migrant – John.

In relation to both children, they are entitled to equal treatment in terms of access to higher education, so any tuition fees charged must be the same as those charged for nationals of France in Helen's case and Netherlands nationals in Dermot's case. They must also have access to any loan provisions made for nationals in relation to those fees. Maintenance grants are, however, explicitly excluded from the provisions, so cannot automatically be granted to non-nationals. In *R (Bidar)* v *London Borough of Ealing* (2005) the ECJ held that EU citizens lawfully resident should receive equal treatment to nationals in relation to maintenance grants. However, there are limits to this, and EU migrant students are required to prove a real link with the host state before the most generous provisions of social advantages, including maintenance grants, are afforded to them. It was therefore lawful to impose a residence requirement of three years in the case of **Bidar** or even five years in the case of **Förster v Hoofddirectie van de Informatie Beheer Groep** (2009). Both Helen and Dermot will therefore struggle to secure any maintenance grants or loans available to host country nationals. This may seem odd, in particular in relation to Dermot whose family are based in the Netherlands. However, it seems that Member States have required a real link with residence and the ECJ has done nothing to challenge that association.

Make your answer stand out

■ Consider Fiona's situation in more detail in the context of cases such as *Sala* or in relation to possible derived rights from her children.

■ Comment further on the real link test and its appropriateness. See, for example, O'Brien, C. (2008) Real links, abstract rights and false alarms, *ECLR*, 29, 605–10.

■ Consider the extent to which Dermot could derive rights from his parents' status and thus get around the real link test applied to migrant students.

■ Outline the facts of *Baumbast* a little more – this seems particularly relevant here.

Don't be tempted to . . .

■ Ignore the fact that all have EU law rights themselves, although more generous rights may be derived.

■ Conclude that because they do not appear to have sickness insurance, they cannot stay – remember proportionality.

■ Presume they cannot stay because they are not workers; self-sufficient EU nationals can stay longer than three months and self-sufficiency is proportionality bound.

■ Base your answer purely on the treaty provisions. You need to consider Directive 2004/38 and case law too.

www.pearsoned.co.uk/lawexpressqa

Go online to access more revision support including additional essay and problem questions with diagram plans, You be the marker questions, and download all diagrams from the book.

EU anti-discrimination law

13

How this topic may come up in exams

EU equality law is a popular examination topic on some EU law courses. Both essay and problem questions are common. Essay questions usually relate to the effectiveness or scope of the provisions or ask for a consideration as to how the law in this area has developed. Problem questions often relate to equality in the employment sphere and ask you to consider whether or not a particular course of action is lawful or not. It is unusual for all the grounds to be covered by one question (although questions may cover more than one); here we have provided two problems dealing with different aspects of the law.

■ Before you begin

It's a good idea to consider the following key themes of EU anti-discrimination law before tackling a question on this topic.

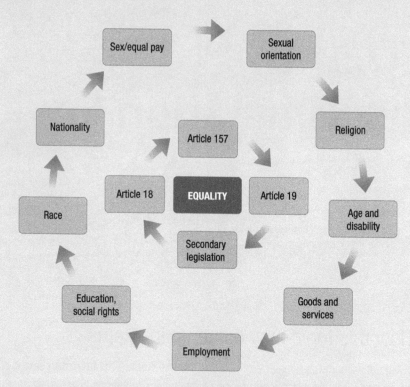

A printable version of this diagram is available from **www.pearsoned.co.uk/lawexpressqa**

❓ Question 1

Julia, Darren and Ben work for a private company in the fictional Member State of Denland, which recently joined the EU. Denland has no national equality law provisions. Julia has just found out that she is paid less than Darren who does exactly the same job she does. He works full time and she works part time. This is the only difference as far as Julia knows. Julia also recently applied for promotion and lost out to Ben. The panel deciding the promotions said that Ben has acquired more experience because he worked full time, and that as he has a family to support he therefore deserves the promotion.

Advise the parties as to:

(a) Whether the difference in pay would be lawful under EU law.

(b) Whether the panel promoting Ben has made its decision based on reasons which would be considered lawful reasons under EU law.

(c) What the position would be under EU law if the employer were to promote Julia in preference to Ben because of the shortage of women in senior posts.

Answer plan

→ Introduction to EU equality law.

→ Briefly outline implementation/enforcement in the national context.

→ Consider equal pay: Article 157 TFEU.

→ Explain your argument using Directive 2006/54 – promotions.

→ Explain positive discrimination.

Diagram plan

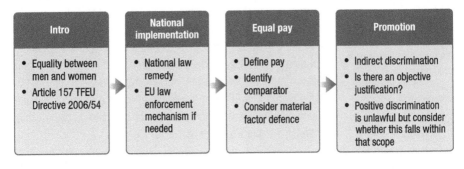

Intro	National implementation	Equal pay	Promotion
• Equality between men and women • Article 157 TFEU Directive 2006/54	• National law remedy • EU law enforcement mechanism if needed	• Define pay • Identify comparator • Consider material factor defence	• Indirect discrimination • Is there an objective justification? • Positive discrimination is unlawful but consider whether this falls within that scope

A printable version of this diagram plan is available from **www.pearsoned.co.uk/lawexpressqa**

Answer

This scenario requires an examination of European Union (EU) equality law, with a particular focus on equality between men and women in the workplace. Denland is a member of the EU, and the provisions relating to equality would form part of the acquis communitaire which they would have to implement and be bound by.[1] Accession would therefore provide people like Julia with a remedy in national law. If, however, as it seems the case here, a country fails to implement the relevant law or fails to do so correctly, it could be subject to enforcement proceedings under Article 258 TFEU. In addition, citizens would be able to rely on those rights deemed to be directly effective in their national courts, and Denland law would have to be interpreted in line with EU law wherever possible under the doctrine of indirect effect. Furthermore, courts in Denland could seek interpretative guidance as to the meaning of the provisions from the ECJ, using the preliminary reference procedure under Article 267 TFEU.[2] In other words, it is worth exploring how EU law impacts on Julia's situation because there would be a variety of ways in which it could be enforced.

The first issue relates to the question of pay. Article 157 TFEU provides for equal pay for equal work and for work of equal value.[3] Pay is further defined as the basic wage or salary or any other consideration in cash or kind which the worker receives directly or indirectly in respect of the employment (Article 157(2) TFEU). The definition has been interpreted liberally by the ECJ in cases such as **Defrenne v Sabena (No. 2)** (1976) and certainly includes hourly pay such as in Julia's case.[4] To bring a claim, Julia would need a comparator of the opposite sex to show she is being paid less. The scenario suggests this is unproblematic as Darren is being paid more per hour than she is. There is little information as to the exact type of work done, but there is no indication in the scenario that there are significant differences in the work carried out – in fact, it rather suggests the same work.[5] The ECJ has, however, left open a possible defence allowing for a material factor to explain the difference in pay which is not related to the sex of the parties.

The fact that Julia works part time only is, however, not such a material factor defence.[6] The issue of part-time and full-time work has been explored in some detail by the ECJ and in most cases it has done so in the context of indirect discrimination. So paying part-time workers less indirectly discriminates against women because they are more likely to work part time. The women concerned would, however, have to show that they are more affected than men and that the difference in pay cannot be objectively justified (**Jenkins v Kingsgate** (1981); **Bilka Kaufhaus v Karin Weber von Harz** (1986)). It is not clear from the scenario whether there is a general policy of paying part-time workers less, in which case Julia would have to show that this affects women predominantly and is not objectively justifiable; or whether the company are trying to use part-time work in her case as an excuse to pay her less, in which case the lower payment is clearly unlawful.

[7] This is a useful signpost. You are now moving on to the next issue. Guiding readers through like this makes it easier for them to read and thus give marks.

[8] Focus on the question; there is no need to go through the other matters that Article 14 covers.

The next issue to consider is the promotion of Ben above Julia.[7] The principle of equal treatment on the grounds of sex can be found in Directive 2006/54, and Article 14 spells out further what this means. Article 14(1)(a) specifically includes a prohibition of discrimination in relation to promotions.[8] The situation Julia finds herself in would therefore be covered by the directive. There is little information given but, from what is available, it is clear that the promotion panel's decision making did not adhere to equality principles. The fact that Ben has a wife and children to support is an irrelevant factor in relation to the promotion and should not have influenced their decision. Taking this factor into account can be seen as indirectly discriminatory against women, as traditionally men have been seen as the breadwinners and the ones to support their families. There appears to be no objective justification in relation to that factor either. Equating full-time work with experience is also controversial.[9] This may also be indirectly discriminatory if the majority of part-time workers are women. As indirect discrimination can be objectively justified, the company would have to show that, by placing greater emphasis on experience gained through full-time work rather than part-time work, they were trying to achieve a legitimate aim. It seems difficult to see how they might do this in the given scenario. The promotion of Ben over Julia thus seems discriminatory if it was affected on the basis of the reasons given in the scenario.

[9] This is your conclusion; you now need to prove it so the examiners can see that it is a considered academic opinion.

[10] As it can be difficult to draw the line between positive action and positive discrimination, a few case examples illustrating the difference will show that you really do understand this area.

The final point relates to the possibility of positive discrimination under EU law. While the TFEU and Directive 2006/54 contain provisions encouraging Member States to promote equality, they stop short of actually allowing positive discrimination. The case of **Kalanke** (1995)[10] is a useful example. A national rule stipulated that where a man and a woman were equally qualified when applying for a position, the woman should automatically be given preference if there was a shortage of women. The European Court of Justice confirmed that this was discrimination on the grounds of sex because it went beyond promoting equality. In contrast, **Marschall** (1997) allowed a provision very similar to the one in **Kalanke.** The difference was that the provision in **Marschall** included a clause stating that, where a male candidate could show grounds which tilted the balance in his favour, the automatic preference for women did not apply. This latter approach was confirmed in **Badeck** (2000) and the position now seems to be that if Julia and Ben are equally qualified and there is no other factor tipping the balance in Ben's favour, Julia can automatically be given the post as a measure of promoting equality.[11] The preference for women, though, cannot be unconditional and there must be equality of qualifications to start off with. The scenario does not provide sufficient information to conclusively say how EU law could apply to this case.

[11] This sentence just refocuses your answer on the problem question at hand and applies the law, showing the examiner that you are answering the question set and are not simply reproducing a generic answer you have learned.

To conclude, Julia would have recourse to EU law provisions.

✓ Make your answer stand out

- Consider material factor defences in a little more detail and think about whether there might be one here.
- Set out more clearly the different provisions relating to direct and indirect discrimination.
- Expand on the implications of the employer being a private company.
- Set out the possible course of action for Julia. Tell her what she should do.

! Don't be tempted to . . .

- Confuse EU law with national law if you are also studying equality law in your national context.
- Write about equality law in general. Focus on the scenario.
- Ignore the point about positive discrimination. You need to engage with this as it is explicitly part of the question.
- Give too much case detail. Just make your point.

Question 2

Critically asses EU equality law provisions.

Answer plan

➜ Introduction to general provisions.

➜ Explain equal pay and sex discrimination.

➜ Consider the Framework Directive.

➜ Consider scope of interpretation.

➜ Examine other ways of promoting equality.

Diagram plan

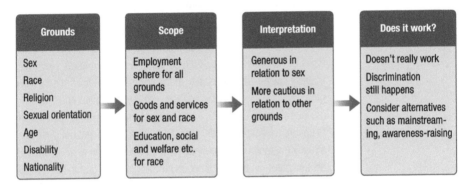

Grounds	Scope	Interpretation	Does it work?
Sex Race Religion Sexual orientation Age Disability Nationality	Employment sphere for all grounds Goods and services for sex and race Education, social and welfare etc. for race	Generous in relation to sex More cautious in relation to other grounds	Doesn't really work Discrimination still happens Consider alternatives such as mainstreaming, awareness-raising

A printable version of this diagram plan is available from **www.pearsoned.co.uk/lawexpressqa**

Answer

[1] Setting out the structure of the essay at the start allows the examiners to see that you have identified the issues needing consideration.

This essay considers the scope of European Union (EU) equality law. It charts the development of provisions from the early inclusion of sex discrimination in the TFEU to the current regime of secondary legislation relating to a variety of grounds and to a context that is wider than the employment sphere.[1] The essay then considers how equality law and policy is implemented across the EU. The argument throughout is that while equality provisions have developed significantly over the years, the EU provisions still very much depend on national implementation and application which in turn is dependent on national contexts

[2] By stating the conclusion early on, you make sure you answer the question set and also that the examiner knows you have a clear argument in mind and are not just writing off the top of your head. This makes for a well-considered answer.

[3] First important point, there is no overall prohibition against discrimination so an examination of individual provisions is required.

[4] Useful to show you are aware of them but you cannot cover everything in detail.

[5] When you are assessing a particular area of law, you can gain extra marks if you are aware of the history of the area. It shows a deeper understanding.

and cultures.[2] As a result, the scope of equality law remains limited in some important contexts and aspects.

There is no general prohibition of discrimination contained in the treaty.[3] Instead, distinct provisions deal with specific areas and seek to promote equality or prohibit discrimination in that area. The most obvious are perhaps the prohibition on discrimination on the grounds of nationality in Articles 18 and 19 TFEU providing the Union with the power to prohibit discrimination across a range of issues, as well as the provisions in Articles 2 and 3 TEU relating to equality between men and women and Articles 153 and 157 TFEU on equality between men and women in the workplace and equal pay. Other provisions, which will not be considered in detail here,[4] include those relating to equal treatment of workers and the self-employed, equal treatment in relation to taxation or equality between producers and consumer under the Common Agricultural Policy.

Many of the prohibitions on discrimination relate to nationality and are therefore logical, given the aims of the EU. Discrimination on the basis of nationality makes little sense in a single market. However, equality law relating to equality of the sexes or non-discrimination on grounds such as race, religion, age, sexual orientation and disability are less obvious. Originally, equal pay was the focus of EU law in order to ensure a level playing field for all Member States and not put those already guaranteeing equal pay for men and women at an economic disadvantage. In spite of its economic origins, the prohibition on sex discrimination soon became part of the fundamental rights in EU law (***Defrenne and Sabena (No. 3)*** (1978)).

Prior to the Treaty of Amsterdam, Article 157 TFEU was the only provision covering this type of discrimination.[5] Since then, treaty amendments and secondary legislation have significantly widened the scope of anti-discrimination law. Articles 2 and 3 TEU now clearly identify equality between men and women as one key aim of the EU; Article 147 TFEU was further expanded to include equal pay for work of equal value and a new provision was added in Article 19 TFEU in the form of an enabling power to make secondary legislation to take appropriate action to combat discrimination based on sex, racial or ethnic origin, religion or belief, disability, age or sexual orientation. Secondary legislation, initially in relation to equal pay only, supported the treaty provisions. Secondary legislation now deals with equality between men and women (Directive 2006/54), race equality (Directive 2000/43) and non-discrimination on the grounds identified in Article 19 TFEU in the area of employment. The scope of the law is therefore quite broad,[6] covering a variety of factors and dealing with the area where discrimination is most likely to occur: employment, but also casting its net wider to cover areas such as social protection, education and access to goods and services in some more limited circumstances (for example, in relation to race).

[6] Come back to the question whenever an opportunity arises.

Generally, the ECJ has taken a wide interpretation in matters relating to equality between men and women.[7] This may in part be due to the fact that in order to protect those affected, it had initially only what is now Article 157 TFEU to rely on, and only expansive interpretations would afford any real protection. Concepts such as pay have therefore been interpreted liberally (***Barber v Guardian Royal Exchange Assurance*** (1990); ***Defrenne v Sabena (No. 2)*** (1976)). Inclusions of part-time workers in equal pay provisions as well as the introduction of equal pay for work of equal value have also been influential in the development of equality law, even if the gender pay gap still remains significant in most EU Member States.

[7] Interpretation is vital in determining the scope. Even widely drafted legislation can be interpreted narrowly and vice versa!

Interpretation in relation to the other provisions has been a little more cautious. ***Tadao Maruko v Versorgunsanstalt der deutschen Bühnen*** (2008) provides an illustration. A claim for a survivor's pension benefit by a same-sex partner was turned down on the basis that the benefit was not paid to parties who were not married. The ECJ noted that same-sex registered partnerships in Germany were increasingly equated with marriage, but, rather than holding that they should be treated as equivalent for the purposes of pension rights, the ECJ remitted the case back to the national court to decide whether in this case registered partners should have spousal rights. It could have been bolder in its interpretation in order to ensure equality of treatment. An even more restrictive judgment can be found in ***Sonia Navas*** (2006), which related to the scope of the term 'disability'. The term was held not to include sickness, so protection from dismissal on the grounds of disability did not cover someone who was dismissed because they were suffering from an illness that did not amount to a disability.

The scope of EU law has widened considerably but it is still subject to national implementation and interpretation, and this has caused problems. High-profile cases questioning the implantation of age discrimination provisions in **R (Incorporated Trustees of the National Council on Ageing (Age Concern England)) v Secretary of State for Business, Enterprise and Regulatory Reform** (2009) or the definition of discrimination on the grounds of disability as in the **Coleman** case (2008) highlight the complexities. Provisions on discrimination on the grounds of sexual orientation or religion and belief are culturally sensitive and application can be tricky. Equality is also an area where law is only one factor. In order to eliminate inequalities, a culture shift is needed, attitudes need to change and a legal framework, especially one as distant to most of its subjects as the EU law, cannot hope to achieve equality on its own. The EU has recognised this to some extent and has utilised other methods in order to try to help the legal provisions succeed in their aim. A range of policy tools, such as mainstreaming of non-discrimination into all EU policies, measuring of discrimination and evaluating of progress, awareness-raising and training activities and encouraging the development of voluntary EU-wide initiatives, as well as supporting national equality bodies, further encourage an overall principle of equality within the EU.[8] In conclusion, then, there is still work to be done but the scope of EU equality law is significantly wider than it was in the original treaties, and the focus now needs to shift from merely providing protection from discrimination to actively promoting equality.

[8] Showing your awareness of policy matters as well as legal matters shows a really contextual and comprehensive approach to this area and will gain extra marks for analysis as well as knowledge and understanding.

✓ Make your answer stand out

- Discuss other methods of promoting equality, such as 'mainstreaming', in more detail.
- Consider the scope of provisions outside the employment sphere in more depth.
- Consider the difference between protection from discrimination and promotion of equality further to build a stronger argument.
- Include some academic commentary, such as Bell, M. and Waddington, L. (2003) Reflecting on inequalities in European Equality Law, *EL Rev*, 2893, 349–69 or Masselot, A. (2007) The State of Gender Equality Law in the European Union, *ELJ*, 152.

? Question 3

Louise, who is a devout Christian, has applied for a place on the University of West Yorkshire's Masters degree in comparative law. She has been refused a place and is told that this is because she does not have sufficient qualifications. However, her friends Peter and Steven have been accepted and both did less well in their first degree and did not state their religious preference on the application form.

Eric and Gavin have been in a relationship for three years. Eric, who is from Jamaica, works as a customer service agent in a bank. Recently, he has noticed that people stop their conversations as he approaches. He has heard comments such as 'well, he should really be a cleaner, not one of us' and 'he should just go home'. In addition, right-wing literature has been anonymously left on his desk and a group of colleagues have started asking him about his views on immigration and what it means to be 'British'.

To take his mind off things Gavin takes Eric to an exclusive golf resort, but on arrival they are told that there has been a mistake with the booking and no rooms are available. Gavin, however, overhears the receptionist telling a colleague that there are plenty of rooms free that weekend but they don't want 'their kind' in the hotel.

Advise Louise, Eric and Gavin on their rights in EU law.

Answer plan

→ Introduction to relevant law.

→ Louise and Gavin have no remedy – Framework Directive does not apply outside employment.

→ Eric – the Race Equality Directive covers harassment.

→ Possible sex discrimination for Louise?

→ Possible race discrimination for Eric and Gavin at the hotel?

→ Summarise advice.

Diagram plan

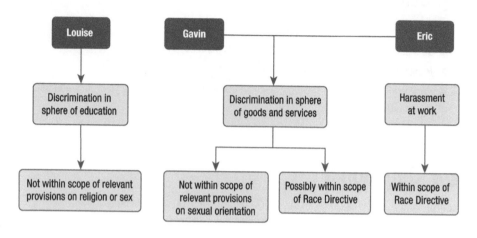

A printable version of this diagram plan is available from **www.pearsoned.co.uk/lawexpressqa**

Answer

[1] The examiners can see from this that you have correctly identified the legal issues and the provisions applying to them, so this is a very positive start which will give the examiner confidence in your answer.

This problem question requires the application of EU equality law and, in particular, a consideration of the Framework Directive (2000/78) and the Race Equality Directive (2000/43) enacted under Article 19 TFEU.[1]

Article 19 TFEU enables the EU to make secondary legislation to promote equality and prohibit discrimination on a number of grounds, including those at issue here: religion, race and sexual orientation. Two directives are of particular interest in relation to the scenario. The first is the Framework Directive, which covers all the grounds mentioned in Article 19 that are not dealt with elsewhere and the second is the Race Equality Directive covering discrimination on the grounds of race in relation to employment, social protection, education and access to public goods and services. This answer will deal with them in turn.

[2] Here the legal issues can be dealt with quickly and there is no point in spending a long time discussing a provision which does not apply. The discussion would lose you marks because it would be irrelevant.

The Framework Directive provides that there shall be no discrimination, direct or indirect, on the grounds of religion and sexual orientation, among others. However, the Framework Directive's scope does not extend outside the employment sphere. As such, it provides no protection for Louise in relation to her religious belief.[2] Furthermore, Gavin and Eric are not protected from discrimination by the hotel on the grounds of their sexual orientation. Until the EU equality law extends beyond matters related to employment in relation to religion and sexual orientation, there is no remedy available. While a proposal for such a law exists (COM (2008) 462 final), we are some way off that becoming law.[3]

[3] This shows your wider reading and knowledge and should thus lead to additional marks.

Directive 2004/113 relates to equal treatment between men and women in relation to goods and services. This extends the traditional scope beyond employment matters, but it does not extend far enough to help Louise even if she can show that Steven and Peter were given preference because of their sex, as it does not include education (Article 3(3) Directive 2004/113).[4]

[4] Citing authority like this without giving further detail is absolutely fine. You have made your point and explained the provision above in your own words already, so the examiners know you know the law.

Finally, we must consider Eric's position. The Race Directive clearly covers his position as he is experiencing difficulties at work. Article 2(3) of the Directive includes harassment in the definition of discrimination and stipulates that it is unlawful 'when an unwanted conduct related to racial or ethnic origin takes place with the purpose or effect of violating the dignity of a person and of creating an intimidating, hostile, degrading, humiliating or offensive environment'.[5] Eric must therefore show that the behaviour of colleagues at work amounts to harassment. The behaviour appears to be clearly linked to his race and does cause an intimidating and degrading environment.[6] It thus appears that the colleagues' actions are unlawful in EU law and the employer can thus be held vicariously liable for those actions.

[5] You could use a statute book here to get the wording right (if you are allowed to use one in exams) or you could paraphrase.

[6] Always remember to apply the provisions to the scenario at hand: otherwise, you will not pick up the marks available for analysis and application, which is actually the main part of what examiners are looking for.

The Race Directive is the only provision with a potentially wide scope. As already stated, it covers education as well as access to services. Although Gavin and Eric have no remedy in relation to discrimination suffered because they are gay, it is possible that they have an action based on race discrimination. It is not clear from the scenario whether or not Gavin is black and on exactly what grounds the hotel has made its decision.[7] However, if Gavin and Eric can show that they were discriminated against on the grounds of Eric's race (or on the grounds of both their race), they may be successful in EU law. Although the Race Directive refers to public services and there is therefore some question as to whether it applies to services for the public delivered through the private sector such as hotels, Directive 2004/113 mentioned above refers to public and private services, and the Commission has insisted that the scope of the two Directives in this respect is the same (COM (2003) 657 at page 13). There is thus a good chance that if Eric and Gavin can show

[7] Where information is unclear or missing, it gives you scope to speculate a little and show off your legal knowledge, so you do need to deal with the issues: otherwise, examiners will presume you did not know what to do with this point.

race discrimination occurred, the Directive would cover their situation. Case law has, however, yet to define the precise scope of the provisions.

To summarise the advice to the parties: Louise unfortunately has no remedy for any discrimination suffered because access to education is not covered in relation to either religion or sex. Gavin and Eric have no remedy in relation to discrimination on the grounds of sexual orientation. There is proposed legislation which would extend protection into the sphere of provision of goods and services but it is not yet finalised. In relation to race discrimination, it is possible but not certain that Gavin and Eric are protected in relation to the hotel's refusal to admit them. Eric's situation at work is covered and he would be able to claim unlawful harassment based on EU law in his national court (assuming that the EU law had been correctly implemented in the UK).

 ## Make your answer stand out

- Include more information about the proposed extension of the law.
- Use case law examples to illustrate how the behaviour of Eric's colleagues amounts to race discrimination.
- Consider the idea of public services offered through the private sector in more depth.
- Consider writing your advice directly addressing the clients. It will add a bit of interest to your work and show confidence in handling legal material.

! Don't be tempted to . . .

- Confuse EU law with national law. Focus on EU law provisions.
- Presume that because there appears to be discrimination, it will be covered – check the scope of the relevant provisions carefully.
- Presume that the discrimination takes place on one ground only – consider all possibilities.
- Explain EU equality law generally without linking your discussion to this scenario.

www.pearsoned.co.uk/lawexpressqa

 Go online to access more revision support including additional essay and problem questions with diagram plans, You be the marker questions, and download all diagrams from the book.

EU law and human rights

How this topic may come up in exams

Increasingly, EU law courses include explicit coverage of the importance of human rights in EU law. Mostly this focuses on fundamental rights principles as general principles of law which underpin the EU legal framework and the development of the Charter of Fundamental Rights and its legal status. Usually you will see essay questions on this topic; problem questions are relatively rare. Some courses will also explicitly cover issues under the European Convention on Human Rights (ECHR) and Strasbourg jurisprudence. As the focus of this book is EU law, we do not deal explicitly with ECHR matters here.

◼ Before you begin

It's a good idea to consider the following key themes of EU law and human rights before tackling a question on this topic.

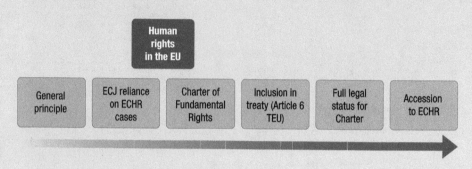

A printable version of this diagram is available from **www.pearsoned.co.uk/lawexpressqa**

Question 1

Assess the importance of fundamental rights as a source of European Union law.

Answer plan

→ Chart the history of human rights in EU law:
  - Unsympathetic at first
  - General principle
  - Developed by Court of Justice of the European Union (CJEU)
  - Eventually gained treaty recognition
  - Charter of Fundamental Rights
  - Accession to ECHR.

Diagram plan

```
                          ┌──────────────┐
                          │    Human     │
                          │    rights    │
                          │   in the EU  │
                          └──────────────┘

┌───────────┐ ┌───────────┐ ┌───────────┐ ┌───────────┐ ┌───────────┐ ┌───────────┐
│  General  │ │ ECJ reliance│ │ Charter of │ │ Inclusion in│ │ Full legal │ │ Accession │
│ principle │ │  on ECHR   │ │Fundamental │ │treaty (Article 6│ │ status for │ │  to ECHR  │
│           │ │   cases    │ │   Rights   │ │    TEU)    │ │  Charter   │ │           │
└───────────┘ └───────────┘ └───────────┘ └───────────┘ └───────────┘ └───────────┘
──────────────────────────────────────────────────────────────────────────────▶
```

A printable version of this diagram plan is available from **www.pearsoned.co.uk/lawexpressqa**

Answer

[1] Set out clearly how human rights fit into the EU legal framework. It shows you know your stuff.

[2] Always make sure your answer is current. Here you are highlighting that you know how the situation has changed since the ratification of the Lisbon Treaty.

EU law is taken from a number of sources of law. The most obvious source are perhaps the provisions contained in the treaties; secondary legislation as well as CJEU jurisprudence provide other obvious examples. In addition, however, a number of general principles underpin European law; one of these general principles is the respect for fundamental human rights.[1] Although the EU Member States are all also signatories to the European Convention on Human Rights (ECHR), the EU itself could not, until recently, sign up to the convention.[2]

3 In the introduction you have highlighted the key developments which act as milestones and now you can move on to explain how we got there.

4 A statement such as this one needs backing up with authorities and examples: otherwise, it looks like you are just making it up!

5 Another bold statement is made here. If you just left it like that without further explanation, you wouldn't pick up many marks because you are not backing up your view.

6 In this case your justification for this statement has gone before – in fact, have a look at the previous comment. The two statements taken together with the explanation and backing up in between make quite a forceful argument.

7 You have made the point that human rights are more explicitly referred to. There is no need to set out the cases in any detail. You probably won't have time to do so. Just list them to show your awareness, though.

8 You should receive marks here for recognising the relatively precarious status of human rights references contained in the judgments.

9 Show your awareness of all the areas you might find references to human rights, and here you should gain marks for recognising the uncertain status of the charter.

Furthermore, the EU did not have its own human rights charter until 2000, and the Charter of Fundamental Rights did not have the same status as the treaties until 2009. This essay thus charts the development of fundamental rights as a source of EU law.[3]

Until 1992, there was no codified human or fundamental rights document applicable to the Member States, so it is to the CJEU jurisprudence that the examination must turn. The early case law relating to individual human rights appeared unsympathetic.[4] In cases such as **Stork v High Authority** (1959) and **Sgarlata v Commission** (1965), upholding Community law was seen as more important than upholding individual rights. This position was, however, not viable in the long term.[5] All founding states were keenly aware of the need to protect fundamental human rights, and the constitutions of Germany and Italy had been rewritten with a focus on such rights. In addition, all the Member States but France were, by 1955, signed up to the ECHR. The CJEU thus had a moral, if not a legal, obligation to uphold fundamental rights.[6] **Stauder v City of Ulm** (1969) is evidence in a shift of emphasis and the court conceded that fundamental rights were 'enshrined in the general principle of the Community'. Once all Member States had signed the ECHR, the CJEU more explicitly referred to fundamental rights jurisprudence, and, in **Hauer v Land Rheinland-Pfalz** (1979), for the first time, it drew extensively and explicitly on the ECHR to help it decide a case.

More recently, in **Wachauf** (1989) the court confirmed that actions of Member States implementing EU law measures must comply with the requirements of fundamental rights. A further string of cases relating to the right to family life enshrined in Article 8 ECHR further shows the importance of the ECHR and fundamental rights generally in CJEU jurisprudence (**Baumbast** (2002); **MRAX** (2002); **Akrich** (2003)).[7]

However, the jurisprudence of the CJEU merely confirms that fundamental rights are an important principle of EU law.[8] Provisions relating to human rights were not contained in any legal or quasi-legal document or codified in any way. However, the greater emphasis placed on these issues is now reflected in the treaty.[9] Article 6 TEU confirms that the EU Charter of Fundamental Rights has the same legal status as the treaty. Previously the charter's status was unclear. Although introduced in 2000 at the same time as the Treaty of Nice, the charter was not part of the treaties and it was not clear just how much reliance could be placed on it. The EU, under the charter, should make law which contravenes the provisions within it, and, where the EU does so, the legal measure can be struck out. To what extent individuals could rely on the charter was, however, a different matter and human rights continued to be considered by the CJEU as a general principle rather than necessarily a charter-derived right.[10]

[10] This is an important point and should pick up marks – you are highlighting the fact that fundamental rights were dealt with as a general principle rather than as a right contained in a treaty or charter. If you had time, you could speculate why.

As well as giving full legal effect to the charter, the Lisbon Treaty, by giving the EU a legal personality, also resolves the question of EU accession to the ECHR. Article 6(2) TEU clearly states that the EU shall accede to the ECHR although, given the developments of fundamental rights as a general principle underpinning EU law and the new legal status of the charter, it might be questioned what can be added. Symbolically, however, accession to the ECHR on the part of the EU will further confirm its commitment to upholding the fundamental rights of its citizens.[11]

[11] By adding this sentence, you are moving away from simply describing and are adding your own analysis, and examiners are generally more interested in analysis than description.

It is worth noting, however, that Poland, the UK and Czech Republic negotiated opt-outs in respect of the charter. The opt-out precludes national courts and the EU's courts from finding that 'laws, regulations or administrative provisions, practices or action' in the countries to which it applies are inconsistent with the charter. In addition, it also stipulates that the part of the charter relating to social and economic rights does not create justiciable rights. Allowing an opt-out calls into question how seriously the EU really does take its charter and the rights enshrined in it.[12] If the rights are fundamental, it seems illogical and wrong to allow countries to opt out of them. Accession to the ECHR has in this respect been less controversial than giving full legal status to the charter. This may be because the Member States are already signatories to the ECHR, and EU accession to this does not change the legal framework applicable.

[12] Highlighting problems with an area of law or with national implementation of EU provisions shows you have really understood the area and shows off your critical thinking skills. The more of this sort of commentary you can include, the better.

Fundamental rights are now well integrated into the EU legal regime, with applicant states having to demonstrate respect for human rights (Article 49 TEU), and it is possible for treaty rights to be suspended in respect of Member States who seriously and persistently offend against human rights principles (Article 7 TEU). It can thus no longer be said that the EU is unsympathetic to fundamental rights.[13]

[13] You have used the same wording early on in relation to case law, and doing so shows you have developed a coherent argument and focuses the reader's attention on how that argument follows logically.

In conclusion, it can be said that the status of fundamental rights has undergone a transformation, from the original status of unwritten

[14] Offering your views on what the future holds shows you have confidence in your argument and a full understanding of the area of law.

guidelines, through express recognition by the CJEU, to the present day where they hold the position of principles underpinning the treaties, as well as being enshrined in the Charter of Fundamental Rights with the same legal effect as treaty provisions. In the future, with the accession of the EU to the ECHR, fundamental human rights are likely to take on even greater significance.[14]

 Make your answer stand out

■ Consider adding some academic commentary, such as Arnull, A. (2003) From Charter to Constitution and beyond: Fundamental rights in the New European Union, *Public Law*, 774 or Jacobs, F. (2001) Human Rights in the EU: The role of the Court of Justice, *EL Rev*, 26, 331.

■ Explain the case law in more depth in order to highlight your points.

■ There are often issues in the news which relate to this. Show off your awareness of current affairs and legal issues by bringing them into your discussion here.

■ Consider the implications of the charter being annexed to rather than being part of the treaty.

! Don't be tempted to . . .

■ Ignore the early development and start with the charter.

■ Presume that the CJEU's influence is not important.

■ Talk mostly about the ECHR: that's not what the question is about.

■ Write about human rights generally: you must focus on the question asked.

www.pearsoned.co.uk/lawexpressqa

 Go online to access more revision support including additional essay and problem questions with diagram plans, You be the marker questions, and download all diagrams from the book.

EU competition law

How this topic may come up in exams

EU competition law is not taught on every EU course and sometimes it is offered as a standalone optional course. You must therefore check the extent to which this area is covered on your course carefully. Both essay and problem questions are popular. Problem questions often focus on whether there has been a concerted practice, or on assessing dominance and then abuse of that dominance. Essay questions can focus on assessment of those same issues or consider the overall aim and nature of competition policy in the EU.

■ Before you begin

It's a good idea to consider the following key themes of EU competition law before tackling a question on this topic.

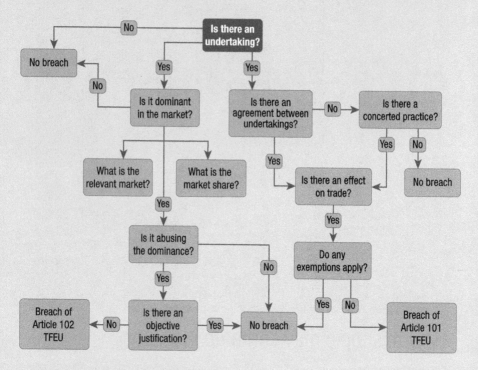

A printable version of this diagram is available from **www.pearsoned.co.uk/lawexpressqa**

❓ Question 1

Beta Ltd produces chemical and organic fertilisers. The European market for fertilisers is dominated by four firms, which between them hold a 70 per cent market share: GO Gmbh 26 per cent, UK Fertilisers Ltd 20 per cent, Euro Dressings 15 per cent, and IFS Spa 9 per cent. The remaining market share amounting to 30 per cent is divided between many small firms. Northern Fertilisers Ltd is one such firm. It holds 4 per cent of the market share.

Last year, demand for organic fertilisers increased appreciably. This, however, has imposed serious pressures on the sales of chemical fertilisers: the major manufacturers identified above were deeply alarmed. The Trade Association of Chemical and Organic Fertilisers Producers published a conference paper as to the marketing of fertilisers at the start of this year. The conference was not open to non-members of the association.

At the end of December last year, GO Gmbh, UK Fertilisers Ltd, Euro Dressings and IFS Spa each announced price rises of 3 per cent in organic fertilisers as from the end of February. In addition, in May this year, the trade association recommended that members offer discounts to wholesalers who refused to stock organic fertilisers.

Advise the firms involved as to their position in EU competition law.

Answer plan

→ Introduction: this is a question concerning concerted practices under Article 101 TFEU.

→ Is there an agreement between undertakings?

→ Is there a concerted practice?

→ Is it likely to affect/distort competition?

→ Conclusions: likely breach of Article 101 TFEU?

Diagram plan

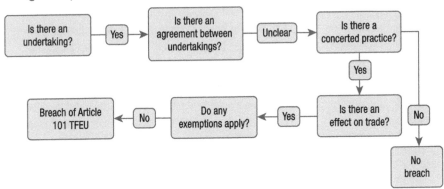

A printable version of this diagram plan is available from **www.pearsoned.co.uk/lawexpressqa**

Answer

[1] Do not worry if you cannot remember this word for word. If you are allowed a statute book in your exam, you could consult that or you can just paraphrase. The principles rather than the exact wording are important.

[2] Restating the question often helps to clarify in your mind what it is you are trying to do but also shows that you have got it right. It should give the examiner confidence that this is going to be a good answer.

[3] If something is as clear as it is here, do not spend time going through and applying definitions. Save your time and effort for areas which are controversial.

[4] You do need to be aware of key cases such as this, but don't worry too much about learning the definition off by heart – something paraphrased along those lines will be fine.

[5] By setting out the question you are considering at the beginning of each little section, you can help focus your mind in the exam and also highlight your structure clearly to the examiner. This should help keep the focus on the question set.

[6] Consider how we have answered the question in the context of the scenario. This should gain marks for application and save time because you are not setting out the law and applying it separately.

This question concerns the application of European Union competition law to the market for fertilisers. It concerns the application of Article 101 TFEU. That Article provides:

> The following shall be prohibited as incompatible with the internal market: all agreements between undertakings, decisions by associations of undertakings and concerted practices which may affect trade between Member States and which have as their object or effect the prevention, restriction or distortion of competition within the internal market.[1]

In order to advise the firms, it must be established whether or not there is an agreement between undertakings in relation to fertilisers and whether, if there is such an agreement, it amounts to a distortion of competition within the internal market. In other words, has the behaviour of the four largest firms with respect to the pricing of organic fertilisers infringed the provisions of Article 101?[2]

It should be noted that 'undertaking' in the context of Article 101 has been interpreted to include legal persons. The companies identified above are therefore included in the scope of the provision.[3] Next, we need to consider whether the companies identified engaged in behaviour which could be subject to the scrutiny of the provisions of Article 101. With respect to the price rises, there is no agreement as such between the four largest firms. However, the circumstances of the rise may be evidence of a 'concerted practice'. The definition of this was given in *ICI v Commission* (1972):[4]

> a form of coordination between undertakings which, without having reached the stage where an agreement properly so-called has been concluded, knowingly substitutes practical cooperation between them for the risks of competition.

Does the behaviour of the largest four firms constitute a 'concerted practice'?[5] The market here may be oligopolistic in nature; there is a large percentage of market share involved, as indicated in the scenario. The trade association meeting in December after which all members imposed the same percentage rise in prices may be evidence of sharing information with respect to the prospective price rises.[6] Is this evidence of a 'concerted practice'? For this to be so, it would be sufficient if the members at that meeting had informed each other of the attitude that each would take on the issue of future price rises. Such knowledge would mean that each firm could regulate its future conduct with respect to price rises, in the security that each possessed foreknowledge of the future conduct of its competitors in such circumstances. In **Ahlström Osakeyhtiö v Commission** (1993), wood pulp producers holding two-thirds of the Union market share announced simultaneous quarterly and identical price rises.[7] It was held that such was not evidence of a concerted practice where the announcement represented 'rational response to the need to limit commercial risk in a long-term market'. In that instance the similarity in the rises was as a result of a high degree of market transparency together with the oligopolistic tendencies of the market. In contrast, an 'agreement' to fix recommended prices and to provide advance notification of deviation to members was held to restrict competition within Article 101(1). It is arguable that with four major producers, the current market with respect to fertilisers shows evidences of oligopolistic tendencies. The General Court may view the announced price increases as parallel behaviour: rational responses by the firms involved to the need to limit commercial risk. Parallel behaviour, while not in itself a concerted practice, provides strong evidence as such.[8] In **ICI v Commission** (1972) the parallel behaviour of three uniform price increases in the oligopolistic market of aniline dyes that were effected virtually simultaneously in 1964, 1965 and 1967 was held to be a concerted practice.

In addition, the trade association recommended that members offer discounts to wholesalers who refused to stock organic fertilisers. Is a recommendation of a trade association covered by the provisions of Article 101(1)? Article 101(1) refers to 'decisions by associations of undertakings'. Is the recommendation of the Trade Association of the Chemical and Organic Fertilisers Producers a decision for the purposes of Article 101(1)? Following **NV IAZ International Belgium v Commission** (1983), a non-binding recommendation of a trade association which is followed by its members would constitute a decision for the purposes of Article 101(1).[9]

Is the behaviour of the four largest firms in the fertiliser market likely for the purposes of Article 101, to 'affect trade between Member States'? Between them, those firms hold a 70 per cent market share within the European Union; it is fairly clear that it would do so. Further, in **STM v Ulm** (1966) the court held the concerted practice would be capable of affecting trade if 'on the basis of . . . objective factors of law or of fact

[7] Even where focusing purely on the scenario as in the paragraph above, you still need to cite your legal authority: otherwise, you will lose marks.

[8] When stating a conclusion like this, it really helps if you can then back it up with an authority, as we have done here.

[9] It is often possible to state the law and apply it at the same time, as shown here.

that the agreement . . . may have an influence, direct or indirect, actual or potential, on the pattern of trade between Member States'. It is sufficient that the concerted practice has either the object or effect of distorting the market for fertilisers with the European Union market. It would, following **STM v Ulm**, not be necessary to prove that the concerted practice had both the object and effect of distorting that marketplace.

[10] As well as setting out what the law is, you should also set out the practical consequences to really show you understand the area of law and thus pick up maximum marks.

Where the court finds under Article 101 that there exists a 'concerted practice', the practice will automatically be void and enforceable.[10] Article 101(2) provides that 'Any agreements or decisions prohibited pursuant to this Article shall be automatically void'. If GO Gmbh, UK Fertilisers Ltd, Euro Dressings and IFS Spa are found to be parties to a concerted practice, for example, they will be fined. However, there is the possibility that Article 101(3) may exempt GO Gmbh, UK Fertilisers Ltd, Euro Dressings and IFS Spa from the provisions of Article 101(1).[11] Were it to be so, the provisions of Article 101(1) would be declared inapplicable, with the result that the parties' behaviour would be considered to be lawful.

[11] Where there are exemptions or derogations, you should always mention their existence even where there is insufficient information to come to a full conclusion. That way, the examiner knows that you know.

If the General Court holds that the February price rise of 3 per cent has been imposed as a result of the fixing of the prices of organic fertilisers between GO Gmbh, UK Fertilisers Ltd, Euro Dressings and IFS Spa, then this is a clear breach of the prohibition of Article 101(1) relating to the 'restriction or distortion of competition within the internal market, and in particular those which: (a) directly or indirectly fix purchase or selling prices'. Such a clear breach of Article 101 in such circumstance would prove extremely difficult to justify.

[12] This is a useful summary of your overall assessment and brings the answer nicely to an end, confirming you didn't just run out of time. It also acknowledges the limited information you had, which is fine.

It therefore seems likely, on the limited evidence available here, that GO Gmbh, UK Fertilisers Ltd, Euro Dressings and IFS Spa are in breach of Article 101 TFEU.[12]

 Make your answer stand out

- Expand on the possible exemptions in Article 101(3).
- Explain the difference between parallel behaviour and concerted practice in more detail with reference to the case law you already cite.
- Define concerted practice more clearly at the beginning and distinguish it from an agreement.
- Consider the application of any exemptions.

✒ Question 2

Article 102 TFEU prohibits undertakings from abusing their dominant position. Critically assess how this concept of abuse has been interpreted by the Court.

Diagram plan

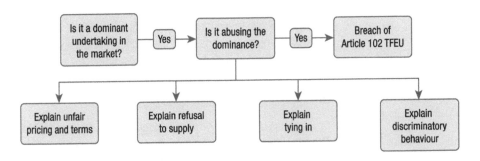

A printable version of this diagram plan is available from **www.pearsoned.co.uk/lawexpressqa**

Answer plan

→ Introduction to Article 102 TFEU.

→ Types of abuse listed in the treaty with an explanation as to how the ECJ has tackled them:

 – Unfair prices

 – Unfair trading conditions

 – Discriminatory treatment

- Tying in
- Refusal to supply.

➡ Conclusions: broad conceptualisation of abuse to avoid distortion of markets.

Answer

[1] At the beginning of an essay, it is useful to identify and set out the area of law the question is asking about. It shows you are on the right track and also helps you get focused.

This essay concerns aspects of European Union competition law.[1] It brings into discussion the concept of the dominance in the market-place and the abuse of that position of dominance by the firms who are players in that particular market. Article 102 TFEU deals with situations of abuse of a dominant position in European Union competition law. Article 102 TFEU gives a non-exhaustive list of specific abuses which are prohibited.

Article 102 provides:

[2] No need to learn this; use your statute book, or paraphrase.

> Any abuse by one or more undertakings of a dominant position within the internal market or in a substantial part of it shall be prohibited as incompatible with the internal market in so far as it may affect trade between Member States.[2]

It is the jurisprudence of the General Court that has identified prohibited abuse in the behaviour of firms which are themselves in a dominant position in the marketplace. This essay will consider the development of that jurisprudence, using the framework adopted for the specified examples of abuse as listed by Article 102.

Unfair prices[3]

[3] Most examiners will be fine with subheadings. It helps structure your argument and makes your points much more clearly and, of course, easy to follow and check that you have included all the key issues.

[4] In this section we have used cases as examples to illustrate our point. Take note, though, how the argument made is still more important than simply listing cases.

On the selling side, excessive prices charged may be unfair. In *United Brands v Commission* (1978),[4] it was held that the price will be excessive if 'it has no reasonable relation to the economic value of the product supplied'. 'Value', the court suggested, might be determined by comparing selling prices and production costs and then determining whether it is *unfair*. In *British Leyland* (1986), the high prices viewed as excessive and discriminatory for type approval certificates imposed to discourage customer imports was held lawful in the content of the manufacturer's policy of maintaining price differentials and compartmentalising the common market. In *United Brands*, there was a reference to 'other ways' in which economists could identify unfair prices. The court considered in that instance, for example, a comparison with the prices of other products or in relation to prices in other areas. With respect to the former, the Commission in **Deutsche Post** (2000) compared cross-border tariffs with domestic tariffs in relation to prices charged for the delivery of mail. With respect to the latter, for example, in **Bodson** (1988), concerning funeral services in France in areas where there were concessions, the court talked of whether the price was 'fair' in comparison to prices in areas in which there were no such concessions.

Unfair trading conditions

In **United Brands**, the company, United Brands, was held to have imposed unfair trading conditions by refusing to allow importers to resell bananas while they were still green. In another example, the Commission reached a settlement with Microsoft in relation to its standard agreements for licensing software to PC manufacturers which had excluded competitors from selling their products. In **AAMS v Commission** (2001),[5] distribution agreements imposed by the dominant wholesaler were held unlawful; they had limited the access to the Italian market by foreign producers of cigarettes.

[5] Just one or two examples will do to illustrate how each of these areas may be an abuse. If it is fairly clear-cut and simple, as here, you do not need to list lots of examples.

Discriminatory treatment

In **United Brands**, for example, the company was charging a price differential of sometimes more that 100 per cent in differing markets. The charge was made on the basis of what the market would bear. So, too, the differing pricing structures for type-approval certificates for left-hand drive cars in British Leyland was held to be discriminatory. In **British Airways v Commission** (2003), BA as a dominant player in the air-travel agency services market had offered UK travel agents a reward scheme for increasing sales of BA tickets. One element contributing to the finding of abuse was that it was possible for two travel agents under the scheme to receive different rates of commission from identical sales.

[6] Before launching in to more examples, set out clearly that you are moving on to a slightly different type of abuse. This gives your answer structure, and also avoids it becoming too descriptive.

Anti-competitive abuse, on the other hand, is where the dominance is used to undermine or eliminate a competitor.[6] Some examples are as follows:

(i) *Tying in.* In **Tetra-Pak** (1994), purchasers of machines for making aseptic cartons were required to purchase cartons exclusively from Tetra-Pak, and in *Hoffmann-La Roche* (1979) customers had to buy most of their requirements from La Roche, in return for which they were given 'loyalty rebates'.

(ii) *Predatory pricing.* Predatory pricing, which is artificially low pricing, sometimes below cost, is adopted to drive a competitor out of the market. Such action may amount to an abuse. In *AKZO Chemie* (1986), a firm dominant in production of organic peroxides was found to have engaged in such pricing practices. However, it was held in *Hoffmann-La Roche* that a distinction should be maintained between trying to win new customers by lowering prices and trying to eliminate a competitor.[7] The judgment of *Compagnie Maritime Belge Transport* (2000) stressed the need to show intent; there was evidence here to show a motive to drive out the only existing competitor in the marketplace.

[7] Rather than just listing cases, justify your choice and always highlight where an issue has been seen to be problematic, as here. It shows off your analytical skills.

(iii) *Refusal to supply.* It is abuse if the refusal to supply reduces or eliminates competition. This was established in *ICI SpA* (1974) where it was intended that its subsidiary would take over production of ethambutol, previously made by competitor Zola. Further, the cessation of supplies of wind instruments by B & H in *Brass Band Instruments (BBI)* v *Boosey & Hawkes* (1988) was intended to prevent BBI entering the market as competitors. In *ICI SpA,* the decision to commence manufacture of ethambutol did not justify the decision to discontinue sales of the raw material in relation to production of the same product to a competitor. In *Radio Telefis Eireann* v *Commission* (1995), the court upheld the Commission decision that a refusal to supply a party where there was no pre-existing commercial relationship was unlawful. The same will apply where there is a refusal to supply because the dominant firm reserves the activities to itself, as in *Italy* v *Commission* (1985), in which BT reserved for itself exclusive rights with respect to its telex forwarding services.

[8] In this conclusion you are really justifying the use of all the examples above and explaining what they show. You need this: otherwise, your answer is just a list of examples and you miss the point of the question.

As can be seen from the examples given above, the concept of abuse in EU competition law is broadly construed so as to capture situations where behaviour of undertakings is likely to impact on and distort competition.[8] Although a list is provided in the treaty provisions of what might constitute abuse, ECJ jurisprudence has further developed the concept and remains flexible enough to deal with other emerging practices which may affect markets in the future.

✓ Make your answer stand out

- Add a more detailed explanation of the difference between exploitative abuse and anti-competitive abuse.
- Consider academic commentary on the application of Article 102 TFEU. For example, Eilmansberger, T. (2005) How to distinguish good from bad competition under Article 82, *CMLR*, 42, 129, or Niels, G. and Jenkins, H. (2005) Reform of Article 82: Where the link between dominance and effects breaks down, *ECLR*, 29, 605–10.
- Explain how and why abuse has been construed so broadly as you go through, rather than leaving that analysis to the conclusion.
- Highlight your argument with reference to recent examples you might have read about in the media. Consult your notes and/or a good quality newspaper to show awareness of developments in this area.

! Don't be tempted to . . .

- Discuss dominance in any detail. You are not asked to consider the meaning of dominance in this question. Just focus on abuse.
- Go through the facts of cases in detail. Just provide enough information for your point to make sense.
- Focus just on one type of abuse. While you do not need to write the same amount about all of them, you do need to engage with them all.
- Stray into a discussion of Article 101 TFEU.

📓 Question 3

Critically assess the scope of exemptions to the competition law provisions found in Article 101(3) TFEU.

Answer plan

→ Introduction: the question relates to exceptions to the prohibition on agreements which distort competition within the internal market.

→ Outline Article 101(3) TFEU, then discuss individual elements:
- Contribute to improving production or distribution or promoting technical or economic progress
- Allowing a fair share of resulting benefits for consumers

- Indispensable restrictions
- Not allowing the possibility of eliminating competition.

Diagram plan

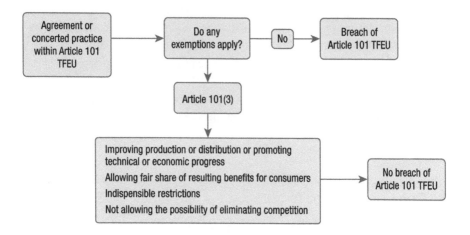

A printable version of this diagram plan is available from **www.pearsoned.co.uk/lawexpressqa**

Answer

This question concerns European Union competition law. Under Article 101(1), agreements between firms are automatically void where they 'affect trade between Member States and which have as their object or effect the prevention, restriction or distortion of competition within the internal market'.

[1] In your introduction, set out the applicable law and issue to show that you have understood the question fully.

Agreements will escape the prohibition of Article 101(1) if they fall within the exemptions of Article 101(3).[1] Exemption decisions were in the exclusive competence of the Commission of the European Communities and given only if the Commission had received notification of an agreement. That system came to an end with Regulation 1/2003.[2] However, the jurisprudence decided under that system is still relevant; it will supply guidance as to the approach to be taken by the domestic courts under the new system of enforcement and in addition to the application of the provisions of Article 101(3) with respect to the

[2] This may seem irrelevant, but you are going to be referring to case law decided under the old regime, so you need to explain that it is still relevant. It also shows your historical knowledge of the area of law.

exemption of agreement that would otherwise be prohibited under Article 101.

Article 101(3) lists criteria which must be satisfied for the agreement to be considered to be exempt. Exemptions may apply with respect to a contribution to improving the production/distribution or to the promotion of technical or economic progress.[3] In *GlaxoSmithKline Services Unlimited* v *Commission* (2006), the court accepted the arguments of Glaxo that the agreement was necessary to support costly and risky global R&D which would encourage innovation and competition. In *Ford/Volkswagen* (1993), the creation of a joint-venture company to develop a multi-purpose vehicle would improve production and promote technical development. In *Transocean Marine Paint Association* (1967), a collaboration by manufacturers and distributors to produce and market marine paints to identical standards to compete with the world-class producers of the same was exempted by Article 101(3);[4] single manufacturers alone were too small to offer adequate stocks. In *Re Vacuum Interrupters* (1980), a joint venture with respect to the development of vacuum interrupters was exempted on the grounds of technological benefits. *CECIMO* (1969) is an example of exemption on the grounds of economic progress in the context of an agreement to regulate trade fairs; rationalisation in this context avoided duplication of time and effort. In *CECED* (2000), an anti-competitive agreement between domestic appliance manufacturers to phase out the production of certain low-energy washing machines was exempted; it would raise production costs for manufacturers who had not developed the more energy efficient models. Set performance standards provided fair returns for the consumer with respect to the higher initial payback costs.

Examples relating to agreements allowing consumers a fair share of the resulting benefits[5] include *VBVB and VBBB* v *Commission* (1984), in which consumers were held not to benefit from the agreement of the parties to fix the retail price of books; no exemption was therefore granted. In *Synthetic Fibres* (1984), the conclusion was an agreement to reduce supply that would benefit consumers and lead in the longer term to a healthier and more competitive industry in the synthetic fibres industry. In *Asnef-Equifax* v *Ausbanec* (2006), an electronic register of credit card information set up by the Spanish banks resulted in a consumer benefit to customers

[3] This is a clear statement of the law which should pick up marks. You can then go on to highlight how that applies by using examples, which is what we do next.

[4] We have given a number of examples here and we think it is useful to do so, just giving a sentence or so about each. It shows you have a wide-ranging knowledge of the case law and understand how this area of law operates.

[5] Refer back to the statement of law at the beginning and tell the examiner what you are exploring further next. This sort of signposting is what gives your answer a good easy-to-follow structure.

in that loans were granted as a result on better terms. Those denied loans due to bad credit ratings would benefit from voiding over-indebtedness.

[6] This is a really good analytical comment to make and shows you are doing more than simply describing case law you have learned by rote.

The criteria identified by Article 101(3) so far have been positive in nature[6] – compliance with the criteria is a positive step in the exemption process. An agreement which accords with the positive criteria must then contain only restrictions which are indispensable to the achievement of the benefits of the agreement. Each clause will be examined to see whether restrictions can be achieved by less restrictive means. In **Carlsberg Beers** (1984), a cooperation agreement of 11 years' duration between Carlsberg Brewery (UK) and Grand Metropolitan was exempted as necessary to enable the former to build up its own independent distribution system and to establish itself within the UK market. In **Pronuptia de Paris GmbH** (1986), the court suggested that some territorial protection might be justified if, overall, the agreement is pro-competitive. In **P & O Stena Line** (2000), an exemption was granted to the parties' joint venture combining operations on a ferry route. In that instance, less restrictive alternatives, such as joint scheduling, would have not resulted in the cost savings and increased frequency of service achievable by the joint venture. In **CECED** the agreement between domestic appliance manufacturers prevented the manufacture of certain types of washing machine; this however, was considered necessary to achieve the benefits of the future production of more energy efficient models.

[7] You have referred to quite a lot of case law already, but where possible draw on other materials such as Commission guidance or academic commentary to help make your point.

[8] Do not worry about learning this word for word. Paraphrasing will do.

The final criteria relates to the possibility of eliminating competition in respect of a substantial part of the products in question. The Commission has explained the relevance of this criterion[7] as 'Ultimately the protection of rivalry and the competitive process is given priority over potentially pro-competitive efficiency gains which could result from restrictive agreements'.[8] The assessment will consider factors such as market share, incentives to compete and actual market conduct of the parties. For example, in **CECED** the Commission found that there was no elimination of competition as a result of the agreement; the parties were able to compete on features such as price, technical performance and brand image. There was, for example, the existence of substantial inter-brand competition in, say, **Re Vacuum Interrupters,** from the Americans and the Japanese.

Make your answer stand out

- The final criteria could be discussed in more depth.
- Summarise the conclusion at the end: it makes it easier for the marker to check that you have dealt with everything and understand the application of the law.
- Add some commentary from academic articles, such as Roitman, D. (2006) Legal uncertainty for vertical distribution agreements: The block exemption Regulation 2790/1999 and related aspects of the new Regulation 1/2003, *ECLR*, 27, 261–8.
- Add comments about why the exemptions are needed and how they are or are not effective in achieving that aim.

! Don't be tempted to . . .

- Explain all of Article 101 TFEU in detail: you need to focus on the question set.
- Focus on only part of the criteria – sometimes it is easy to get side-tracked into focusing on something you feel more confident with.
- Give loads of detail about one or two cases. This essay requires a broader overview, so a few more examples are required, but keep them short.

? Question 4

Plastex Ltd has developed a specialised plastic coating product that can adhere to any surface without the need for adhesive. The sealant product is effective in protecting any surface to which it is applied from corrosion or decomposition. It is extremely popular in DIY shops where there is a big demand for the product.

Other competitor companies also produce similar plastic coating products but Plastex Ltd still retains 45 per cent of the market share in the EU, although only 5 per cent of the total market for plastic coverings in general.

Plastex Ltd supplies the plastic coating product to DIY shops where they agree to sell only the plastic coating product Plastex produces and no other coating material. Low Price Hardware Ltd is a small hardware retailer which wants to stock the plastic coating product as developed by Plastex Ltd. However, Plastex Ltd refuses to supply Low Price Hardware because it would not agree to comply with Plastex's conditions.

Advise Low Price Hardware Ltd (LPH) and Plastex Ltd on the practices adopted in the light of European Union competition law.

Diagram plan

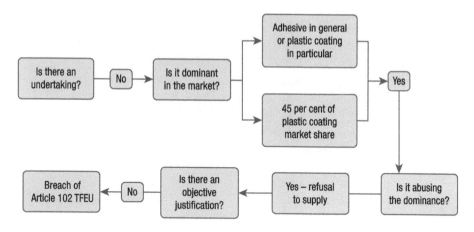

A printable version of this diagram plan is available from **www.pearsoned.co.uk/lawexpressqa**

Answer plan

→ Introduction: question relates to Article 102 TFEU on the abuse of a dominant position in EU law.

→ Establish whether there is dominance in the relevant market:
 – What is the relevant product market?
 – Is there dominance within that market?

→ Has there been an abuse of dominance?
 – Refusal to supply falls within scope of provisions as potentially abusive.

→ Conclusion: breach of Article 102 TFEU.

Answer

[1] This is a great introduction because it highlights what law is under consideration but keeps the focus on the problem question.

This question concerns European Union competition law and the application of Article 102 TFEU in the context of an alleged abuse of a 'dominant position' by Plastex Ltd in the market for plastic coating products.[1]

Article 102 provides:

> Any abuse by one or more undertakings of a dominant position within the internal market or in a substantial part of it

shall be prohibited as incompatible with the internal market
in so far as it may affect trade between Member States.

The word 'undertaking' is interpreted to include any legal person
engaged in a commercial activity. It covers therefore Plastex Ltd,[2]
and the production by it of plastic coating products. Three important
questions must be raised in the present context. The first concerns
the issue of the dominance of Plastex Ltd within the market for plastic coating products. The second concerns an abuse of a position
of dominance.[3] The third question relates to whether an abuse has
affected trade between Member States.

[2] When you have an
uncontroversial issue as here,
do not spend time on it but
do remember to state the law
and how it applies.

[3] Setting out what issues
you need to consider shows
the examiner you have
understood those issues and
can also act as a reminder
if you do later lose your way
a little.

The first issue relates to the dominance of Plastex within the marketplace for plastic coating products. A position of dominance within the
market was defined in **United Brands v Commission** (1978) as:

> A position of economic strength enjoyed by an undertak-
> ing which enables it to prevent effective competition being
> maintained on the relevant market by giving it the power to
> behave to an appreciable extent independently of its com-
> petitors, customers and ultimately of its consumers.[4]

[4] There is no need to learn
this word for word but you do
need to know the case and
this key definition.

To assess whether Plastex Ltd enjoys the economic strength to behave
independently in the marketplace for coating will involve ascertaining
the 'relevant market' in which the competition is claimed to exist. The
relevant product and geographical markets will require examination.

[5] This question states that
you are now moving to apply
the law and acts as a helpful
signpost for the examiner. It
also makes the structure easy
to follow.

How is the 'relevant product market' (RPM) for plastic coating products to be defined?[5] A sub-market can be defined in narrow terms. Is
Plastex Ltd, for example, operating in a market that can be defined by
reference to plastic coating products in particular or within the market
for all sealant products in general? The RPM is assessed in terms
of product substitution. It is one in which the products are substantially interchangeable (**ICI SpA v Commission** (1974)). It involves
an assessment of the cross-elasticity of demand and of supply of the
products, by reference to characteristics, price and the use to which
the products can be put. On the demand side, for example, if the price
for plastic coating products is increased, do consumers buy general
sealants instead?[6] Alternatively, will only the plastic coating products
produced by Plastex Ltd continue to be bought? If the former is the
case, then elasticity of demand for the plastic coating products is
high, if the latter, it is low.

[6] Keep the focus on the
question set and do not be
tempted to set out the law in
detail. You can state the law
in the context of the scenario
as we have done here for
quick and easy marks.

Whether the products are substantially interchangeable will depend on an assessment of the marketplace. In *United Brands*,[7] for example, analysis was undertaken which found that the relevant product market, 'other fruit' could not readily be substituted for bananas; bananas were therefore isolated as a separate market. In *Tetra-Pak* (1994), for example, Tetra-Pak's argument that there were separate markets for aseptic cartons and related packaging machinery and for non-aseptic cartons and packaging machinery was rejected due to the relative ease in that instance with which the manufacturer could switch from one to the other. In *ICI SpA*, the effect of a refusal to supply a company (Zoja), was to eliminate a principal manufacturer of etambutol within the market. Other raw materials could not be substituted for the aminobutanol without difficulty. It was not feasible for Zoja to adapt its production; the relevant product market in these circumstances was therefore the specific chemical, aminobutanol.

[7] You do still need legal authority, though, and case examples work well here to show how the ECJ has applied the same legal provisions.

The marketplace for adhesives in general and the plastic coating products made by Plastex Ltd in particular would have to be researched. In theory, it may be possible to classify the specialised plastic coating product produced by Plastex Ltd as operating in a separate market from the similar plastic coating products produced by other suppliers. In *Brass Band Instruments v Boosey & Hawkes* (1988), in defining the relevant product market, it was held that 'the essential question is whether the sub-market is sufficiently distinct in commercial reality'. In that case, the RPM was the instruments for *British-style* brass bands, not brass instruments in general.

The undertaking must be dominant 'within the internal market or in a substantial part of it'.[8] Plastex Ltd has a 45 per cent of the total market share within the EU, evidence that it is dominant at least within a substantial geographical part of the EU market. The geographical market is one where the 'objective conditions of competition are the same for all traders' (*United Brands*).

[8] By stating the law succinctly like this, you can really focus on the application, which is where most marks are available.

The assessment of whether Plastex Ltd is dominant within the market for specialised plastic coating products account requires a wide-ranging economic analysis of Plastex and its position in the marketplace. Such assessment may in addition need to be taken of the company's financial and technological resources and of any barriers to entry that may exist, such as access to superior technology in relation to this particular product.

What is crucial is not whether Plastex Ltd is found to be in a dominant position but whether they have abused that position.[9]

'Abuse' has been defined in ***Hoffmann-La Roche*** (1979) as:

> An objective concept relating to the behaviour of an under-taking in a dominant position which is such as to influence the structure of a market . . . the degree of competition is weakened and . . . has the effect of hindering the main-tenance of the degree of competition still existing in the market or the growth of that competition.

It could be argued in this instance that the refusal to supply LPH appears to be in retaliation because it would not accept Plastex Ltd's condition that it sells only the plastic coating products produced by Plastex and none other. This would be an exploitative abuse. In ***United Brands***, UB had refused to supply an important wholesaler who had constructed special facilities to store bananas, simply because it had taken part in an advertising campaign for a competitor.

Were Plastex Ltd to be found to be in a dominant position and to have abused that dominance, the national authorities in the UK can require that the infringement be brought to an end. Such authorities have the power to impose fines and periodic penalty payments.[10]

✓ Make your answer stand out

- Deal with refusal to supply as an abuse in more detail with reference to cases, e.g. *Metro-SB-Grossmärkte GmbH & Co KG* v *Commission* (1975); *BBC* v *Commission* (1991).
- Consider the level of fines that could be imposed.
- Apply the law a little more and explain in detail why a separate market might be established, by applying the decided cases more explicitly to the given scenario.
- You should also deal with whether there is an effect on trade explicitly rather than skipping over it and just implying it.

⚠ Don't be tempted to . . .

- Jump to the conclusion of abuse once you have established dominance; these are separate issues and should be treated as such.
- Jump straight to assessing dominance: first you need to establish the relevant market.
- Go through all possible types of abuse: focus on the question.
- Just explain the law without applying it to the scenario. Explain how and why the law applies.

www.pearsoned.co.uk/lawexpressqa

Go online to access more revision support including additional essay and problem questions with diagram plans, You be the marker questions, and download all diagrams from the book.

Bibliography

Arnull, A. (2003) From Charter to Constitution and Beyond: Fundamental Rights in the New European Union, *Public Law*, 774.

Barnard, C. (2013) *The Substantive Law of the EU: The Four Freedoms*, 4th edn, Oxford: Oxford University Press.
Bell, M. and Waddington, L. (2003) Reflecting on Inequalities in European Equality Law, *EL Rev*, 2893, 349–69.

Chalmers, D., Davies, G. and Monti, G. (2014) *EU Law. Cases and Materials*, Cambridge: Cambridge University Press.
Craig, P. (1997) Directives: Direct Effect, Indirect Effect and the Construction of National Legislation, *EL Rev*, 22, 519–38.
Craig, P. (2006) *EU Administrative Law*, Oxford: Oxford University Press.
Craig, P. (2008) The Lisbon Treaty: Process, Architecture and Substance, *EL Rev*, 33, 137.
Craig, P. and De Burca, G. (2011) *EU Law. Text Cases and Materials*, 5th edn, Oxford: Oxford University Press.

Dani, M. (2009) Constitutionalism and Dissonances – Has Europe Paid Off its Debt with Functionalism?, *ELJ*, 25, 324–50.
De Witte, B. (1999) Direct Effect, Supremacy and the Nature of the Legal Order, in P. Craig and G. De Burca (eds) *The Evolution of EU Law*, Oxford: Oxford University Press.
Dougan, M. (2000) The Disguised Vertical Direct Effect of Directives?, *Cambridge Law Journal*, 59(3), 586–612.
Dougan, M. (2004) What is the Point of Francovitch?, in T. Tridimas and P. Nebbia (eds) *European Union Law for the Twenty-First Century: Rethinking the New Legal Order*, Oxford: Hart Publishing.
Dougan, M. (2006) The Constitutional Dimension of the Case Law on Union Citizenship, *EL Rev*, 31, 613.
Dougan, M. (2007) When Worlds Collide: Competing Visions of the Relationship Between Direct Effect and Supremacy, *CMLR*, 44, 931.
Drake, S. (2005) Twenty Years after Von Colson: The Impact of Indirect Effect on the Protection of the Individual's Community Rights, *EL Rev*, 30, 329–48.

Eilmansberger, T. (2005) How to Distinguish Good from Bad Competition under Article 82, *CMLR*, 42, 129.

Eleftheriadis, P. (1998) Begging the Constitutional Question, *Journal of Common Market Studies*, 36, 255–272.

European Union Agency for Fundamental Rights (2010) Homophobia, Transphobia and Discrimination on Grounds of Sexual Orientation and Gender Identity, *2010 Update Comparative Legal Analysis*, Luxembourg: Publication Office of the European Union.

Jacobs, F. (2001) Human Rights in the EU: The Role of the Court of Justice, *EL Rev*, 26, 331.

Lenaerts, K. and Corthaut, T. (2006) Of Birds and Hedges: The Role of Primacy in Invoking Norms of EU Law, *EL Rev*, 31, 287.

Masselot, A. (2007) The State of Gender Equality Law in the European Union, *ELJ*, 152.

Niels, G. and Jenkins, H. (2005) Reform of Article 82: Where the Link between Dominance and Effects Breaks Down, *ECLR*, 29, 605–10.

O'Brien, C. (2008) Real Links, Abstract Rights and False Alarms: The Relationship Between the ECJ's 'Real Link' Case Law and National Solidarity, *EL Rev*, 643.

O'Leary, S. (1999) Putting Flesh on the Bones of European Citizenship, *EL Rev*, 24, 68.

Petersen, J. and Shackleton, M. (eds) (2006) *The Institutions of the European Union*, 2nd edn, Oxford: Oxford University Press.

Rawlings, R. (2000) Engaged Elites Citizen Action and Institutional Attitudes in Commission Enforcement, *ELJ*, 6(1).

Rittberger, B. (2005) *Building Europe's Parliament. Democratic Representation Beyond the Nation-State.* Oxford: Oxford University Press.

Roitman, D. (2006) Legal Uncertainty for Vertical Distribution Agreements: The Block Exemption Regulation 2790/1999 and Related Aspects of the New Regulation 1/2003, *ECLR*, 27, 261–8.

Sangiovanni, A. (2013) Solidarity in the EU, *Oxford Journal of Legal Studies*, 1–29.

Shaw, J. (2000) *Law of the European Union*, London: Palgrave Macmillan.

Toth, A.G. (1992) The Principle of Subsidiarity in the Maastricht Treaty, *Common Market Law Review*, 29, Issue 6, 1079–1105.

Tridimas, T. (2003) Knocking on Heaven's Door: Fragmentation, Efficiency and Defiance in the Preliminary Reference Procedure, *CMLR*, 40, 9–50.

Usher, J. (2003) Direct and Individual Concern – an Effective Remedy or a Conventional Solution, *EL Rev*, 28, 575.

Ward, I. (2009) *A Critical Introduction to EU Law*, 3rd edn, Cambridge: Cambridge University Press.

Weatherill, S. (1996) After *Keck*: Some Thoughts on How to Clarify the Clarification, *CMLR*, 33, 885.

Weatherill, S.R. (2005) Better Competence Monitoring, *EL Rev*, 30(1), 23–41.

Weatherill, S. (2009) Current Developments in European Law: Free Movement of Goods, *International and Comparative Law Quarterly*, 58, 985–93.

Index

Tried and tested

What law students across the UK are saying about the **Law Express** and **Law Express Question&Answer** series:

'I personally found the series very helpful in my preparation for exams.'
Abba Elgujja, University of Salford

'Law Express are my go-to guides. They are an excellent supplement to my course material.'
Claire Turner, Open University

'This is the best law Q&A series in my opinion. I think it's helpful and I will continue to use it.'
Nneka H, University of London

'These revision guides strike the right balance between enough detail to help shape a really good answer, but sufficiently brief to be used for last-minute revision. The layout is user friendly and the use of tables and flowcharts is helpful.'
Shannon Reynolds, University of Manchester

'I find them easy to read, yet very helpful.'
Rebecca Kincaid, University of Kent

'The information is straight to the point. This is important particularly for exams.'
Dewan Sadia Kuraishy, University of Manchester

'In the modules in which I used these books to revise with, generally the modules I found the most difficult, I got the highest marks in. The books are really easy to use and are extremely helpful.'
Charlotte Evans, Queen Mary University of London